I0881207

THE RENEWED CHURCH

The Second Vatican Council's Enduring Teaching about the Church

INTRODUCTIONS TO CATHOLIC DOCTRINE

This series provides readable scholarly introductions to key themes in Catholic doctrine, written by preeminent scholars from around the world. The volumes of the series are suitable for college, university, and seminary courses, as well as for educated readers of all ages who seek to grow in their understanding of the Catholic faith.

PUBLISHED VOLUMES

Avery Cardinal Dulles, SJ, *Magisterium, Teacher and Guardian of the Faith*
Daniel A. Keating, *Deification and Grace*
Steven A. Long, *The Teleological Grammar of the Moral Act*
Charles Morerod, OP, *The Church and the Human Quest for Truth*
Kenneth D. Whitehead, *The Renewed Church*

THE RENEWED CHURCH

The Second Vatican Council's Enduring Teaching about the Church

KENNETH D. WHITEHEAD

EX CORDE ECCLESIAE
VERITATIS SPLENDOR
·AVE·
MARIA
UNIVERSITY

Sapientia Press
of Ave Maria University

Sapientia Press
of Ave Maria University
5050 Ave Maria Blvd.
Ave Maria, FL 34142
888-343-8607

Cover Image: Pope John Paul II, Vatican City, Rome 1970s: Pope John Paul II (Karol Wojtyla, second from the right) and Pope Paul VI during the general audience in Vatican. (Photo by Wojtek Laski/Getty Images)

Cover Design: Eloise Anagnost

Printed in the United States of America.

Library of Congress Control Number: 2009932878

ISBN-13: 978-1-932589-53-5

To Dan and Mary,
Jerry and Jeanne, Joan,
and in memory of Tom

Contents

Introduction

IF THEY were listening carefully to what the new pope was saying, some people were perhaps surprised when one of the first things Pope Benedict XVI spoke about following his election to the chair of Peter was the need—and his intention—to carry on with the implementation of Vatican Council II. In his very first message to the cardinals the day after his election, the new pope called for what he described as "an authoritative *rereading* of the Second Vatican Council" (emphasis added). He then went on to state:

> [A]s I prepare myself for the service that is proper to the Successor of Peter, I also wish to confirm my determination to continue to put the Second Vatican Council into practice, following in the footsteps of my predecessors and in faithful continuity with the 2,000-year tradition of the Church. This very year [2005] marks the 40th anniversary of the conclusion of the Council (8 December 1965). As the years have passed, the Conciliar Documents have lost none of their timeliness; indeed, their teachings are proving particularly relevant to the new situation of the Church and the current globalized society. (Initial Message of Pope Benedict XVI to the Cardinals, April 20, 2005)

How did it come about that practically the first thing the new pope wanted to talk about was an event, the Second Vatican Council, that had occurred some forty years earlier? And what was the point of his talking about after all this time, of all things, the "conciliar documents," noting that they had lost "none of their timeliness," that their "teachings" were "proving particularly relevant"? What did all this have to do with the prospects for the new pontificate? What, indeed, was the "authoritative rereading of the Second Vatican Council" that Benedict mentioned all about?

Nobody who had followed his career should have been surprised that Pope Benedict XVI would speak about the Second Vatican Council in this fashion. Similarly, anybody who had paid close attention to the words and actions of the late Pope John Paul II in the course of his long pontificate would have realized that he too constantly spoke about the Second Vatican Council in the same terms. Immediately following *his* election to the papacy in 1978, Pope John Paul II had declared:

> [W]e wish to point out the unceasing importance of the Second Vatican Ecumenical Council, and we accept the definite duty of assiduously bringing it into effect. Indeed, is not that universal Council a kind of milestone, as it were, an event of the utmost importance in the almost two thousand year history of the Church, and, consequently, in the religious and cultural history of the world? (To the Cardinals and to the World, October 17, 1978)

Pope John Paul II's references to and pronouncements on the Council were frequent. As only one example among the very many that we could cite, in an address to the Plenary Assembly of the Sacred College, delivered on November 9, 1979, the Polish pope affirmed:

> Obedience to the teachings of the Second Vatican Council is obedience to the Holy Spirit, who is given to the Church in order to remind her at every stage of history of everything that Christ said, in order to teach the Church all things (cf. Jn 14:26). Obedience to the Holy Spirit is expressed in the authentic carrying out of the tasks indicated by the Council, in full accordance with the teaching set forth therein.
>
> These tasks cannot be treated as if they did not exist. It is not possible to make the Church go back.

More than a quarter of a century later, near the end of his pontificate, John Paul II was still saying the same thing. In his Spiritual Testament published in the English edition of *L'Osservatore Romano* on April 13, 2005—after the pope's death—he wrote, "I am convinced that it will be long granted to the new generations to draw from the treasures that this 20th-century Council has lavished upon us."

So what was it, then, about this Council, which Pope John Paul II considered had lavished treasures upon us, obedience to which was equivalent to "obedience to the Holy Spirit"? The bare facts about this Council, the twenty-first in the series of ecumenical councils the Catholic Church has convened in the course of her two-thousand-year history, are that Blessed Pope John XXIII, supposedly elected at age seventy-seven as a "transition pope," greatly surprised the world instead by calling for "*un concilio*," a council. That was in January 1959. After extensive preparations, and for four straight years (1962–1965), the more than 2,500 Catholic bishops of the world at that time—today there are more than 4,000 Catholic bishops—gathered each October in Rome to spend some three months deliberating and deciding together about a large number of questions concerning the Church, her teachings, policies, problems, practices, and worship. The Council issued sixteen documents in all—the "conciliar documents" that Pope Benedict XVI thought had "lost none of their timeliness" and that continue to govern and direct various aspects of the Church's life today.

Both John Paul II and Benedict XVI, in fact, can be considered, above all, to be "men of the Council." The Council formed the lives and ecclesiastical careers of both of them. Both served prominently *at* the Council. The then only recently appointed archbishop of Kraków, Poland, Karol Wojtyla, intervened in a number of important ways in the course of the Council's work, sometimes in the name of all the Polish bishops, and sometimes individually in his own right. He became increasingly influential toward the end of the Council, when he served on one of the committees working on the draft of what became Vatican II's Pastoral Constitution on the Church in the Modern World, *Gaudium et Spes.*

At the Council, Father Joseph Ratzinger was a *peritus*, or theological expert and advisor, and he was an unusually influential one, especially considering how young he was at the time (in his early thirties); but then he had the providential good fortune of being a *peritus* for Joseph Cardinal Frings of Cologne, Germany, who was one of the major movers and shakers among the Council Fathers. Among the other issues on which he worked, the young Father Ratzinger was one of the two principal drafters of the really beautiful theological text that constitutes the first part of Vatican II's Decree on the Church's Missionary Activity, *Ad Gentes Divinitus.*

A fair number of people who have followed and admired both John Paul II and his longtime prefect of the Congregation for the Doctrine of the Faith, Cardinal Ratzinger, like many on the liberal side who have been critical or have expressed their disapproval of one or both of them, often do not realize the degree to which both of these men must be considered, fundamentally, "men of the Council." John Paul II was widely thought to be a "restorationist," coming from "backward" Poland, wedded to certain traditions, and trying to turn back the clock by bringing back aspects and practices of the Church that had come to be dismissed by many as "preconciliar."

Cardinal Ratzinger, for his part, was almost universally considered in later years to be "the enforcer," a man insisting upon narrow doctrinal purity in his role as prefect of the Congregation for the Doctrine of the Faith at a time when it was thought by many—erroneously—that Vatican II had deliberately downplayed Catholic doctrine in favor of opening up the Church to the world. A preoccupation with doctrine was considered to be narrow and somewhat anachronistic and was, again, thought to be "preconciliar." Certainly, acting publicly to correct or discipline erring theologians was hardly in the spirit of the times, and it was thus considered to be more a feature of the "old Church," which Vatican II had supposedly done away with (it was also, of course, considered to be unjust and "harsh"—the latter adjective a favorite word often used to describe the official actions of Cardinal Ratzinger). The cardinal was deplored if not despised by many merely for doing what was obviously his job, namely, correcting some of those who had quite openly abandoned the authentic Catholic faith in some areas in order to embrace ideas that had come to be thought more suitable and up-to-date. He was regularly given pejorative labels such as "Grand Inquisitor," "head of the thought police," or "*Panzerkardinal*" and was widely considered to be badly out of tune with Vatican Council II.

These characterizations of both of these churchmen who became popes were quite commonly made by observers coming from both the "left" and the "right" (if we may employ these political terms, at least figuratively, even though they do not accurately describe the typical divisions among practicing Catholics; often enough they are no better than caricatures). Throughout their entire ecclesiastical careers, though, neither Karol Wojtyla nor Joseph Ratzinger was either of the "left" or of the "right." Rather, they were "orthodox Catholics"; that is, they actually believed and affirmed the faith as proposed by the Church, quite apart from the typical assumptions about the faith of, say, modern secular liberals—or, indeed, even perhaps those of typical Catholic traditionalists, who sometimes noticed that these supposedly "conservative" churchmen invariably actually did cite and act on what was contained in the documents of Vatican II. Believing and affirming the faith as proposed by the Church, both Wojtyla and Ratzinger constantly had recourse to Vatican II in practically everything they said or did; they were not in any doubt that the Council was, in fact, an authentic ecumenical council of the Catholic Church.

Both were also well aware, of course, that not everything had worked out for the Church in the postconciliar era in the way that the Council Fathers had envisaged and hoped. Many problems followed the Council, and some of them even grew out of it. Nevertheless, both of these popes coming after the Council were also well aware that a general council of the Catholic Church necessarily speaks *for* the Church—and for Christ—in a unique way. As pope, John Paul II thus regularly accentuated the positive about the Council, regardless of what might have gone wrong in the postconciliar era. Since his election, Benedict XVI has pretty much done the same thing. It is no exaggeration, in fact, to say that both of these pontificates basically have been, and are, *inspired* by Vatican Council II.

More than forty years later, we should still be looking back at what was so important about the Council. We really do need to know what Vatican II actually said and did; we need to know this not only in spite of, but indeed *because of,* the stark decline in Catholic faith and practice that has roughly coincided with the postconciliar years. Most people are quite well aware of this. Vatican II is not the primary cause of this decline, however, as some believe. On the contrary, the decline has come about in spite of what the Council decided and ruled. It has largely come about, in fact, because of *infidelity* to the Council—that is, of infidelity to the Church. This is a very big subject, which we shall touch upon in more respects than one in this book but which obviously extends far beyond what any council may or may not have done.

Another very important Vatican II voice, theologian, and *peritus,* Father Yves M.-J. Congar, O.P., one of the most influential of all the *periti* at Vatican II, once actually quoted French president General Charles de Gaulle as stating that Vatican Council II was "the most important event in the twentieth century."

That's not the most important religious or ecclesiastical event in the twentieth century; that's the most important event, period. This judgment may seem rather startling upon first hearing, but we should try to understand what de Gaulle was driving at. If the Catholic Church indeed represents the authentic extension in history of the words and works of Jesus Christ, the redeemer of mankind, as the Catholic Church believes and teaches; if the salvation of the world is indeed intimately if mysteriously tied in to this ancient institution that has now survived and grown down through the vicissitudes of some twenty centuries to become also the *oldest* continuously existing institution in the world today, at the same time as it continues to grow and spread, and is now virtually worldwide in scope and thus also is probably the *largest* single institution in the world today in terms of members; if God's plan for mankind is indeed linked in a mysterious way with the fortunes of this enduring, but in some ways very human, institution, as Vatican II held and taught in more ways than one—if these things are true, and the Church teaches that they certainly are true, then when this utterly unique institution, the Catholic Church, decides to convoke the twenty-first in her long series of general or ecumenical councils—roughly one for each century since her founding—this has got to be an event of very great importance indeed by any standard. Thus, *sub specie aeternitatis* (as Charles de Gaulle was judging), the renewal of the Catholic Church, mandated by the Second Vatican Council beginning in the twentieth century, perhaps was the most important event in that century just past.

Even though many of the dreams, hopes, and intentions of Blessed Pope John XXIII in convoking the Second Vatican Council have not been fully realized—or have *yet* to be fully realized—it is important to recall why he thought a council to be important and necessary in the first place. Blessed John XXIII gave three reasons why he called the Council.

The first reason, as he said in his famous and still often quoted opening address to the Council, *Gaudet Mater Ecclesia* ("Mother Church Rejoices"), delivered on October 11, 1962, was that "the greatest concern of the Ecumenical Council is this: that the sacred deposit of Christian doctrine should be guarded and taught more efficaciously." So far from Vatican II being a "nondoctrinal" council focused merely on new ideas and initiatives and openings to the world, the preservation and effective proclamation of Christ's truths, as taught by the Church, was Pope John's very first reason for calling the Council.

The faith of the Church needed to be renewed, he thought, in order that it might be more effectively disseminated in the world by means of a new evangelization. He wanted the Church to reach out more positively to a world always very much in need of Christ's saving truths. Pope John considered the Church's faith to be solidly established and beyond dispute, and so for him it was a matter of getting the word out more effectively. He did not anticipate the wave of doctrinal dissent that came in during the postconciliar era and is, unfortunately, still with us in many respects today. Thus, one of the less successful utterances of Blessed John XXIII in his epochal opening address to the Council was his observation that "frequently . . . the Spouse of Christ prefers to make use of the medicine of mercy rather than that of severity. She considers that she meets the needs of the present day by demonstrating the validity of her teaching rather than by condemnations."

If only. This particular formulation of John XXIII did not prove to be as fruitful or as prophetic as some of the other things he announced in his marvelous Opening Speech to the Council. If the jovial and saintly pope considered the renewal and spread of the Catholic faith to be the first of his reasons for convoking an ecumenical council, his second reason was to launch a renewed effort to seek reunion with other Christians not in communion with the Catholic Church. As a member of the Vatican diplomatic service, Archbishop Angelo Giuseppe Roncalli had earlier worked in the East—in Bulgaria and Turkey—with Eastern Orthodox Christians, and he was scandalized by Christian disunity, especially in the face of the growing secularization of the modern world. After he was elected pope in 1958, he was determined to do something about it, and so he made it one of his principal reasons for calling the Council. Relaunching the quest for Christian unity would, in fact, prove to be one of the major achievements of Vatican Council II.

Finally, as his third reason, good Pope John wanted an adaptation and updating (*aggiornamento* in Italian, "bringing up to date") of the Church's practices and discipline in order that Christians and the Church might meet the challenges of the modern world more effectively. Forty-plus years after the Council, it has surely been this *aggiornamento* of Pope John XXIII's, including the various practical reforms carried out at the behest of the Council—and including, especially, the reform of the sacred liturgy—that has had the greatest impact on most Catholics. Some people even think that "change," whether they are in favor of it or opposed to it, was what the Council was really mostly all about.

This brings us to the question of what the Council really did do—as contrasted with what many people think "the spirit of Vatican II" stood for. For, as everybody knows, there has been a good deal of confusion following the Council, not to speak of a number of false starts, and so it is especially important to understand and keep in mind what the Council did do that remains permanently valid.

As already noted, the Council issued sixteen documents in all, and it is these documents that today constitute the Council's basic legacy to the Church. These conciliar documents remain both vital and operative today. They are regularly referred to and relied on by Church authorities today, especially by the popes, and they have with equal regularity formed the basis of such epochal postconciliar developments as the revision of the Church's Code of Canon Law, approved in 1983, and the drafting of the indispensable *Catechism of the Catholic Church*, promulgated in 1992. Even as the memories of the Council itself recede into history, the Council's documents continue to be alive and valid. What were, then, some of these Vatican II documents that Pope Benedict XVI, upon his election, declared to be "particularly relevant to the new situation of the Church" and in need of a "rereading"?

In this book, we are going to glance first at the unfolding of the Council itself, how it got set up and was able to produce and issue the sixteen documents that it did. To describe and comment on all sixteen of these documents, however, would take a volume larger by far than the present one. Hence we shall be able only to list and summarize most of them, looking only briefly even at some of the more important ones among them. What we will then concentrate on in the greater part of this book, however, will be those Vatican II documents dealing with the Church herself. These include the Council's great Dogmatic Constitution on the Church, *Lumen Gentium*, and its epochal Pastoral Constitution on the Church in the Modern World, *Gaudium et Spes*. Nothing is more important for Catholics today than to understand what the Church teaches about herself in these two documents. We will also take a look at the Council's other document on the Church herself, namely, the relatively neglected Decree on the Eastern Catholic Churches, *Orientalium Ecclesiarum*. These three Vatican II documents together afford us an unparalleled opportunity to come to understand what the Catholic Church really is, and what she does.

Following this "rereading" of the Second Vatican Council's enduring teaching about the Church herself, we shall then try to sum it all up by briefly setting forth its continuing relevance and significance for us today, now more than forty years after the end of the Second Vatican Council itself.

CHAPTER ONE

The Second Vatican Council and Its Documents

I.

THE FORTIETH anniversary of the opening of the Second Vatican Council came on October 11, 2002. October 1962, forty years earlier, was a time of great tension in world affairs: the opening weeks of the Council coincided with nothing less than the historic Cuban Missile Crisis, when the Communist government of the Soviet Union tried to place missiles aimed at the United States in nearby Cuba; and the United States then went to the very brink of war by instituting a "quarantine" (blockade) of Cuba and announcing its intention of halting and boarding Soviet vessels on the high seas to search for missiles and related military equipment. Blockading actions of this type had always been considered overt acts of war in international law.

Only the extreme caution and restraint through this whole crisis that was exercised by both American president John F. Kennedy and Soviet premier Nikita S. Khrushchev kept the world from plunging into a war between the two great powers that could well have ended with a fatal nuclear exchange.

Those who remember the Cuban Missile Crisis, or who have read about it, or who even have seen the movie *Thirteen Days* based upon it, know that this was the closest the world ever came to mutual nuclear annihilation. And amid the tensions that reigned while Khrushchev and Kennedy exchanged messages seeking for a formula that would allow each of them to draw back from the brink without a loss of face, it seems that Pope John XXIII, in the midst of all that he was doing to get the Second Vatican Council under way, was also heavily involved in the negotiations to resolve this crisis. The pope issued a statement—confidentially requested of him by both sides, separately—that proved to be instrumental in reconciling the positions of the American and the Soviet leaders.

According to the pope's biographer, the late Peter Hebblethwaite, in his *Pope John XXIII: Shepherd of the Modern World*, John XXIII drafted a statement addressed to both leaders, beginning, "I beg heads of state not to remain insensitive to the cry of humanity: peace, peace!" This statement ended up being printed on the front page of the official Soviet newspaper *Pravda* on October 26, 1962. "This was unheard of," Hebblethwaite correctly wrote. "It meant that Khrushchev was preparing his retreat. Pope John XXIII's intervention helped to let him off the hook. He could present himself as a lover of peace." Khrushchev was later quoted as saying that "the pope's message was the only gleam of hope."

This, then, was the very same month that also marked the opening of the Second Vatican Council. So it was not just a time of grave international tensions and "rumors of war" (Mt 24:6; Mk 13:7). It was also a time of great hope as well, in part because of the contagious spirit of the pope who begged the world leaders to give peace a chance and who had also summoned the Second Vatican Council. Many of us still remember—nor are we likely to forget!—the heady days of the convoking and convening of the Council by Blessed Pope John XXIII. This writer vividly remembers in particular the thrill that accompanied reading the press accounts of Pope John's opening address to the Council, *Gaudet Mater Ecclesia*. Among other things, the pope declared that the Catholic Church,

> raising the torch of religious truth by means of this ecumenical Council, desires to show herself to be the loving mother of all,

> benign, patient, full of mercy and goodness toward the brethren who are separated from her. To mankind, oppressed by so many difficulties, the Church says, as Peter said to the poor who begged alms from him: "I have neither gold nor silver, but what I have I give you; in the name of Jesus Christ of Nazareth, arise and walk!" (Acts 3:6)

In the nature of things, of course, it would have been impossible to sustain for very long the joy and hope, and, indeed, the euphoria, that accompanied the opening of the Second Vatican Council on the note established by John XXIII. Biographer Peter Hebblethwaite aptly remarked of the jovial—and now by the Church officially judged to be the saintly—pontiff that his sunny and invariable optimism was, in fact, quite regularly "refuted by events." And so in many ways this would prove to be true of the Council as well. But few of us were disposed to be critical at the time. It seemed appropriate that the Twenty-first Ecumenical Council of the Catholic Church should have gotten off to such a fine and memorable and universally applauded start!

There followed the four successive, exciting years, 1962 through 1965, during which the more than 2,500 Catholic bishops from all around the world met together for several months each fall in the *aula* of St. Peter's Vatican Basilica in Rome in order to debate and decide about the affairs of the Church and about how the Church should approach the modern world and what Catholics should be doing. These debates took place under intense public and media scrutiny, since interest in the novelty of an ecumenical council of the Catholic Church was great around the world. High hopes were invested in the Council in various quarters. It would be fascinating today to follow the developments of the Council through all of the four years that it sat. One thing of special interest for believing Catholics would be the way in which the very pronounced "human element" at the Council was so prominent and so visible. In many ways the gathering resembled the conventions of a political party or the processes and give-and-take of a legislature, and the doings of ecclesiastical factions and major Council figures were often sensationally reported to the world in the media accordingly. Unfortunately, however, too many people took the Council to be *nothing more* than a political-type gathering!

This was a mistake. Although the human beings who were the Catholic bishops at the Council necessarily had to proceed by means of many of the human processes and procedures that we normally associate with politics, the Church is *not* in essence a political body; nor does the majority "rule" in the Church in the way that it is supposed to rule in "democratic" bodies. The bishops of the Catholic Church are not elected officials answerable to a democratic electorate or engaged in carrying out the wishes of their people; their authority comes to them from the original commission of Jesus Christ to his apostles, transmitted to their successors in an unbroken line down through the centuries by the laying on of hands by other bishops. Moreover, the Catholic bishops are strictly obliged to preserve and hand on in their turn the essential and authentic Catholic tradition that they have received.

More than that, the decisions the Catholic bishops solemnly make at an ecumenical council are supposed to enjoy the ratification of the Holy Spirit in a tradition that goes back to the primitive Council of Jerusalem described in the New Testament's Acts of the Apostles: "It has seemed good to the Holy Spirit and to us" (Acts 15:28).

And indeed, almost amazingly, the results of all the recorded activity, agitation, bargaining, "politics," rivalries, and even turmoil that characterized the Second Vatican Council turned out in the end to be the sound, sane, and serene sixteen documents that the Council Fathers verifiably and undeniably produced. The believing Catholic cannot but imagine, therefore, that the Holy Spirit too must indeed have played the role at the Second Vatican Council that Catholic teaching has traditionally affirmed concerning the outcomes of all of the Church's ecumenical councils.

Unfortunately, however, no good contemporary history of the Second Vatican Council currently exists in English that might enable today's interested reader to follow all the developments and events through all four years of the Council. The principal recent history of the Council, published between 1995 and 2001, is a five-volume work edited by Professor Giuseppe Alberigo of the University of Bologna and written by multiple authors of various nationalities; it was issued first in Italian and later translated into the major European languages; a version of it exists in English published by the leftist publishers Orbis Books.

But this very "liberal" history, which celebrates the often invoked "spirit of Vatican II" rather than the actual documents produced by the Council, is biased, tendentious, inaccurate, and often just plain wrong. A searching and severe critique of it can be found in a book written by Archbishop Agostino Marchetto of the Roman Curia and published by the Vatican press (translated into English by the present author).

Thus, there is no good complete contemporary history of the Council in English. A sound and accurate history of the Council in English would represent a project that awaits an able Catholic historian or historians who have not yet come forward. Readers interested in the Council today must still rely on the popular histories that came out shortly after the Council, most of them "instant histories" based on reportage produced at the Council—and most of them also written from a decidedly "liberal" perspective. I refer to such books as the pseudonymous Xavier Rynne's *Vatican Council II*, consisting of the four successive volumes of the author's reporting on the Council that appeared originally in the *New Yorker* magazine during the Council years; and the massive *Drama of Vatican II* by Henri Fesquet, consisting of translations of this author's almost daily reporting on the Council while it was in session, published in the Parisian newspaper *Le Monde*. A fair number of diaries and memoirs have also been written by some of those who were at the Council; these works are often still available in libraries. Then there is the excellent and perceptive but also very brief early history of the Council published by Father Ralph M. Wiltgen, S.V.D., entitled *The Rhine Flows into the Tiber: The Unknown Council*. This book has remained in print and is well worth reading. Otherwise, however, there is not all that much available today on the actual history of the Council.

All this represents another reason why it is important to "reread" the approved Vatican II documents themselves, as Pope Benedict has suggested, since only then can it be clearly seen that the Church was *not* abandoning or repudiating her tradition in any essential way, as some commentators seem to have thought at the time, and as many people apparently think still.

In this book, we can only review some of the highlights, mostly anecdotal, concerned with the development of the Council's documents on the Church. These highlights do, however, serve to convey the flavor of the conciliar years, which were mostly years of positive approval of what was going on for the Catholic Church in Rome during the Council. It was only later that troubles began to be noticeable; only later did the often confused aftermath of the Council ensue. And it was not until the only slightly later "revolutionary" 1960s, and on into the 1970s, in fact, that it suddenly seemed that everything in the Church was changing, sometimes even beyond recognition—and all this along with the many, many changes in society at large that were occurring at approximately that very same time.

It is not an insignificant fact, for example, especially as regards how the post–Vatican II Church would develop, that the Church's twentieth-century general Council and its immediate aftermath also happened to coincide with the civil rights revolution in America. It was in August 1963, just prior to the Second Session of the Council, that Martin Luther King delivered his famous "I Have a Dream" speech to a gigantic rally at the Lincoln Memorial in Washington, D.C. The next year or two—during which the Council also was in session each fall—were the crucial years of the massive popular demonstrations that would soon lead to the end of racial segregation in America. Agitation against "the powers that be" turned out to "work" as far as American society was concerned; so it seemed to many of the agitators—a fact that was not lost on some of those in the Church who had their own agendas for the postconciliar years.

The years of the Council also coincided in America with the beginnings of the popular agitation against the Vietnam War that would eventually bring that conflict to a bitter end as well. Here again, popular demonstrations, operating from below, were eventually able to force change upon a seemingly stubborn and immovable American government. Both the civil rights and the antiwar movements gave many people in this country as well as abroad the impression that "power" and "authority" could and should be confronted and changed from below by popular agitation. In Europe, of course, these same years saw the rise of leftist student revolutionary activism and even the organization of extremist groups that engaged in the kinds of abductions, assassinations, and bombings that have become more familiar to us recently with the rise of today's jihadism and terrorism in the Muslim world.

As a result of developments such as these in the late 1960s and early 1970s, not a few of those working for "change" in the Church came to see rebelliousness, defiance, disobedience, and agitation as suitable methods to be used also against the Church's hierarchy—seen by the rebels as a "power" similar to the secular political and institutional power that they thought needed to be tamed or curbed. At the same time, the frequent haplessness and ineptitude so often exhibited by the leaders of challenged institutions simply incited the "reformers" to bolder efforts: "Up against the wall!" they cried out against anyone in authority.

Similarly, the ecumenical Council that announced and promised change in the Catholic Church also coincided, unfortunately, with the beginnings of what came to be called "the sexual revolution" in the Western world as a whole. This meant that the rebellious spirit that had already infected so many in the Church would manifest itself also in a particular way in dissent from Catholic teaching on sexual morality—and also in departures in practice from the norms of that morality.

Contrasting what an increasingly decadent secular culture now openly sanctions in the way of sexual behavior and practices with the Church's attempts to uphold her traditional moral teachings, many Catholics have unhappily opted for the culture's viewpoint instead. The Church's teachings have increasingly come to be seen as simply retrograde, hidebound, and wrong; and it has become progressively more difficult for the Church to try to maintain her teachings in the face of widespread dissent and disobedience from within her own ranks. Bishops and pastors—not to speak of parents of college students!—often simply no longer knew how to react when confronted with instances of the "new morality" among Catholics and within the Church. Only with the outbreak of the clerical sex abuse scandals in the first months of 2002, though, did it become apparent how thoroughly Catholic sexual morality had become eroded in the postconciliar era in the minds of too many Catholics, including, sadly, even some priests and bishops.

None of these outcomes, though, was in the minds of the Catholic bishops in 1962 when they convened amid the splendid surroundings and solemn pageantry of St. Peter's Vatican Basilica to deliberate about and legislate for the future of the Church and of the faith. Certainly none of these outcomes was in the mind of Blessed Pope John XXIII—who, by the way, most decidedly *did not*, as too many people erroneously believe to this day, convoke the Second Vatican Council in order to bring the Church into greater conformity with the modern world. Rather, it was the other way around. In the words of the pope's apostolic constitution *Humanae Salutis* of December 25, 1961, the pope explained that the Council had been convoked in order to bring "the modern world into contact with the vivifying and perennial energies of the *Gospel*"!

Blessed John XXIII actually—and correctly—saw the modern world as being "in a grave state of spiritual poverty." He saw the Church, by contrast, as being "vibrant with vitality." The saintly pope's aim was not so much to open up the windows of the Church in order to let in the air of the modern world—a figure of speech that has been ceaselessly repeated and believed throughout the entire postconciliar period—as it was to open up the windows of the Church in order to let out the light of Christ to shine more brightly into the darkness of the modern world!

In point of fact, John XXIII's longtime secretary, Monsignor Loris Capovilla, flatly denied that the pope ever said anything at all about "opening the Church's windows." The whole—still widely popularized—idea that the point of the Council was somehow supposed to be to open up the windows of the Church to the vivifying breezes of the modern world was an idea originally launched by the dissident Swiss theologian Father Hans Küng, who later, in 1979, on account of his many aberrations and even outright heresies, was finally officially declared by a judgment of the Congregation for the Doctrine of the Faith to be no longer "a Catholic theologian."

However, speaking at a U.S. bishops' press panel in 1962 in Rome in connection with the Council—according to Father Ralph M. Wiltgen, S.V.D., author of the book we have already mentioned, *The Rhine Flows into the Tiber: The Unknown Council*—Hans Küng claimed that when asked in a private conversation why he had called the Council, Pope John XXIII had gone to the window, opened it up, and said, "To let some fresh air into the Church."

This anecdote was immediately picked up by the media and was widely repeated, then and since; but we need to contrast what a reporter as dubious as Hans Küng says with the *official* reasons John XXIII gave for calling the Council, as set forth in his *Humanae Salutis*. We have noted already that, according to this latter document, the purpose of the Council was to bring the Gospel more effectively to the world (not the world to the Church).

It was rather "under the impetus of divine providence," according to John XIII, writing in the same document, that he had felt the "urgency" of calling a council; he really believed that it was by divine inspiration that, as he had told some seventeen rather surprised cardinals in the Roman Basilica of St. Paul Outside the Walls in January 1959, less than three months after his election to the papacy, he was *obliged* to call an ecumenical council!

One of his principal aims, he later made clear in the same *Humanae Salutis*, was to complete the work of Vatican Council I, which back in 1870 had very clearly defined the place of the pope in the Church. According to Vatican I, the pope both enjoyed what that Council called a "primacy of jurisdiction" over the whole Church of Christ and also possessed a divinely assisted capability of defining Catholic doctrine on faith and morals "infallibly," that is, without error.

However, the work of Vatican I had been interrupted by the outbreak of the Franco-Prussian War in Europe before this 1870 Council could properly complete its work by defining the place of bishops, priests, religious, and laity in the Church. As John XXIII saw it, an important task of Vatican II was to do for all these others making up the Church of Christ what Vatican I had done for the pope, thus completing the Church's process of self-understanding begun at the earlier Council.

It was also an important aim of John XXIII, perhaps *the* most important aim of his, to renew and bring up to date the life of the Church and of her members—what the pope called *aggiornamento*, using the Italian word for "bringing up to date." It was a favorite word of Pope John's; he was already using it while he was still patriarch of Venice in the 1950s. In the wake of the Council, the idea of *aggiornamento*, or updating, came to dominate all the other purposes for which the Council had been called.

At the same time, though, in practice, *aggiornamento* often came to mean whatever anybody thought the Church ought to be doing in order to be more "up-to-date"—without necessarily having any reference to what the Council itself had decided and set forth in its official documents. Too often, ominously, *aggiornamento* became equated in the minds of some with doing exactly what St. Paul had once so solemnly taught that Christians should never do; that was when the apostle wrote that Christians should "be not conformed to this world" (Rom 1:5). Following the Council, too many Catholics unfortunately decided that the point of the Council was, apparently, to be "conformed" to the modern world!

A final expressed aim of John XXIII for convoking the Council, as set forth in *Humanae Salutis*, was to remove all possible obstacles to the achievement of reunion with Christians not in full communion with the Catholic Church. In other words, it was very much a part of Blessed John XXIII's original agenda to promote what, in fact, became a notable feature of the postconciliar era, namely, a more serious participation in Christian *ecumenism* on the part of the Catholic Church. We have already seen how Pope John XXIII set forth in summary form all these same aims and reasons for calling the bishops of the Church to assemble in Rome in his memorable opening address to the Council; he explained these aims more fully in his *Humanae Salutis*. In judging the Council, we should never lose sight of what its aims actually were, as Blessed John XXIII so clearly laid them out.

II.

The Catholic bishops had come to Rome from all over the world to discuss and presumably to approve the material put together by Pope John's Preparatory Commissions; it consisted of seventy-plus ready-made *schemata*, or draft documents. Probably many if not most of the bishops initially agreed with Pope John that the Council would have little more to do than to approve the voluminous material prepared and assembled in Rome for them by the Preparatory Commissions.

This was not to be, however. On the first working day of the Council, October 13, 1962, the official conciliar agenda called for the election of members to the various Conciliar Commissions, successors to the Preparatory Commissions. The elected members of these Conciliar Commissions were supposed to go over the prepared *schemata* and then consider any amendments proposed by the Council Fathers in the course of their discussions and debates. After this, the Council's decrees and other decisions could then be voted upon. The whole process would presumably be neat and uncomplicated. Some 180 names had been drawn up by the Roman Curia to be members of these Conciliar Commissions. If past practice and precedents were any guide, it was again assumed that these names would pretty much be rubber-stamped by the Council Fathers.

But when the secretary general of the Council, Archbishop Pericle Felici, announced that the assembly would then proceed to the election of the members of the Conciliar Commissions, Achille Cardinal Liénart of Lille, France, a member of the Council's seven-member Council of Presidents, arose and read a prepared statement in which he suggested that, instead of voting immediately for the Commission members being proposed, the Council Fathers should instead adjourn, arrange to meet with each other in national or regional groups, and then prepare lists of proposed Commission members of their own on the basis of these consultations. In this way, the Commissions could be said to be genuinely "conciliar" and not just bodies chosen on the basis of the lists drawn up by the Curia in Rome.

Joseph Cardinal Frings of Cologne, Germany, arose immediately after the French cardinal of Lille had made his proposal and seconded the procedure being proposed. He said that he was speaking in the name of all the German-speaking bishops in the matter. Vigorous applause greeted this announcement. These two cardinals, a Frenchman and a German, belonged to a group of like-minded bishops coming mostly from Western European countries that became known at the Council as the European Alliance. This very well-prepared European Alliance of bishops had apparently tapped into a rich vein of opinion among the Council Fathers and had thus made itself very well known at the Council, and even dominant, at the very outset. It quickly became clear what the overwhelming sentiments of the Council Fathers apparently were; they wanted to draw up and elect their own lists of the members of the Conciliar Commissions—although in the atmosphere that prevailed, any contrary opinions would very likely have gotten lost in the rush to approve what was being proposed.

After some brief uncertainty on the part of the Council presidents, and some consultations back and forth, it was decided that the Liénart proposal could indeed be adopted; and thus, on its first working day, the Second Vatican Council did adjourn as suggested, so that Council Fathers could consult with one another on the makeup of the lists of proposed Conciliar Commission members. Certainly the members of the European Alliance already had their preferred lists drawn up, as the eventual membership on the Conciliar Commissions would show.

The following week, after some feverish consultations over the weekend, the Council proceeded to the election of its Conciliar Commission members on the basis of lists drawn up among the Fathers themselves, rather than on the basis of those prepared in advance by the Preparatory Commissions under the influence of the Roman Curia. The latter body probably never completely recovered in the course of the entire Council from the way it had gotten shoved aside on the very first day of the Council by the organized and determined group of Council Fathers who made up the European Alliance. Henceforth the curial elements would be fighting a largely defensive battle for their points of view—and with the added disadvantage that the major media reporting on the Council heavily favored the initiatives of the liberals and the liberal viewpoint. In the media's reporting on the Council proceedings, European Alliance members and their allies were regularly assigned white hats, while conservative bishops associated with the Roman Curia or reflecting its typical views were given black hats.

The change in the Council's procedures, engineered at the outset by the European Alliance, thus changed the course of the Council itself. Henceforth, it became clear, the Council's agenda would be *its* agenda, not one drawn up by curial bodies or dictated by the pope. There was never any real evidence, of course, that the popes, in spite of allegations and insinuations often made, ever really *wanted* to "dictate" to the Council anyway; rather, most of the evidence pointed to the conclusion that the popes genuinely wanted the Council to act as a real deliberative body consisting of the bishops of the Catholic Church. So the developments registered in the first week of the Council showed that it would be precisely that. Whatever the accomplishments—or the failures—of the Second Vatican Council, they would have to be considered genuinely the accomplishments or failures *of* the Council. It was going to be a true deliberative assembly.

But since it was also a general council of the Catholic Church, its formal acts and documents, when ratified by the successor of Peter, would enjoy the guidance and guarantee of the Holy Spirit. Pope John XXIII was not fundamentally mistaken about the overall role of the Holy Spirit at a general council of the Catholic Church. And once this particular Council got off and running, it would turn out that there would be a considerable amount of material for the Holy Spirit to guarantee. The makeup of the Conciliar Commissions meant that much of the preparatory material would be thrown out or greatly modified in the course of the First Session, and this was quickly and sometimes unceremoniously done. Beginning with the Second Session, and with a new pope from out of the conciliar ranks now sitting on Peter's chair overseeing it all—Blessed John XXIII having died in the summer of 1963—the Council was off and running.

Having pledged to carry on with the Council upon his accession to the papacy, Paul VI, in his opening address to the Second Session, was able to summarize the principal aims or objectives of the Council, as Blessed John XXIII had originally conceived them. He summed them up in four main points:

1. **The self-awareness of the Church.** This meant achieving a greater understanding of the inner nature of the Church—what she is and what she *does*. The pope thought that the Church was especially in need of this greater self-awareness or self-understanding in order to deal with the complexities of the modern world. In the event, this particular aim of the Council was surely realized in an important sense in *Lumen Gentium*, as well as in some of the other Council documents.

2. **The renewal of the Church.** This aim, of course, had probably been the principal aim of Pope John XXIII. Paul VI hoped that this desired renewal of the Church could be brought about "not by turning upside down the present way of life or breaking with what

is essential and worthy in her tradition." This hope would turn out not to have been very realistic, as events in the postconciliar period would soon show. Nevertheless, the optimism of Paul VI here was very typical of the conciliar years themselves.

3. **The bringing together of all Christians in unity.** Christian unity was certainly one of the principal aims of John XXIII. Paul VI was equally committed to seeking it. In his speech, he addressed the non-Catholic observers at the Council directly, stating that their presence there stirred great hope in his heart as well as sadness concerning the present separation. "If we are to blame in any way for that separation," he added, inaugurating the series of contemporary Catholic "apologies" that John Paul II would later apparently never tire of offering, "we humbly beg God's forgiveness, and ask pardon too of our brethren who feel themselves to have been injured by us." Paul VI, like John Paul II later, apparently really believed that such gestures were not only necessary but might really lead to reunion soon with some of the Christians outside the visible boundaries of the Catholic Church.
4. **The dialogue of the Church with the contemporary world.** "Dialogue," of course, was one of Pope Paul VI's favorite themes. He treated it extensively in the first encyclical he issued on August 6, 1964, *Ecclesiam Suam*, and he would go on to promote dialogue significantly during his pontificate. Also in connection with this fourth point, he pointed to some of the vacant benches in the *aula* of St. Peter's, noting that they belonged to bishops unable to attend the Council, and he added that "religious liberty, like other fundamental rights of man, is being crushed by principles and methods of political, racial, and anti-religious intolerance." This reference applied in particular to Communist countries since, at the time of the Council, the Iron Curtain still extended across Europe, and the pope's reference was to those bishops from some of the countries behind the Iron Curtain who had not been able to attend the Council.

Forty years later, it has become clear to us that events were set in motion at the Council that eventually did help bring the Iron Curtain down; but it has not been equally clear that "dialogue" itself has always merited the importance that Paul VI, among others, assigned to it. However that may be, Pope Paul VI himself was pretty sure at the time where he thought the Council should be going. Even with the perspective of forty years, it is not easy for us to say that either he or John XXIII should have spoken or acted much differently than they did speak and act. Hindsight is easy, and we can now see where some of the things the Council was so enthusiastic about actually led, no matter how well motivated they may have been at the time. It is not hard to see today, for example, that some of the thinking at the Council was perhaps overly idealistic and overly optimistic. However, neither the pope who launched the Council nor his successor who carried it on could possibly have foreseen how it was all going to turn out. Like St. Paul, they could only "walk by faith and not by sight" (2 Cor 5:7), and we certainly have to give them credit for doing that, since we too are obliged to do the same.

III.

At the very beginning, the Second Vatican Council was not as well organized as it should have been. As we have mentioned, Pope John XXIII had originally given the task of preparing for the Council to a number of Preparatory Commissions, which had in turn consulted bishops, heads of religious orders, Catholic universities, and other institutions around the world. More than two thousand responses consisting of proposals, position papers, and lists of questions were eventually received back in Rome and collected into fifteen large bound volumes. This material was then reduced by the Preparatory Commissions to some seventy-two *schemata*, or draft texts. It was an enormous amount of material to be dumped upon the bishops coming to the Council to read, absorb, and decide about. In their reminiscences of the Council, some bishops vividly remembered the burden of all this "documentation," which they scarcely had time to read at all, much less absorb.

This was perhaps a foretaste of the experience that many bishops would have in the postconciliar years with the soon heavily bureaucratized national episcopal conferences that were set up nearly everywhere after the Council, providing the bishops with mountains of material at every meeting that they were somehow supposed to read, absorb, and decide about.

As early as March 1962, some seven months before the opening of the Council, the archbishop of Mechelen-Brussels, Léon-Joseph Cardinal Suenens, in a conversation with the pope, asked: "Who is working on an overall plan for the Council?"

"*Nessuno,*" promptly replied Pope John XXIII. "Nobody."

This was typical. Pope John trusted the Holy Spirit: if it was God's will, the bishops at the Council would be guided to do the right thing. Blessed John told Cardinal Suenens: "The pope's first duty is to listen and keep silent to allow the Holy Spirit free play." But since Cardinal Suenens was a practical man, he was still concerned about the manifold difficulties of discussing, as he put it, seventy-two *schemata de omni re scibili et quibusdam aliis* ("seventy-two drafts concerning all things known and a few other things besides"). Faced with this question, the pope agreed that it would be desirable to have an overall plan. So he asked Cardinal Suenens to draw one up.

The Belgian cardinal was only too glad to oblige. He very quickly presented the pope with a mercifully brief outline that laid out in broad general terms both what the Council ought to consider and what it ought not to consider. He noted:

> The announcement of the Council has raised great hopes among the faithful and in the world at large. It must respond to this double level of expectation: this, it seems to me, means that it must deal with a double range of subjects. The first would deal with the Church *ad extra*, that is, the Church as it faces the world of today outside. The second would deal with the Church *ad intra*, that is, the Church in itself, but with the aim of helping it better respond to its mission in the world.

Cardinal Suenens thought it "would be a great and painful disappointment for the Church and the world if the Council were to get bogged down on minor matters," and he frankly told the pope that "eight tenths of the *schemata*, in their present form, do not strike me as 'Council material.'" He favored "mercilessly" cutting everything that was secondary and referring much of the material contained in the *schemata* to postconciliar commissions rather than weighing down the deliberations of the bishops at the Council with too many issues and too much detail.

As it happened, the Council was going to get into a great many subjects and perhaps in greater detail than Cardinal Suenens evidently thought desirable. But he was giving advice to a pope who, prior to the opening of the Council, still thought that the whole conciliar process could be wrapped up in one session. At Pope John's beatification process, Agostino Cardinal Casaroli testified that "Pope John thought all the conciliar problems could be solved in the space of two months." Pericle Cardinal Felici, who served as secretary general for the Council itself, added that the pope thought that the Council "could be finished in a single session—two months—or, at the very most, given the difficulties that had emerged in the preparatory commissions, two sessions."

Very probably, Cardinal Suenens was addressing the pope's expectations in this regard when presenting his plan to the latter. What proved to be of permanent importance in this original plan was the basic idea of addressing the Church's internal, or *ad intra*, concerns and relationships on the one hand and her external, or *ad extra*, concerns and relationships on the other. However, Blessed John XXIII did not immediately adopt the Belgian prelate's plan. At first he seems to have put it in a drawer. He evidently really was quite averse to interfering in the conciliar process in any way that might stifle the Spirit. There were other indications that this was precisely how he viewed the matter. Some writers of a more liberal bent have even suggested that he did not want to stir up opposition in the Roman Curia of the day by bringing forward the work of a non-Italian cardinal.

Nevertheless, it was the basic Suenens plan that would eventually indicate the path down which the Council was in fact going to proceed. This came about in part because the cardinal not only gave a copy of the plan to the pope himself. He also sent copies to "cardinal friends" of his, as he styled them, including the archbishop of Milan, Giovanni Battista Cardinal Montini, soon to be elevated to Peter's chair as Pope Paul VI. It was the latter who, also concerned from its very first days about the Council's apparent lack of direction, wrote a letter about this to the Vatican secretary of state, who was also president of the Council's Secretariat for Extraordinary Affairs, Amleto Cardinal Cicognani. In this letter, Cardinal Montini relaunched the basic Suenens idea for the organization of the Council's work. In several succinct paragraphs, he recommended that the work should be immediately centered around one sole theme, namely, "Holy Church" (*la Santa Chiesa*). He thought this emphasis was necessary in order to bring out the role and power of the bishops "in continuity with the First Vatican Council." That Council had described the role and power of the pope but then had been "interrupted." But "in view of the maturity reached by the doctrine of the Church since the encyclical *Mystici Corporis*"—issued in 1943 by Pope Pius XII—Cardinal Montini thought the time was ripe to develop the Church's self-understanding to the fullest. Concentration on the Church, he thought, should lead back to Christ, of whom the Church is the "emanation and continuation." The primacy and infallibility of the pope should be reaffirmed, but above all, "the mystery of the Church" should be brought out, what the Church is. All this would occupy a First Session, he thought.

A Second Session would be needed, in Cardinal Montini's opinion, in order to deal with what the Church *does*—basically, what Cardinal Suenens had styled *ad intra* matters. Finally, a Third Session would be needed "to deal with the relationship between the Church and the world which surrounds it," even including, Cardinal Montini specified, "the enemies of the Church"—the *ad extra* matters of Cardinal Suenens. Afterward, "postconciliar commissions should be set up . . . so as to assure the actual execution of the decrees and good intentions produced by the great effort of renewal."

This was a remarkably accurate prediction of just how the Council would unfold. It should also be evident that what the future pope thought should be the Council's main area of concentration, namely, the Church herself, turned out to be what the Council did, in fact, focus upon most markedly. Vatican II was preeminently a council on the Church. This is also the area of concentration of the present book. Cardinal Montini not only addressed his letter setting forth his views on this to the then key figure in the Roman Curia under the pope, the secretary of state, Amleto Cardinal Cicognani. He also sent a copy of it to Cardinal Suenens himself, whom he identified in the letter as having made the "suggestion" for the "structure" of what the Milan cardinal was now proposing. This time, however, there was no question of a non-Italian "outsider" presuming to direct the Council.

Besides, in October 1962, when the letter was sent, just about everybody took it for granted that Giovanni Battista Cardinal Montini would before long be the next pope. The Italian papers had speculated about his possible election even earlier, during the conclave of 1958, although he was not yet then a cardinal. One of Pope John XXIII's first acts, in fact, had been to name him one. But he already occupied such a prominent place in the ecclesiastical scene of the day that any letter from him was bound to get attention. Moreover, the letter was both perceptive and practical in grasping both the immediate needs of the Council and its long-term task, and then suggesting a way for the Council to move forward.

Of course, the Montini-Suenens plan meant putting aside any idea of just leaving things to the Holy Spirit or, especially, of completing the Council's work in just one session. As things turned out, of course, there would be four sessions instead of the three that Cardinal Montini had projected, but the Council certainly would go on largely to fulfill his hopes and expectations in advancing the Church's self-understanding, especially in its great Dogmatic Constitution on the Church, *Lumen Gentium*; in setting forth both what the Church *is* and what she *does*; and then also in laying out in a number of other documents how she must relate to and interact with the world around her.

Cardinal Montini's letter to Cardinal Cicognani, which proved to have been so enormously influential in establishing the agenda that the Council eventually followed, remained unknown until Cardinal Suenens presented a copy of it to the Paul VI Institute in Brescia (Paul VI's birthplace) in September 1983, on the occasion of a colloquy on his pontificate. None of the initial reporters or historians of the Council refer to it or apparently knew about it. It became widely known only when it was included in Dom Alberic Stacpoole's 1986 volume, *Vatican II Revisited: By Those Who Were There.*

In the meantime, the original plan of Cardinal Suenens had been circulated among a number of other influential cardinals, including those on the Council's Central Preparatory Commission, of which Cardinal Suenens himself was a member, as he would later serve as one of the Council's "moderators." This circulation of the Suenens plan was apparently not without effect. The First Session of the Council had failed to bring to any conclusion any of the various subjects that had been brought forward and debated. In many ways, the Council seemed to be floundering at first. Near the end of the first session, on December 4, 1962, therefore, Cardinal Suenens delivered a loudly applauded address to the whole body in which he laid out how all the *schemata* under consideration needed to be reworked within the framework of his two basic categories of *ad intra* and *ad extra*. He stressed that the Council must focus on its own central concerns and set aside secondary matters that would unduly prolong its sessions. Prior to his speech, Cardinal Suenens had assured himself through Archbishop Angelo Dell'Acqua of the Secretariat of State of the basic support for his plan of Blessed John XXIII, whose health was beginning to deteriorate at this point.

In a pastoral letter to his Milanese flock published the very next day after the speech of Cardinal Suenens, Cardinal Montini of Milan in effect publicly endorsed the plan of his Belgian colleague when he wrote that "there is an immense amount of material which is excellent but heterogeneous and uneven. It could have been considerably reduced and better classified." The following day, December 6, 1962, it was announced that the seventy-plus *schemata* then being considered were being reduced to twenty. (This original preconciliar material, by the way, was more voluminous than all of the documents and decrees issued by all twenty of the previous general councils of the Catholic Church!)

Thus, it seemed that the original Montini-Suenens "team" had moved at just the right psychological moment in order to provide direction to a Council that had lacked it up to that point. It would turn out that the three subsequent sessions of the Council would proceed pretty much as the two cardinals had indicated that they should. Later on, as evidence of the first conciliar and postconciliar turmoil began to be evident, Cardinal Suenens, as one of the members of the liberal European Alliance most prominently in view, fell out of favor, relatively speaking, with Pope Paul VI (his imprudence a little later on in bringing up the birth control issue on the Council floor at a time when the pope had clearly said that the subject was reserved to a papal commission did not help). But that did not change the fact that the Belgian cardinal, who was a flamboyant figure and in his day considered *papabile*, or capable of being elected pope, by some, worked very effectively with the Italian cardinal Montini to get the Council organized along lines that both of them agreed upon at the time.

It was not without importance, of course, that when the Council resumed its work at the Second Session in the fall of 1963, the new pope was none other than the former Cardinal Montini himself, who could now be depended upon to direct the Council in the way he wished to see it go. During the First Session in 1962, Cardinal Montini had been uncharacteristically passive and silent for so definite a personality. Cardinal Suenens himself described him as *très réservé* ("very reserved"). He addressed the Council only twice as a cardinal during the First Session. One of his speeches was on the liturgy, where he tried to steer a middle course between making what he called "arbitrary innovations" and doing nothing.

No doubt during that First Session, Cardinal Montini was as conscious as anybody could be that, very likely, he would be chosen to be the next pope, if and when the failing John XXIII passed on. He thus probably did not wish to take positions that could be perceived as "one-sided" or "partisan," when very soon he might be obliged to appear and function as the impartial "father" of the entire Council—above the fray. Most people at the time, however, understood that his basic orientation on many of the issues facing the Council was basically "progressive." Indeed, he was closer to most of the members of the liberal European Alliance of bishops in his characteristic views than he was to most of the other Italian bishops of his day.

The key to how the Council should proceed, though, was certainly to be found in the plan that Cardinal Suenens and Cardinal Montini had jointly put together and promoted. It would fall to the remaining three sessions, always eventful, and occasionally tumultuous, to carry out the work the Council was destined to produce. While it would be both interesting and instructive to follow the carrying out of all that work in detail, we will here in this book mostly view it in terms of the documents that the Council in fact produced and that we are undertaking to "reread," at least in part.

IV.

By the time the Fourth Session of Vatican Council II opened on September 14, 1965, all of the subjects on which the Council would officially pronounce and issue documents had already been brought forward and debated, sometimes intensively and occasionally even exhaustively, during the preceding three sessions. Two documents were completed and issued at the end of the Second Session, the Constitution on the Sacred Liturgy, *Sacrosanctum Concilium*, and a second one on the modern media, the Decree on the Means of Social Communication, *Inter Mirifica*. For reasons that are not entirely clear, the Church quite regularly uses this rather curious term, "the means of social communication," to refer to the modern media; perhaps it is a translation back from the Latin. The fact that the Constitution on the Sacred Liturgy was issued so relatively early in the course of the Council's work meant that the reform of the Church's liturgy mandated by this document actually got under way while the Council itself was still sitting.

Three more documents were completed by the end of the Third Session and hence were issued in 1964; they included the most important single document produced by the Council, the Dogmatic Constitution on the Church, *Lumen Gentium*. Then, in addition to this, there was the Decree on the Catholic Eastern Churches, *Orientalium Ecclesiarum*. Both of these two documents, bearing as they do upon the Church's teaching about herself, will be examined later in these pages. The third document issued in 1964 was the very important Decree on Ecumenism, *Unitatis Redintegratio*; it dealt with the subject of Christian unity, which both Pope John XXIII and Pope Paul VI had declared to be one of the major reasons for holding the Council in the first place. Thus, a total of five documents had been issued by the Council prior to the Council's final session in 1965.

None of the remaining eleven documents that would be approved and promulgated by the end of the Fourth Session, however, originated during that session. Some of them, such as the documents on revelation and the Church in the modern world, had been under consideration from the very first session on. Others—among them the very controversial ones on religious liberty and non-Christians—had been parts of the original *schema* on ecumenism that got separated and developed into separate documents in their own right in the course of the sometimes heated conciliar debates on these two particular topics.

Five of these eleven documents issued in the course of the Fourth Session—those on bishops, religious, the training of priests, Christian education, and non-Christians—were approved on October 28, 1965. Two more of them—those on revelation and the lay apostolate—were approved on November 18, 1965. The final four—on the missions, the ministry and life of priests, the modern world, and religious liberty—were voted in as part of the Council's permanent legacy to the living Church on December 7, 1965, the day before the Council itself ended. The entire 1965 session was obviously a very busy time for the Council Fathers, resulting in a remarkable number of documents, though it cannot be emphasized too strongly that most if not all of these documents had been discussed and debated to a greater or lesser degree throughout the entire Council, and hence these documents were in no way hastily written or without careful, and, indeed, prolonged, thought being given to them.

In retrospect, in fact, it is quite clear that the Council was generally very slow to make up its mind and express it in the form of a completed and official document binding henceforth upon the Church. We have already noted how no document at all was issued during the First Session. The young German theologian and *peritus* for Joseph Cardinal Frings of Cologne, Father Joseph Ratzinger, was even memorably quoted at the time as having observed that "the great, astonishing, and genuinely positive result of the First Session" was the fact that it issued no documents. This, according to Father Ratzinger, represented "the truly epoch-making character of the Council's First Session." He undoubtedly meant that only the mature deliberations of the conciliar process itself could have resulted in documents that were *worth* issuing.

But the relatively leisurely pace at which the Council produced its first five documents over three years meant that the Fourth Session, which was the final one, would be characterized by the issuance of a veritable blizzard of documents. Yet each of the eleven documents produced in 1965 proved to be worthy of the Council's attention in its proper sphere—and worthy of ours today. Some are obviously more important than others; but not a single one should really be passed over by Catholics serious about their faith and desirous of adhering to the *authentic* Catholic faith as expounded by this general Council of the Church.

Generally speaking, all of the Council's documents can be classified under the two basic headings identified by Cardinals Suenens and Montini during the First Session: first, there were those documents that concern the Church's internal membership, mission, and affairs and that did come to be designated by the Latin term *ad intra*; and second, there were those that concern the Church's external relationships with, and mission to, the world, which similarly came to be called *ad extra*.

This distinction between *ad intra* and *ad extra* documents in one sense even went back to Blessed John XXIII's original idea about the nature and purpose of the Council. In a radio-television address delivered on September 11, 1962, Pope John had said that the Council's task was to concern itself with what he considered to be the twofold vitality of the Church. There was, first, her *ad intra* vitality that was found in her membership, organization, and structures—but, especially, in what he called "the treasures of illuminating faith and sanctifying grace." Then there was her vitality *ad extra*, pertaining to helping supply the wants and needs of the world, including those of people outside the Church, as exemplified in her many works such as schools, hospitals, orphanages, and the like. As we have seen, this twofold distinction, through the efforts of Cardinals Suenens and Montini, eventually did become an integral part of the Council's organization and output. All sixteen Council documents can indeed be classified under one or another of these two categories. We lay them out herewith, along with the date each was issued by the Council, as follows:

Ad Intra	*Ad Extra*
Constitution on the Sacred Liturgy, *Sacrosanctum Concilium*, December 4, 1963	Decree on the Means of Social Communication, *Inter Mirifica*, December 4, 1963
Dogmatic Constitution on the Church, *Lumen Gentium*, November 21, 1964	Decree on Ecumenism, *Unitatis Redintegratio*, November 21, 1964
Decree on the Catholic Eastern Churches, *Orientalium Ecclesiarum*, November 21, 1964	Declaration on Christian Education, *Gravissimum Educationis*, October 28, 1965
Decree on the Pastoral Office of the Bishops in the Church, *Christus Dominus*, October 28, 1965	Declaration on the Relation of the Church to Non-Christian Religions, *Nostra Aetate*, October 28, 1965
Decree on the Up-to-Date Renewal of the Religious Life, *Perfectae Caritatis*, October 28, 1965	Decree on the Church's Missionary Activity, *Ad Gentes Divinitus*, December 7, 1965
Decree on the Training of Priests, *Optatam Totius*, October 28, 1965	Pastoral Constitution on the Church in the Modern World, *Gaudium et Spes*, December 7, 1965
Dogmatic Constitution on Divine Revelation, *Dei Verbum*, November 18, 1965	Declaration on Religious Liberty, *Dignitatis Humanae*, December 7, 1965
Decree on the Apostolate of Lay People, *Apostolicam Actuositatem*, November 18, 1965	
Decree on the Ministry and Life of Priests, *Presbyterorum Ordinis*, December 7, 1965	

Each one of these Vatican II documents in its own right, as we have stressed, is well worth the "rereading" that Pope Benedict XVI recommended. In this book, however, we are going to be able to manage a careful and fairly detailed rereading of only those documents bearing upon the Council's teaching on the Church herself, namely, *Lumen Gentium*, *Gaudium et Spes*, and *Ecclesiarum Orientalium*. We can and should, however, first briefly describe and summarize the more important of the other documents as well, and this will be the task of the next two sections of this chapter.

V.

The Vatican II document that has surely had the most visible effect on most Catholics almost everywhere is undoubtedly the Council's Constitution on the Sacred Liturgy, *Sacrosanctum Concilium*. The reform of the sacred liturgy mandated for the Roman rite of the Catholic Church by this document has probably affected more Catholics in more ways than all of the other enactments of the Council put together. *Sacrosanctum Concilium* ("Sacred Council"), the first document approved by the Council, set the liturgical reform in motion by observing that "Mother Church earnestly desires that all the faithful should be led to that full, conscious, active participation in liturgical celebrations which is demanded by the very nature of the liturgy, and to which the Christian people, 'a chosen race, a royal priesthood, a holy nation, a redeemed people' (1 Pet 2:9; 4:5), have a right and obligation by reason of their baptism" (*SC* 14).

If you are still asking why the Council made all the changes in the liturgy that were made, the answer is contained in the above quoted passage from *Sacrosanctum Concilium*: the Council Fathers wanted "full, conscious, and active" participation in the liturgy by the faithful. What exactly was meant by this "full, conscious, and active participation" in the liturgy, however, was never spelled out or made very clear by the Council itself; and it has not, in fact, been made entirely clear up to the present day. Thus, whether the decision to mandate a reform of the liturgy was a wise and necessary decision on the part of the Council Fathers is a question that has not yet been entirely settled in the minds of some people.

But there is no question at all that the basic decision to reform the liturgy was indeed made by the Council: it happened. Vatican Council II very definitely *did* mandate a reform of the Roman liturgy. *Sacrosanctum Concilium* did state quite plainly and unmistakably that the Council "desires that . . . the rites be revised carefully in the light of sound tradition, and that they be given new vigor to meet present-day circumstances and needs" (*SC* 4). The authorities of the Church, duly and properly, carried that reform out, whatever we may think of the results (especially since the reform was unfortunately not, in fact, always carried out as "carefully in the light of sound tradition" as had been stipulated).

But because a reform of the liturgy *had* been mandated by the Council, Catholics who, sometimes with good reasons, expressed their disagreement with or disapproval of the reform as actually carried out, sometimes saw their loyalty to the Church generally questioned by some bishops and pastors. This was an unfortunate development.

But it was equally unfortunate that a small number of Catholics opposed to the Council's enactments *did* prove disloyal: the only schismatic-type movement arising out of Vatican II turned out to be that led by French archbishop Marcel Lefebvre, whose followers reject the liturgical reform along with a number of other Vatican II decisions. Because at least some Catholics have in fact continued to prefer the former "Tridentine Mass," as it is now called (with less than entire exactitude, however), the popes, by the issuance by Pope John Paul II of a special indult in 1988, and an extension of that permission by Pope Benedict XVI in 2007, have allowed the celebration of this old Mass to be continued in accordance with the 1962 Roman Missal under certain conditions. The popes have allowed this primarily in order to prevent more tradition-minded Catholics from joining a schismatic-type group that continues to celebrate the Tridentine Mass illicitly. In effect, the "indult" Tridentine Mass has become the equivalent of another "rite." Since Vatican II did mandate a general reform of the liturgy, however, it remains unlikely that anything other than the reformed Roman liturgy will constitute normative worship in the Western Church.

In the opinion of most knowledgeable observers, the Church at the time of the Council probably was long overdue for a proper reform of the liturgy. Some of the liturgical accretions of centuries had begun to be a burden, and, too often, even the Mass was celebrated in a rote or routine fashion. As is rather well known, however, the actual reform that was carried out has certainly not been an unalloyed success in every respect either. Too many people, including not a few pastors and bishops, never understood what *Sacrosanctum Concilium* was really all about, and too many among them, apparently, decided that the fact that the Church was officially making changes in her liturgy and worship meant that henceforth "change" could indeed be considered the new order of the day. As a result, not a few changes not necessarily mandated or even envisaged by the Council got incorporated into the mix, often in accordance with various "theories" about the liturgy, some of which have been less than helpful.

Some of the changes proved unsettling to many of the faithful as well, particularly as regards the move from Latin to the vernacular Mass (decided upon, definitively, only *after* the Council, when most of the bishops' conferences around the world opted for the vernacular and petitioned Rome to allow it—as the Council *had* allowed it in principle [see *SC* 36.2], provided that both Rome and the local bishops approved).

The misunderstandings and misapplications of the actual enactments of Vatican II, in accordance with a supposed "spirit of Vatican II," however, were particularly evident in some of the liturgical excesses and abuses that have been widely encountered in the postconciliar era. This, in fact, is precisely one of the other reasons why we need to go back now and reread the actual documents issued by the Council, as Pope Benedict XVI indicated in his initial address to the cardinals: we need to remind ourselves what the Council really did call for in the way of liturgical reform.

It turns out that *Sacrosanctum Concilium*, for example, is a very sane and balanced and even beautifully written document, which still today provides a wonderful account of what the Church's liturgy is and what a reform of it should be—or should have been. It is a shame that the liturgical renewal mandated by the Council has gotten such a bad reputation in some quarters, because it should have been otherwise, and, God willing, it will yet be otherwise.

Only now, more than forty years after the Council—and, especially, over the past ten years or so, since the advent of Jorge Cardinal Medina Estevez, followed by his successor Francis Cardinal Arinze, at the head of the Congregation for Divine Worship and the Discipline of the Sacraments in Rome—can it be said that the reformed vernacular liturgy is coming to approximate what Vatican II called for in the first place. In particular, with the issuance of a new, revised General Instruction on the Roman Missal (GIRM) in 2001, followed by a reorganization of the International Commission on English in the Liturgy (ICEL), we are now able to look forward, in the next few years, to an adequate and accurate translation into English of the Roman liturgy. After so many years, this should prove to be a great boon for the Church and the faith, for, as *Sacrosanctum Concilium* reminds us:

> [I]t is the liturgy through which, especially in the divine sacrifice of the Eucharist, "the work of our redemption is accomplished," and it is through the liturgy, especially, that the faithful are able to express in their lives and manifest to others the mystery of Christ and the real nature of the true Church. (*SC* 2)

Yet *Sacrosanctum Concilium* was only the first of the documents issued by the Council. Vatican II's writ ran far beyond questions merely of liturgy and worship alone, although it is not without significance that this was the first and perhaps one of the most far-reaching of all the Council's documents. As another example of one of the Council's more important documents, let us take the Council's Decree on Ecumenism, *Unitatis Redintegratio*, approved on November 24, 1964.

Most people are very well aware that the Catholic Church at Vatican II significantly changed her approach to Christians outside her visible boundaries. Before the Council, the Church took a position that basically called for waiting rather passively for a "return" of the lost sheep into Christ's true fold, the Catholic Church. The trouble was that most non-Catholic Christians, unlike their ancestors, had never belonged to the Catholic Church in the first place, so they could never contemplate any such "return"—and only a trickle of converts ever did, as a matter of fact, "return."

The Council thus decided to adopt a more active policy whereby the Church, like the Good Shepherd in the parable, would henceforth go out in search of the lost sheep (cf. Mt 18:12). To effect this change of approach, the Council Fathers picked up on a point they had already decided upon in their Dogmatic Constitution on the Church,

Lumen Gentium; the point was that non-Catholic Christians, though lacking the fullness of truth and most of the sacraments, usually nevertheless possessed at least some "elements of sanctification and truth," even if they did not possess all of the sacraments or the truth of Christ in its fullness—in other words, their Christian glass was not just half empty; it was half *full*; for they possessed *some* "elements of sanctification and truth." So the idea was to emphasize what they did possess and what all Christians still agreed on, not what those who had ceased to be in communion with the Catholic Church now lacked or what they disagreed with the Church about.

Building on this basic idea, the Council Fathers issued their Decree on Ecumenism, *Unitatis Redintegratio* ("Restoration of Unity"). This document declared at the outset that

> [t]he restoration of unity among Christians is one of the principal concerns of the Second Vatican Council. Christ the Lord founded one Church and one Church only. However, many Christian communions present themselves to men as true inheritors of Jesus Christ; all indeed profess to be followers of the Lord but they differ in mind and go their different ways, as if Christ himself were divided. Certainly, such division openly contradicts the will of Christ, scandalizes the world, and damages that most holy cause, the preaching of the Gospel to every creature. (*UR* 1)

Unitatis Redintegratio developed a set of ecumenical principles whereby Catholics might henceforth participate in ecumenical dialogue and, under certain circumstances, engage in joint prayer or worship with non-Catholic Christians, aimed at helping to clear away the obstacles to Christian reunion. The principles developed by the Council included avoiding blame or harsh judgments against separated brethren; engaging in honest and sincere dialogue with them in order to see what agreements might possibly be reached; engaging in common charitable works; and praying together when possible.

As a result of the adoption of these ecumenical principles, the Catholic Church, over the last forty years, has pretty much *taken over the leadership of the worldwide ecumenical movement* among Christians. You can verify this by consulting the section in the latest *Catholic*

Almanac entitled "Ecumenism and Interreligious Dialogue," where a running record is kept of all the current interfaith dialogues, joint ecumenical declarations, agreed statements, and the like that have taken place since Vatican II. Christian unity may not have been achieved as yet—although the Catholic Church may be close to reunion with some of the Ancient Churches of the East that have been separated for some sixteen hundred years—but it is remarkable nonetheless what agreements have been reached between churches formerly at loggerheads with each other.

At the same time that Vatican II launched the Church into today's organized ecumenical activity, it is of interest—as it is somewhat ironic—that *Unitatis Redintegratio* happens to be the Vatican II document that brings out most clearly the fact that the Catholic Church has in no way relinquished her claim to be the one, true Church of Christ. The document states in this regard that

> it is through Christ's Catholic Church alone, which is the universal help toward salvation, that *the fullness of the means of salvation* can be obtained. It was to the apostolic college *alone*, of which Peter is the head, that we believe Our Lord entrusted *all* the blessings of the New Covenant, in order to establish on earth the one Body of Christ into which *all those should be fully incorporated* who belong in any way to the people of God. (*UR* 3; emphasis added)

Yet *Unitatis Redintegratio*, which has had such a significant effect on Catholic practice in the postconciliar era, is still only one more of the sixteen documents issued in all by the Council. Other Council documents are perhaps of equal or even greater significance. Let us take, as yet one more example, the Council's Dogmatic Constitution on Divine Revelation, *Dei Verbum*, approved on November 18, 1965. *Dei Verbum* ("Word of God") is the second of the Council's three great "constitutions." It is an enormously important document that explains the Church's contemporary understanding of sacred Scripture, following upon more than two centuries of modern biblical scholarship that has "demythologized" Scripture (to employ the term coined by one of the most distinguished modern German practitioners of biblical scholarship, Rudolph Bultmann) to the point where many people no longer believe in the Bible as divine revelation—that is, as God's word to mankind. Many people, including too many Christians, have long been in varying degrees of disarray, perplexity, or doubt because of the questions raised and doubts cast upon the credibility of sacred Scripture generally by modern biblical scholarship and the attitude of mind it fosters.

However, this has not fundamentally been a problem for the Catholic Church—just as the theory of evolution too, regardless of how modern science may explain it, has never posed the same kind of problem for Catholic believers that it apparently poses today for many Bible Christians. Though it remains very *mysterious* that God should have chosen to reveal himself to mankind in the way that he has—or, indeed, should have chosen to save us in the way that he has, as recorded in the Bible—the fact remains that the Bible *is* the Word of God, as the Catholic Church firmly believes and teaches, and this is precisely and plainly reaffirmed in this Vatican II document, *Dei Verbum*: "We must acknowledge that the books of Scripture, firmly, faithfully, and without error, teach that truth which God, for the sake of our salvation, wished to see confided to the sacred Scriptures" (*DV* 11).

Fully cognizant of the questions raised by modern biblical scholarship, but also possessed of knowledgeable and sophisticated answers to these questions that are in no way incompatible with truly established modern scientific knowledge, this major conciliar document concisely but accurately validates the Church's traditional understanding of the meaning and authority of sacred Scripture. Following rather intense debates on the Council floor concerning questions of Scripture and Tradition that go all the way back to the Protestant Reformation and its claim that the faith is based only on *sola Scriptura*, or Scripture alone, *Dei Verbum* instead defines that "sacred Tradition and sacred Scripture make up a *single sacred deposit of the Word of God*, which is entrusted to the Church" (*DV* 10; emphasis added). Thus, the living Church stands behind Scripture and properly *interprets* it for the benefit of the faithful.

Importantly, *Dei Verbum* also states conclusively that "the Christian economy . . . since it is the new and definite covenant, will never pass away; and no new public revelation is to be expected before the glorious manifestation of Our Lord Jesus Christ (cf. I Tim 6:14 and

Tit 2:14)" (*DV* 4). As has traditionally been said, God's revelation to us of himself and his plan for us "ended with the death of the last apostle." *Dei Verbum*, in effect, endorses and upholds this truth.

It is also of special interest that it is in this Vatican II document that the Magisterium of the Catholic Church has officially adopted and confirmed what nineteenth-century English cardinal John Henry Newman famously formulated and described as "the development of doctrine." Revealed Christian truth does not change, but it does "develop" in the sense that it can be better stated and understood and applied. The actual words of the Council's text state that "the tradition that comes to us from the apostles makes progress in the Church, with the help of the Holy Spirit. There is *growth in insight* into the words and realities that are being passed on" (*DV* 8; emphasis added).

Dei Verbum, it is important to add—especially considering how so many wrongly imagine that the Council somehow downgraded or made optional the importance of the "official" teachings of the Church—also plainly taught that "the task of giving an authentic interpretation of the Word of God, whether in its written form [Scripture] or in the form of Tradition, has been entrusted to the living teaching office of the Church *alone*" (*DV* 10; emphasis added). It is the teachings of the Church's Magisterium, or teaching authority, not scholarly or theological opinions, that should form the basis of the faith for Christians.

VI.

Sacrosanctum Concilium, *Unitatis Redintegratio*, and *Dei Verbum*, which we have now reviewed, are, as Pope Benedict XVI suggested, obviously very important Church documents; but there is yet another Vatican II document of perhaps even greater overall importance in some ways, namely, the Council's Declaration on Religious Liberty, *Dignitatis Humanae* ("Human Dignity"), dated December 7, 1965. This document is undeniably one of the greatest of the achievements of the Second Vatican Council. As its Latin title makes clear, it deals not just with religious freedom as such but also with one of the greatest problems confronting mankind today, namely, the recognition and protection of basic *human dignity*.

Human dignity is under steady and unrelenting assault today from a number of quarters, including especially from some of our Frankenstein-monster-type scientists engaged in such evils as embryonic stem-cell research and cloning—not to speak of the widespread procedures employed in artificial reproduction and in vitro fertilization themselves, considered to be wholly beneficent because they help women conceive—but without regard to the fact that human embryos are unavoidably manipulated and often destroyed, thus making these procedures unquestionably immoral in spite of their wide acceptance in our society today. It has come to be widely believed that what we can do technically, we may do morally. Human dignity—and violations of it—is practically the last thing anybody apparently thinks of in these cases. However, this is also true in the case of the massive falling away in our society from any inherent respect for human dignity that is evidenced today by widespread legalized abortion, euthanasia, and assisted suicide.

Then there are today's terrorists of whatever motivation, including not only fanatic jihadists placing their roadside bombs but also teenagers willing to strap bombs around their waists in order to blow themselves up inside buses or crowded pizza parlors—or, let us say, to fly hijacked passenger airliners into skyscrapers. Questions of human dignity are scarcely ever even raised in these contexts nowadays, any more than they were normally raised when the world took to practicing aerial bombardment.

Human dignity was equally under assault at the time of the Council. Then it was the totalitarian regimes of the day, German Nazism and Italian Fascism, only recently defeated at the time of the Council, while, of course, there was still in existence then the very strong and still apparently flourishing regime of Soviet Communism. All these oppressors of human dignity helped convince the Council Fathers that the urgent question of religious freedom—the freedom of human beings to live and act in accordance with their consciences—had to be addressed and answered by the Magisterium of the Church. *Dignitatis Humanae* essentially answered that very question. This Vatican II document declares that

> the human person has a right to religious freedom. Freedom of this kind means that all men should be immune from coercion on the part of individuals, social groups, and every human power, so that, within due limits, nobody is forced to act against his convictions in religious matters in private or in public, alone or in association with others. The Council further declares that the right to religious freedom is based on the very dignity of the human person as known through the revealed Word of God and by reason itself. (*DH* 2)

Thus, the essence of this human right declared by the Council is to be free from "coercion," and its basis is the dignity of the human person. Having lived under a Communist regime, Pope John Paul II tirelessly reaffirmed the principles of religious liberty expounded by *Dignitatis Humanae.*

It is not without interest that, as Pope Benedict himself recently observed, it was the American bishops at Vatican II who were quite instrumental in securing the passage of *Dignitatis Humanae*—just as the American Jesuit theologian Father John Courtney Murray was very influential in preparing the draft of it.

In spite of its great importance, however, the document has not been uniformly appreciated by all Catholics. Some Catholic traditionalists, looking back at certain nineteenth-century teachings of Blessed Pope Pius IX and Pope Leo XIII—teachings that dealt with the duties of the state and public officials in Catholic countries toward the true religion—have made the claim that this Vatican II Declaration on Religious Liberty actually departs from the Catholic tradition and is heretical. In fact, of course, the document addresses a wholly different question from the one that preoccupied the nineteenth-century popes struggling to preserve the freedom of the Church from Europe's then newly minted anticlerical governments. The question that *Dignitatis Humanae* addresses is rather the basic right of the human person to be "immune from coercion" in his beliefs and convictions, as we have explained.

Such freedom from coercion accords with the Church's long tradition. The Church has always taught that even though the revealed faith of the Church is held to be God's truth, its adoption, as well as adherence to it, must always stem from the voluntary, free act of a human person: "Truth can impose itself on the mind of man only in virtue of its own truth, which wins over the mind with both gentleness and power" (*DH* 1). Even in the Middle Ages, the Church forbade efforts to coerce Jews or other non-Christians into accepting conversion.

At Vatican II, the Church declared, as we have now seen, that this freedom from coercion must be "based on the very dignity of the human person as known through the revealed Word of God and by reason itself" (*DH* 2). It would be hard to imagine a greater cause in which the Church at Vatican II could have been enlisted.

Yet it is still somewhat ironic that, just as Vatican II's clearest statement that the Catholic Church remains the one, true Church of Christ happens to be found in the Council's Decree on Ecumenism, as we pointed out above, so the Council's clearest statement that Christians are strictly obliged to form their consciences in accordance with the teaching of the Church comes in this document on freedom from coercion in matters of belief and conscience. Here the Council stated, in one of the most important single statements it made, that

> in forming their consciences, the faithful must pay careful attention to the *sacred and certain teaching* of the Church. For the Catholic Church is by the will of Christ *the teacher of truth*. It is her duty to proclaim and teach *with authority* the truth which is Christ and, at the same time, to declare and confirm by her authority the principles of the moral order which spring from human nature itself. (*DH* 14; emphasis added)

The Catholic Church is, quite simply, "the teacher of truth." This is what the Second Vatican Council said about the binding and obligatory nature for the faithful of the Church's authoritative teachings; they are to be accepted and acted upon in our lives because they are *true*. This is guaranteed by the very fact that it is the Church that teaches them. As Jesus said long ago to his apostles in a statement intended to apply both to them and to their successors, the bishops of the Catholic Church, some 2,500-plus of whom were the Council Fathers who issued this particular teaching about the Church as the teacher of truth in 1965: "He who hears you hears me" (Lk 10:16).

But the adherence of our mind and will to the teachings of the Church that constitutes our faith must always be a *free act*. *Dignitatis*

Humanae even states that religious beliefs that are *false*—not in accord with what the Magisterium of the Church teaches, or even contrary to it—must nevertheless be respected because of the *human dignity* of those who hold these beliefs, even of those who do not adhere to the true religion. The Church at the Council could not have been more clear on this point.

Not all of the Council's documents are perhaps equal in importance to a document such as *Dignitatis Humanae.* Yet another one of Vatican Council II's documents that has its own importance in its own particular sphere is the Council's Declaration on Christian Education, *Gravissimum Educationis,* promulgated on October 28, 1965. It is one of the shortest of the Council's sixteen documents (only the Decree on the Means of Social Communication, *Inter Mirifica,* is shorter). However, in view of what the Council called "the paramount importance of education in the life of man and its ever-growing influence on the social progress of the age," the Council Fathers did not believe the topic could be omitted from their conciliar deliberations and decisions.

Unlike such earlier Church documents on education as Pope Pius XI's 1929 encyclical on Christian education, which tended to focus primarily on the institutions of the family, the Church, and the state, *Gravissimum Educationis,* in keeping a major emphasis of Vatican II, again focuses initially on "the dignity of the human person." As related to education, it is the dignity of the human person that (1) gives "all men of whatever race, condition, or age . . . an inalienable *right* to education" (*GE* 1) and (2) gives to all the baptized "a right to a *Christian* education" (*GE* 2; emphasis added).

The declaration defines education by stating that "true education is directed toward the formation of the human person in view of his final end and the good of that society to which he belongs and the duties of which he will, as an adult, have a share" (*GE* 1).

Another emphasis of the document is the importance it gives to the role of parents in the education of their own children—almost as if the Council had foreseen the decline in standards and morality in modern schools and the rise of the modern home-schooling movement. According to *Gravissimum Educationis,* parents must "be recognized as being primarily and principally responsible for the education of their children. The role of parents in education is of such importance that it is almost impossible to provide an adequate substitute" (*GE* 3). Only after insisting upon this fundamental point does the declaration go on to speak of society's, of the school's, and of the Church's responsibility for education.

Gravissimum Educationis recognizes that it is "the duty of the state to ensure that all its citizens have access to an adequate education"; at the same time, "the public authority . . . whose duty it is to protect and defend the liberty of its citizens is bound according to the principle of distributive justice to ensure that public subsidies to schools are so allocated that parents are truly free to select schools for their children in accordance with their conscience. . . . There must be no monopoly of schools which would be prejudicial to the natural rights of the human person" (*GE* 6). A distinctly traditional note is struck, though, in the declaration's insistence upon "the right of the Church freely to establish and conduct schools of all kinds and grades, a right which has also been asserted time and time again in many documents of the Magisterium" (*GE* 8).

It is of interest that one individual Doctor of the Church, St. Thomas Aquinas, is singled out for mention in this document—one of the two mentions of him in the documents of Vatican II, the other being in *Optatam Totius*, the Decree on the Ministry and Life of Priests (*OT* 16). These mentions of the Angelic Doctor are among the rare occasions when any individual is singled out in official Church teaching documents. St. Thomas is commended for his "method" in achieving what the declaration styles "the convergence of faith and reason" in seeing and expounding the truth of the Catholic faith (*GE* 10).

Another one of the Council's shorter documents is the Declaration on the Relation of the Church to Non-Christian Religions, *Nostra Aetate* ("Our Age"). This document was approved amid intense controversy on October 28, 1965. It was controversial primarily because it was the document in which the Council attempted to deal with the burning question of the Church's relationship with the Jews. During World War II, the Council Fathers had all lived through the very recent horror of the Nazi holocaust against the Jews—Adolf Hitler's unhappily all-too-successful attempt to carry out a "final solution" to a perceived "Jewish problem" by killing most of the Jews of Europe in extermination camps. This was a matter that rested heavily upon the European conscience at the time of the Council. Many bishops were determined that the Council should issue a statement making unmistakably clear that anti-Semitism formed no part of Catholic teaching.

The degree to which past negative Christian sentiment against the Jews had all that much to do with the kind of virulent and violent ideological anti-Semitism practiced by the frankly pagan Nazis, however, has perhaps too often been exaggerated, then and still today; but after Hitler showed what could be carried out, and was carried out, in the name of anti-Semitism, anti-Jewish sentiment of any kind could no longer be part of any Christian teaching and action, even by implication. Unfortunately, however, the fact is that an animus against the Jews has existed in Christianity and has surfaced at various times, including in modern times; this is undeniable. This animus was often based in particular upon the fact that it was within the ambit of the Jewish nation that Jesus Christ, himself a Jew and the son of a Jewish mother, was crucified; but some Catholics also have bought into what might be called "cultural" prejudice against the Jews, who could not be assimilated to Christian society in the ages of faith and were "different."

Precisely because the Church and the Christian faith sometimes got blamed for the horrors of Hitler's holocaust against the Jews—it took place, after all, in "Christian" countries—some Council Fathers were determined to put the Council plainly on the record with a strong statement condemning any form of anti-Semitism or violence against the Jews. Yet other Council Fathers opposed any such move, however, some because they feared such a statement could lead to persecution of Christians in the Middle East, where various Arab and Muslim governments opposed to the creation of the modern state of Israel already had a clear record of imposing various disabilities on non-Muslims. The establishment of the state of Israel in 1948 had already aroused considerable Arab and Muslim opposition, in fact, and many Catholic bishops did not want to get the Church involved in trying to deal with this, one of the "hottest" of all political "hot potatoes" (as it still is today). Besides, Blessed John XXIII's Council was not supposed to be "condemning" anybody, even apparently anti-Semites.

The first draft of a conciliar statement on the Jews originally formed part of the Council's *schema* on ecumenism, but then it got separated out because it was not thought pertinent to the question of relations between Christians. Yet because there still remained opposition among the bishops to any statement exclusively on the Jews and Judaism alone, the idea emerged of issuing a conciliar statement on the subject of the Church's relations with non-Christian religions generally, including the Jews and Judaism. In the end, this was how the issue was dealt with by the Council with its issuance of *Nostra Aetate*—although the document remains heavily oriented toward the Jewish question.

Drawn up and debated and approved under the glare of the most intense publicity generated in the course of the Council—the document was considered by organized Jewish groups especially to be a test of whether the Church was serious about expunging even the suggestion of anti-Semitism from her record—*Nostra Aetate* was applauded by many when it was approved because it did serve to clear up many ambiguities and uncertainties regarding the Church's attitude toward the original Chosen People.

Others, however, considered that the document did not go far enough. However that may be, the operative teaching of *Nostra Aetate* surely did exclude any possible basis for any kind of "Christian" anti-Semitism, as follows:

> Even though the Jewish authorities and those who followed their lead pressed for the death of Christ (cf. John 19:6), neither all Jews indiscriminately at that time, nor Jews today, can be charged with crimes committed during his passion. It is true that the Church is the new people of God, yet the Jews should not be spoken of as rejected or accursed as if this followed from Holy Scripture. Consequently, all must take care, lest in catechizing or in preaching the Word of God, they teach anything which is not in accord with the truth of the Gospel message or the spirit of Christ.
>
> Indeed, the Church reproves every form of persecution against whomsoever it may be directed. Remembering, then, her common heritage with the Jews and moved not by any political consideration, but solely by the religious motivation of Christian charity, she

> deplores all hatreds, persecutions, displays of anti-Semitism leveled at any time or from any source against the Jews. (*NA* 4)

Reflecting the Council's great emphasis generally on the subject of *human dignity*, this document too went on to teach that "there is no basis . . . for any discrimination between individual and individual, or between people and people, arising either from *human dignity* or from the rights which flow from it. Therefore, the Church reproves, as foreign to the mind of Christ, any discrimination against people, or any harassment of them, on the basis of their race, color, condition in life, or religion." (*NA* 5; emphasis added)

Nostra Aetate also stated for the record the Church's developed teaching concerning her attitude to non-Christian religions generally, and this is well worth quoting here:

> The Catholic Church rejects nothing of what is true and holy in these religions. She has a high regard for the manner of life and conduct, the precepts and doctrines which, although differing in many ways from her own teaching, nevertheless often reflect a ray of that truth which enlightens all men. Yet she proclaims and is in duty bound to proclaim without fail, Christ, who is the way, the truth, and the life (Jn 14:6). In him, in whom God reconciled all things to himself (2 Cor 5:18–19), men find the fullness of their religious life. (*NA* 2)

In going over the six conciliar documents that we have just reviewed, we cannot fail to see both the variety and the range of the Vatican II documents, as well as their vital importance, even today. It is easy to understand why Pope Benedict XVI thought that these documents deserved a "rereading." However, we shall not examine any further here those conciliar documents that remain—with the exception of the three on the subject of the Church that we shall be examining more closely in the following chapters. Most of the remaining conciliar documents that we have not discussed—those on bishops, priests (two documents), religious, and the apostolate of the laity—represent *ad intra* documents on the Church's internal life and mission that are all to some extent based upon, or heavily influenced by, the teachings articulated in the Council's great Dogmatic Constitution on the Church, *Lumen Gentium.* This key document, of course, we shall be examining in some detail, beginning in the next chapter.

Of the other remaining documents that we have not discussed, the two on the media and on the Church's missionary activity are *ad extra* documents that remain highly pertinent, the former, *Inter Mirifica*, being perhaps the Council's most neglected document. It is quite generally scorned and belittled by modern media practitioners, if they bother to take any notice of it at all. This is the case even though the basic message of the document is that modern media reporting ought to be based on *truth*, and its presentations should always be within the context of the moral order. How anyone could object to this is hard to understand, but it is perhaps a measure of the kind of moral decadence that has overtaken our society today that many people *do* object to it.

As for the Decree on the Church's Missionary Activity, *Ad Gentes Divinitus*, it sets forth a sound theology for the Church's conduct of her missionary efforts around the world. It really awaits proper implementation, however, since a downgrading of the importance of the missions and, to some extent, of the very idea that the Church should even be "preach[ing] the Gospel to the whole creation" (Mk 16: 15) has been one of the notable casualties of the postconciliar downgrading of the doctrine of the faith as true and necessary for salvation. Hopefully, this present situation will prove to be a temporary one in the perspective of the long history of the Church, which has always been zealously missionary. When genuine missionary fervor returns, *Ad Gentes* should be able to come into its own. Its beautifully written chapter 1, expounding what it calls "Theological Principles" for the missions, is actually one of the best concise summaries of the content of the Catholic faith as a whole to be encountered anywhere; it is of great significance, perhaps, that one of the principal drafters of this beautifully written chapter was none other than the young Council *peritus* Father Joseph Ratzinger. The Catholic faithful who turn to this document will not fail to find their faith nurtured and strengthened thereby.

CHAPTER TWO

Lumen Gentium

I.

VATICAN COUNCIL II'S Dogmatic Constitution on the Church, *Lumen Gentium*, is the most important single statement that the Catholic Church has ever made about herself in the nearly two thousand years of her life on this earth. The document's Latin title, *Lumen Gentium*, means "Light of the Nations" and refers, of course, not to the Church herself but to Jesus Christ, who is the light of the nations. Since, however, in the opening words of this dogmatic constitution itself, "the light of Christ . . . shines out visibly from the Church" (*LG* 1), the theme of Christ's light got incorporated into the title by which this most important and most profound of all the Council's sixteen documents has been known since it was approved by the Council Fathers by an overwhelming vote of 2,121 votes in favor and only 5 opposed. It was promulgated on November 21, 1964, at the end of the Council's Third Session.

In the very first paragraph of *Lumen Gentium*, the Church in Council proposes, "for the benefit of the faithful and of the whole world, to set forth, as clearly as possible, and in the tradition laid down by earlier councils, her own nature and mission" (*LG* 1). The document largely and even abundantly succeeds in accomplishing this declared aim, as we shall see. Few or no Church teaching documents have contributed more to the Church's own self-understanding.

At first reading, however, the document may not exactly appear to be drawn up "in the tradition laid down by earlier councils." There are no *definitions of doctrine*, for example, although the constitution is styled "dogmatic." Nor does the document contain any of the solemn canons with anathemas attached that earlier councils produced so readily.

Instead, in keeping with Blessed John XXIII's original intention that the Second Vatican Council should approach its work in a positive vein, *Lumen Gentium* consists of a narrative in eight chapters that essentially *describes* the Church and her members from various standpoints—although the document actually avoids the term "members," preferring terms such as "the faithful," or those "called" to belong to the Church (*LG* 13, 19, and passim), or those "incorporated" into her (*LG* 14).

The Dogmatic Constitution on the Church eventually does get around to describing the visible, sacramental, sacerdotal, and hierarchical worldwide "organization" headed by the pope and the bishops in communion with him as successors of Peter and the other apostles of Christ. It describes this "organization" as well as this has ever been done, as a matter of fact. In many accounts, of course, it is this same visible "organization" that is often taken to *be* "the Church."

But Vatican II wanted to get beyond the popular notion that the Church is somehow defined or delimited by her hierarchy or clergy or simply by her visible or hierarchical structure. The Church's sacred hierarchy is described, of course, and as thoroughly and accurately as anywhere else in the Church's teaching corpus, and often using the very words of Vatican I, Trent, or Florence. Thus, no "new" Church emerges in the formulations contained in this document, as some have imagined (or perhaps even have hoped).

Nevertheless, *Lumen Gentium* consciously aimed to go beyond the way in which the Church was typically seen and described; and thus, in one way or another, the Dogmatic Constitution on the Church treats or touches upon nearly every other theme or topic pertaining to the Church contained in the other documents produced by the Second Vatican Council: it treats bishops, priests, religious, laity, revelation, missionary activity, ecumenism, non-Christian religions, religious liberty, freedom of conscience, and yet other points of doctrine covered by the Council in the other documents it issued. At the same time, these other documents that Vatican II produced on many of these same topics reflect and elaborate upon the way in which *Lumen Gentium* treats the nature and mission of the Church. The document is quite freely and frequently referenced as an authority in many of the subsequent documents issued by the Council.

Strictly speaking, then, the document does not "define" any new doctrine. It does, however, contain and restate a number of already defined Church doctrines, such as the Immaculate Conception, the Assumption, the primacy and infallibility of the pope, and so on. It makes quite clear, contrary to the views of some modern revisionist theologians, that the Catholic Church was indeed *founded* by Jesus Christ (cf. *LG* 5, 8, and 14). It also makes clear that Christ, the eternal head of the Church, is the one sole Mediator between God and man (cf. *LG* 8). Of equal importance, it expressly identifies the holy Eucharist as "the source and summit of the Christian life" (*LG* 11).

It also unmistakably affirms as well that the Catholic Church is "the *sole* Church of Christ which in the Creed we profess to be one, holy, Catholic, and apostolic" (*LG* 8; emphasis added). In other words, in *Lumen Gentium*—as elsewhere also, for example, in *Unitatis Redintegratio*—Vatican II makes very clear what has always been claimed by the Church, namely, that she is "the one true Church of Christ." This particular truth is even reiterated in a number of ways and places in the document (e.g., in *LG* 7, 13, 15, and 23). *Lumen Gentium*'s claim to be the "sole" Church of Christ, however, was not formulated and included in the text without considerable debate at the Council, especially as regards the following paragraph:

> This Church, constituted and organized as a society in the present world, *subsists in* [*subsistit in*] the Catholic Church, which is governed by the successor of Peter and by the bishops in communion with him. Nevertheless, many elements of sanctification and truth are found outside its visible confines. Since these are gifts belonging to the Church of Christ, they are forces impelling toward Catholic unity. (*LG* 8; emphasis added)

The use of the phrase "subsists in" in the above paragraph occasioned spirited debate at the Council and has been much commented on since (and sometimes much misunderstood as well). Similarly, the statement that "many elements of sanctification and truth are found outside [the] visible confines" of the Catholic Church was not included in the final text without considerable discussion and argument. This latter concept, though, is one of the most important of the Vatican II doctrinal developments, entailing enormous consequences for Christian ecumenism and the quest for Christian unity. Some of these consequences did not fail to get worked out in greater detail in some of the Council's other documents.

For the recognition—even while the claim that the Catholic Church was the one true Church was being reaffirmed—that other Christian churches and communions might nevertheless possess *some* Christian truths, or "elements," as the Council called them, was immediately recognized as calling for a whole new approach by the Catholic Church to ecumenism and to the quest for Christian unity. For what the phrase "subsists in" entailed and allowed for, among other things, was an ecclesiology of *degrees*; bodies outside the Catholic Church might possess *elementa ecclesiae* (such as one or more of the sacraments) without being in full possession of *all* the elements of the Church as founded by Christ. Only the Catholic Church possesses *all* the elements in their fullness.

In practice, this was going to mean that the postconciliar Church, while not abandoning or watering down any of her traditional claims, would be actively seeking dialogue and greater understanding of existing differences with other Christian bodies rather than simply waiting passively for these erring separated brethren to see the light and return to the true fold.

As for the phrase "subsists in," the original conciliar *schema* that became *Lumen Gentium* had said quite simply that the Church in the process of being so elaborately described simply "is" the Catholic Church; but as was explained by the Council's Theological Commission at the time, after much debate, the "is" was replaced by "subsists in"—so it was explained—"so as to be more consonant with ecclesial elements found elsewhere."

But using "subsists in" instead of simply saying "is" has occasioned controversy and misunderstanding virtually from the time the phrase first appeared in a Church constitution up until now. It has even been interpreted by some as indicating that the Catholic Church is no longer strictly claiming that she is the one true Church of Christ; it has been taken as admitting, rather, that the "one Church of Christ" might possibly in some sense also "subsist in" other or perhaps in a combination of Church bodies, including non-Catholic bodies.

This is not the teaching of *Lumen Gentium.* Although this dogmatic constitution has certainly nuanced our understanding of the *way* in which the Catholic Church remains the one true Church of Christ, the fact that she does so remain is still intact: the Church's essential teaching has not changed. What the choice of "subsists in" was intended to convey is precisely the opposite, namely, that the one Church of Christ subsists *only* in the Catholic Church, while outside her boundaries there exist only "elements of sanctification and truth," as *Lumen Gentium* 8 so carefully specifies. Some of these *elementa ecclesiae* are listed later on in *Lumen Gentium* 15, as follows:

> There are many who hold sacred Scripture in honor as a rule of faith and of life, who have a sincere religious zeal, who lovingly believe in God the Father Almighty and in Christ, the Son of God and the Savior, who are sealed by baptism which unites them to Christ, and who indeed recognize and receive other sacraments in their own churches or ecclesiastical communities. Many of them possess the episcopate, celebrate the Holy Eucharist, and cultivate devotion to the Virgin Mother of God. There is, furthermore, a sharing in prayer and spiritual benefits; these Christians are indeed in some real way joined to us in the Holy Spirit for, by his gifts and graces, his sanctifying power is also active in them and he has strengthened some of them even to the shedding of their blood.

In spite of the cogent justification it offers for the position it takes, though, this part of *Lumen Gentium* has nevertheless been very widely misunderstood. The necessity for taking up again the whole "subsists in" question has continued to be felt, and, in a document issued by the Congregation for the Doctrine of the Faith as recently as

September 14, 2000, it was taken up again. The document in question is entitled *Dominus Iesus*: On the Unicity and Salvific Universality of Jesus Christ and the Church. This CDF document itself proved to be highly controversial and was again wrongly interpreted by some as signaling that the Catholic Church was going back on her ecumenical commitment that was made at Vatican II.

Dominus Iesus, issued in 2000, notably pertains to the Council's documents on ecumenism, missionary activity, revelation, and non-Christian religions; and it proved to be a crucial clarifying document issued at the beginning of the new millennium. But it also pertains, and significantly, to our present constitution on the Church. In it the CDF specifically attempted to clarify *Lumen Gentium*'s use of "subsists in" by stating that

> [w]ith the expression *subsistit in*, the Second Vatican Council sought to harmonize two doctrinal statements: on the one hand, that the Church of Christ, despite the divisions which exist among Christians, continues to exist fully only in the Catholic Church, and, on the other hand, that "outside her structure, many elements can be found of sanctification and truth," that is, in those churches and ecclesial communities which are not yet in full communion with the Catholic Church. But with respect to these, it needs to be stated that "they derive their efficacy from the very fullness of grace and truth entrusted to the Catholic Church."
>
> Therefore, there exists a single Church of Christ, which subsists in the Catholic Church, governed by the successor of Peter and by the bishops in communion with him. The churches which, while not existing in perfect communion with the Catholic Church, remain united to her by means of the closest bonds, that is, by apostolic succession and a valid Eucharist, are true particular churches. Therefore, the Church of Christ is present and operative also in these churches, even though they lack full communion with the Catholic Church, since they do not accept the Catholic doctrine of the primacy, which, according to the will of God, the bishop of Rome objectively has and exercises over the entire Church. (*DI* 16–17)

Thus the CDF's *Dominus Iesus* is only one of the clarifications that have had to be issued in the postconciliar period because of the misunderstandings of what Vatican II really said. The documents issued by the Council were mostly very clear and should not have been misunderstood to the extent that they have been misunderstood. Nevertheless, special interests have obviously been at work since the Council, and they have often prevented a proper understanding of what in fact was decided at the Council. This proved to be preeminently true of some of the truths enunciated in *Lumen Gentium.* This dogmatic constitution does not rely upon a string of abstract propositions or isolated definitions. Rather, it incorporates the truths it expounds into a smooth organic narrative that succeeds not only in telling us what the Church is but in bringing out the unique richness of her many-sided reality.

The Fathers of Vatican II quite consciously elected to begin this magnum opus on the Church with a chapter entitled "The Mystery of the Church." Yes: mystery. The word recurs not only in the title but repeatedly in the text (e.g., *LG* 5, 39, 44, and 63). What was meant by "mystery" was explained during the Council by one of the Council Fathers, Bishop Emilio Guano of Livorno, Italy, speaking on October 2, 1963: "This word ['mystery']," he said, "is taken from sacred Scripture; it seems suitable for expressing the fact that the external visibility of the Church, like the holy human nature of Christ, both conceals and reveals the inner divine reality of the Church, a reality which surpasses all knowledge."

In other words, although the Church as an institution is quite visibly and immediately present in the world as an institution, she also possesses, for the sake of our salvation, an invisible divine and transcendent nature. Pope Paul VI referred to this in his opening address to the Council's Second Session, on September 29, 1963, when he said that "the Church is a mystery, a mystic reality, steeped in the presence of God." That is, the Church is more than can be defined in propositions or described in words, although—what should be superfluous to state—it is an integral part of her nature to make use of mystery as well as of propositions addressed to the mind, as in this present Constitution on the Church.

Nor was the choice of the term "mystery" to frame Vatican II's teaching about the Church merely a matter of speaking. On the contrary, as we shall see, the emphasis on what Paul VI styled the "mystic reality" of the Church has important implications for how *Lumen Gentium* has treated such questions as Church membership and those "elements of sanctification and Christian truth . . . found outside [the] visible confines" of the Church.

Furthermore, *Lumen Gentium* does plainly teach not only that the Church is the sole Church of Christ with the *fullness* of Christ's truth and means of grace but also that the Church is necessary for salvation (cf. *LG* 14). It then goes on to explain how the truths and graces of Christ granted to the Church can nevertheless be extended beyond her visible boundaries. This, indeed, is one of the most mysterious of realities in the total mystery of the Church.

Because the Church, *Lumen Gentium* declares, "is the kingdom of Christ *already present in mystery* . . . Christ inaugurated the kingdom of heaven on earth and revealed to us his mystery" (*LG* 3; emphasis added). The Church then perpetuates and carries on this kingdom down through history. The visible Catholic Church, known to history and present in the world, is continuous with "the kingdom" preached by Jesus—although the full identity of the latter is still in the process of being realized. It is therefore not yet complete, but, as *Lumen Gentium* itself states farther on, the Church will achieve "perfection only in the glory of heaven" (*LG* 48).

Parallel with the theme of "mystery" in *Lumen Gentium* is the idea of sacrament. In the very first paragraph of the document, it is stated that "the Church, in Christ, is in the nature of a sacrament—a sign and instrument, that is, of communion with God and of unity among men" (*LG* 1). The Church is the "sign and instrument," that is, that Christ uses to perpetuate his word and his work in the world. This sacramental theme recurs later on, where the Church is again described as "a visible sacrament" (*LG* 9); finally, quite simply, she is described as "the universal sacrament of salvation" (*LG* 48).

The Vatican II Constitution on the Liturgy, *Sacrosanctum Concilium*, had already taken up the theme of the Church as a sacrament ahead of *Lumen Gentium*, notably in its first chapter, where, quoting the old Roman Missal, it declares that "it was from the side of Christ as he slept the sleep of death upon the cross that there came forth the wondrous sacrament of the whole Church" (*SC* 5).

Now, sacraments, as we know from the *Catechism of the Catholic Church*, are "efficacious signs of grace, instituted by Christ and entrusted to the Church, by which divine life is dispensed to us" (*CCC* 131). They are visible signs that contain and convey the graces they signify. As every properly catechized Catholic should know, there are seven sacraments in the Church: baptism, confirmation, Eucharist, penance, anointing of the sick, holy matrimony, and holy orders. So in describing, by analogy, the Church herself as a sacrament, *Lumen Gentium* is saying not only that all sacraments come through the Church but that this fact represents another all-important dimension of the Church understood as mystery. The original New Testament Greek word *mysterion*, in fact, is translated into Latin not only as *mysterium* but also as *sacramentum*. The Eastern Churches even call the seven sacraments "the holy mysteries" (cf. *CCC* 774).

The decision of the Fathers of Vatican II to frame their description of the Church in terms of mystery and of the Church's own essential sacramental nature aptly expresses profound truths about the nature and mission of the Church that it was precisely their aim to set forth. In the same vein, they made prominent use of the various symbols and metaphors, most of them scriptural, that have traditionally been employed to characterize the Church. These include the Sheepfold of Christ the Good Shepherd, the Tilled Field or Vineyard of the Lord, the House of God, the New Jerusalem, and the Bride of Christ (cf. *LG* 6). Throughout *Lumen Gentium*, not surprisingly, the Church is referred to as the Body of Christ, as it is so often in the New Testament itself.

In short, in relying upon Scripture and Tradition to supply an abundance of names by which the Church has been known, the first chapter of *Lumen Gentium* succeeds quite well in conveying the basic message that the Church is indeed a manifold mystery and that many aspects of her life and teaching are most properly understood in that light. If the Church were not a mystery, would she be the Church Christ intended her to be?

II.

The well-known symbol or metaphor of the Church that has most prominently come to be identified with Vatican Council II is surely the term "the People of God." This is the title of the second chapter of *Lumen Gentium*. Many of the more liberal interpreters of the Council were not slow to seize upon this metaphor of the People of God. It quickly became a popular slogan and was often taken as the basic theme of Vatican II and of *Lumen Gentium*, sometimes to the exclusion of almost everything else the Council did or said. Promoting agendas supposedly favoring the People of God came to be considered the essence of what Vatican II was all about.

Probably as many of the errors and false starts that followed in the wake of Vatican II came from the misunderstanding or misinterpretation of this metaphor as from any other single source. It was regularly—and erroneously—taken to mean some kind of "democratization" of the Church, as if the Church were now some "big happy family" in which everybody now enjoyed "equality," the distinctions between hierarchy, clergy, religious, and laity becoming deliberately blurred. Henceforth whatever Church authority might see fit to decide or decree, for example, came to be thought of as of little moment; what "the people" thought was now what was supposed to count. "The people are the Church" became an often repeated (and mindless) popular slogan. Not infrequently the phrase was taken to mean "the people" against the hierarchy or the pastors!

The well-known liberal Vaticanologist, the late Peter Hebblethwaite, for example, in his biography *Paul VI: The First Modern Pope*, wrote with a naïveté surprising in one supposedly so knowledgeable in Church affairs when commenting on the arrangements being made in the immediate postconciliar years to implement the Council: "Where were the laity?" he asked. "Declared the People of God by the Council, with a radical equality in grace before the Lord, they nevertheless had no place in the decision-making processes of the Church"—as if "radical equality in grace" necessarily entailed a role in the "decision-making processes of the Church." This is an assumption that the radical feminists too have been too often prone to make. But the "decision making" in the Church necessarily carried out by her appointed leaders hardly equates with the grace of the Holy Spirit conveyed through the Church to the faithful; this, again, is to treat the Church as *only* an "institution."

What *Lumen Gentium* actually says about the People of God, however, differs substantially from, if it is not diametrically opposed to, such typical popular ideas or interpretations of the Council. For one thing, the concept of the People of God *includes* the hierarchy and the clergy and the religious; they too belong to the People of God and are "members" of the Church, after all! The People of God are not just the laity! At the simplest level, *Lumen Gentium* notes that "God willed to make men holy and save them, not as individuals without any bond or link between them, but rather to make them into a people who might acknowledge him and serve him in holiness" (*LG* 9).

Thus, God first called Israel as a messianic people and made a covenant with them; and then, with the new covenant in his blood, Christ constituted the New Israel, the Church: "a chosen race, a royal priesthood, a holy nation . . . who in times past were not a people, but now are the People of God" (1 Pet 2:9–10).

As we might have surmised, then, the idea of the People of God, as set forth in *Lumen Gentium*, is primarily a *religious* idea, not a populist or "democratic" one. Its sources are in Scripture, and it was this religious idea that was primarily in the minds of the Council Fathers. "The people are the Church" only in the sense and to the extent that "they repent and believe in the Gospel" (Mk 1:14) and then are "incorporated into the Church by baptism" (*LG* 10). The document states quite plainly, echoing John XXIII's aim for the Council as a whole, that "the Church, clasping sinners to her bosom, at once holy and always in need of purification, follows constantly the path of penance and renewal [*renovatio*]" (*LG* 8).

However, "all men are called to belong to the new People of God," the Council declares further, which "while remaining one and one only, is to be spread throughout the whole world and to all ages in order that the design of God's will may be fulfilled" (*LG* 13). Moreover—and this is another aspect of the mystery of the Church—"the faithful scattered throughout the world are in communion with each other in the Holy Spirit" (*LG* 13). Again, this new People of God,

> although it does not actually include all men, and at times may appear as a small flock, is, however, a most sure seed of unity, hope,

> and salvation for the whole human race. Established by Christ as a communion of life, love, and truth, it is taken up by him also as the instrument for the salvation of all; as the light of the world and the salt of the earth (cf. Mt 5:13–16), it is sent forth into the whole world. . . . Destined to extend to all regions of the earth, it enters into human history, though it transcends at once all times and all racial boundaries. (*LG* 9)

Thus, the phrase "the People of God," in other words, is nothing else but another description of *the Catholic Church*, treated in this case as yet one more—and very basic—aspect of her "mystery." Vatican II was determined to present the Church in the many aspects she possesses but especially in her "mystery," as expressed in the title of the first chapter of *Lumen Gentium*. The People of God concept is one important aspect of this mystery. The People of God are those who benefit from the means for their sanctification and salvation provided to the Church by Christ. In view of the importance of these means, it should not be surprising that the seven sacraments of the Church are enumerated and described at this point in the text; and they are described from a scriptural and historical—and Christocentric—perspective.

It is at this point too that the important issue of Church *membership* is treated. *Lumen Gentium*'s treatment of this particular subject is one of the most important things that Vatican II accomplished. It is good to quote here some of the Council's actual words on the subject:

> Fully incorporated into the Church are those who, possessing the Spirit of Christ, accept all the means of salvation given to the Church, together with her entire organization, and who—by the bonds constituted by the profession of faith, the sacraments, ecclesiastical government, and communion—are joined in the visible structure of the Church of Christ, who rules her through the Supreme Pontiff and the bishops. (*LG* 14)

This definition of Church membership brings us back to what is so often pejoratively styled "the institutional Church." Yet what else should anybody have expected? The kind of "belonging" described here obviously goes along with the visible, sacramental, sacerdotal, and hierarchical Church that the Catholic Church indubitably is. The text quoted here is followed by a passage that notes that it is not enough merely to "belong"—one must also "persevere in charity." Those who fail in this latter task are "not saved," as a matter of fact, according to Vatican II. Such is the doctrine that this document teaches. Moreover:

> All children of the Church should remember that their exalted condition results not from their own merits but from the grace of Christ. If they fail to respond in thought, word, and deed to that grace, not only shall they not be saved, but they shall be the more severely judged. (*LG* 14)

Thus, salvation is *not* guaranteed by Church membership. What the latter provides is the prospect and hope of salvation, along with the graces from Christ through the sacraments of the Church to enable one to achieve it.

It should thus be clear that Vatican II's teaching here corresponds to the traditional Catholic teaching regarding Church membership. What the Council then goes on to establish, however, represents an important development in this traditional Catholic teaching. This development can be seen in the Council's use of the phrase "*fully* incorporated into the Church" (emphasis added). Such a full incorporation into the Church as an attribute of true membership in her implies the possibility that there are those who are perhaps in some sense "members" of the Church yet who are not "fully" so. In other words, there are *degrees* of Church membership. We saw this in the discussion of *subsistit in.* And, indeed, *Lumen Gentium* goes on to say quite explicitly that:

> The Church knows that she is *joined* in many ways to the baptized who are honored by the name of Christian, but who do not, however, profess the Catholic faith in its entirety, or have not preserved unity or communion under the successor of Peter. (*LG* 15; emphasis added)

These Christians, the Dogmatic Constitution on the Church goes on to say (*LG* 15), "are indeed in some real way joined to us in the Holy Spirit." This is another manifestation of the mystery of the Church. Once again, we find ourselves coming back to those "elements of sanctification and truth . . . found outside [the] confines" of the visible

Church. For the use of the word "joined" here again implies that non-Catholics who are "validly" baptized, that is, baptized "in the name of the Father, and of the Son, and of the Holy Spirit," already possess by virtue of that baptism an incipient kind of "membership" in the true Church of Christ, the Catholic Church.

In fact, it would seem that the Church has always held this position by refusing to rebaptize (or by baptizing only "conditionally") those recognized to have been already validly baptized in the name of the Father, and of the Son, and of the Holy Spirit. Vatican II, though, brought out this point as an explicit development of the Catholic doctrine concerning Church membership.

It is not that the Church has abandoned St. Cyprian of Carthage's famous dictum that there is no salvation outside the Church (*extra Ecclesiam nulla salus*). Popes Innocent III and Boniface VIII, along with the Fourth Lateran Council, among other Church authorities, including a pope as recently as Blessed Pope Pius IX, have solemnly reaffirmed this dictum. The important thing is what it means and how it is to be understood. Although it is not actually quoted in this chapter of *Lumen Gentium*, its meaning is included in what the text does say, namely, that the Church "is necessary for salvation" (*LG* 14). As far as validly baptized non-Catholic Christians are concerned, then, it would seem that they are not to be considered "outside the Church" in a way that would see them necessarily deprived of salvation. The graces of Christ through the Church, in other words, can be mysteriously extended to them by their baptism.

This whole notion, of course, has important ecumenical implications. It points, inevitably, to the ideas of "full communion" or merely "imperfect communion"—ideas that were worked out more explicitly in the Council's Decree on Ecumenism, *Unitatis Redintegratio*.

In this perspective, though, St. Cyprian's dictum might better be explained by saying that Christ's salvation comes—though "mysteriously"—*through* the Church. All salvation, if it is salvation, comes from Christ in any case. Yet since Christ has established his Church as the "sign and instrument" of it—as the "sacrament" of it, in other words—the Church truly, though mysteriously, participates in salvation where salvation is in fact effected.

The second chapter of *Lumen Gentium* on the People of God goes on to teach, without going into detail or providing any explanation—although extensive references to previous teaching documents of the Church concerning Church membership are provided in footnotes—that the mystery of salvation in and through Jesus Christ can extend even beyond the ranks of the baptized. In a teaching that has become very well known, the dogmatic constitution declares:

> Those who through no fault of their own do not know the Gospel of Christ or his Church, but who nevertheless seek God with a sincere heart, and, moved by grace, try in their action to do his will as they know it through the dictates of their conscience—those too may achieve eternal salvation. Nor shall divine Providence deny the assistance necessary for salvation to those who, without any fault of theirs, have not yet arrived at an explicit knowledge of God, and who, not without grace, strive to lead a good life. (*LG* 16)

Here again, this teaching, though newly formulated by the Council, is quite traditional. Blessed Pope Pius IX, for example, wrote almost as a matter of course that

> those who are invincibly ignorant of our most holy religion, and who carefully observe the natural law and its precepts placed by God in the hearts of all men, and, disposed to obey God, lead an honest and upright life, can, with the help of the divine light and grace, merit eternal life; for God has perfect knowledge, examines and judges the minds, the souls, thoughts and deeds of all men, and does not permit, in his sovereign goodness and mercy, any man not culpable of willful sin to be punished with eternal torment. (Pope Pius IX, Letter *Quanto Conficiamur Moerore*, dated August 10, 1863)

Lumen Gentium has thus enunciated no new doctrine in teaching that some who appear to be "outside" the visible Church can nevertheless be saved. The Council's teaching concerning salvation and Church membership has merely developed an old doctrine and placed the question of the possible salvation of non-Catholics within the context of the Church's overall salvific work—which is Christ's salvific work. Meanwhile, *Lumen Gentium* does not neglect the negative of all this, namely, the lot of those who do not "seek God with a sincere heart." Human beings are free to reject God. They can suffer the loss of their souls in spite of the grace of Christ offered to all through the Church.

This has always been the teaching of the Church, of course. *Lumen Gentium* does not dwell unduly on the possibility of the loss of one's soul, but it does explicitly refer both to the temptations of the Evil One and to the possibility of "ultimate despair" (*LG* 16). As we shall see later on, though, the whole question of the "last things" does constitute one area where this great dogmatic constitution perhaps falls a bit short of saying everything that should have been said. Nevertheless, the text does not try to ignore or evade the topic; much further on, it refers again to the devil and to the "eternal fire" (*LG* 48). The text also plainly states that "they could not be saved who, knowing that the Catholic Church was founded as necessary by God through Christ, would refuse either to enter it, or to remain in it" (*LG* 14).

In view of the urgent importance of salvation in Christ, and of the indispensable role of the Catholic faith in qualifying and preparing souls for that salvation, this second chapter of *Lumen Gentium* on the People of God concludes with an exhortation to the effect that "each disciple of Christ has the obligation of spreading the faith to the best of his ability" (*LG* 17). Just, as we shall see, as *Lumen Gentium* will summon "all" to holiness of life, so it summons "all" to bear witness to and spread the faith of Christ. The text had already made clear that "the holy People of God spreads abroad a living witness to him" (*LG* 12), and here we see the truest significance of the concept of the People of God as this was truly taught by the Council: this holy people was not at all seen as some supposed "democratic" element within the Church aiming to "balance" the hierarchy and the clergy; rather, it was seen as the bearer to the world of the Church's faith, which, long since, Jesus had commanded be preached "to the whole creation" (Mk 16:15).

All these themes would be expanded upon and amplified in the Council's later Decree on the Apostolate of Lay People, *Apostolicam Actuositatem*, and the Decree on the Church's Missionary Activity, *Ad Gentes Divinitus*—both decrees approved by the Council in 1965, a year later than *Lumen Gentium*. Meanwhile, though, *Lumen Gentium*, since it was an earlier document, had already taken up and laid out important themes that the later Council documents would then elaborate upon and develop further. Some of the most important themes of Vatican II received "double treatment" in this way. *Lumen Gentium,* though, will usually be found to be the primary document.

The concept of the People of God, in particular, should be understood primarily as referring to all those who profess their faith in Christ in the Church and who are therefore necessarily the principal ones obliged to bear witness to the faith and promote it in a world today perhaps more than ever in need of the truth and grace of Jesus Christ.

III.

In *Lumen Gentium*'s third chapter, entitled "The Church Is Hierarchical," we finally arrive at the kind of description of the "institutional Church" with which we are most familiar. The Council Fathers deliberately placed the chapters on the mystery of the Church and the People of God before the chapter on the hierarchy in order to make clear that the latter does not constitute the *essence* of the Church and also to show that the hierarchy has been constituted *in service* to the deeper mystery of the Church in her essence and as God's assembled holy people. Jesus told his apostles that their authority was not given to them to enable them to lord it over others but rather to enable them to serve (cf. Mt 20:25–28). So should it be with the Catholic bishops, the successors of the apostles, in the Church today.

The organization and governance of the Church, though necessary—and instituted by Christ himself in the sense that he appointed and commissioned the apostles—is still of lesser importance than what the Church is, namely, the Body of Christ and the extension of his word and his work in the world and down through history. It was one of the conscious aims of *Lumen Gentium* to bring this out unmistakably.

At the Council, one of the young bishops who insisted upon treating the People of God ahead of the hierarchy in the *schema De Ecclesia* that became *Lumen Gentium,* in an intervention delivered in October 1963, was none other than Karol Wojtyla, then administrator, later archbishop, of the diocese of Kraków in Poland. His argument was that the whole should be treated before the part.

Lumen Gentium's chapter 3 immediately points out the obvious, namely, that "in order to shepherd the People of God and to increase its numbers without cease, Christ the Lord set up in the Church a variety of offices which aim at the good of the whole body." The holders of these offices, the text goes on to specify, "are invested with a sacred power" (*LG* 18). Though all souls are equal in the sight of God, and equal in grace before the Lord, as the document had earlier pointed out, some distinctions are still important and necessary among the People of God on earth. Some among this People of God must indeed be set apart through the sacrament of holy orders in order to fulfill the special functions in the Church, especially sacramental, by which she helps bring sanctification and salvation to all.

The document identifies these essential Church officeholders as the ancient ones of bishops, presbyters (or priests), and deacons. From the earliest records we possess concerning the primitive Church, these three offices were present. Christ founded the Church on the apostles, who in due course appointed priests and deacons as helpers. The New Testament itself attests to this (cf. Acts 6:1–4; 14:23). All these Church "officeholders" are set apart by the sacrament of holy orders in order to carry out the threefold task first confided to the apostles of teaching, ruling, and sanctifying in the Church.

And just as there is a fullness of Church membership, as we saw in the previous section of this chapter, so there is a "fullness of the sacrament of Orders" (*LG* 21 and 26). The bishops, Vatican II plainly teaches, enjoy that fullness, and are the successors of Christ's apostles. Indeed, Vatican II said about itself:

> This sacred synod, following in the steps of the First Vatican Council, teaches and declares with it that Jesus Christ, the eternal pastor, set up the Holy Church by entrusting the apostles with their mission as he himself had been sent by the Father (cf. Jn 20:21). He willed that their successors, the bishops, namely, should be shepherds in the Church until the end of the world. In order that the episcopate itself, however, might be one and undivided, he put Peter at the head of the other apostles, and in him he set up a lasting and visible source and foundation both of the faith and of communion. This teaching concerning the institution, the permanence,

> the nature, and import of the sacred primacy of the Roman pontiff and his infallible teaching office, [this] sacred synod proposes anew to be firmly believed by all the faithful. (*LG* 18)

Thus, it is all here: everything that the Church has traditionally taught about the primacy, infallibility, and universal jurisdiction of the pope as the successor of the apostle Peter and head of the whole Church on earth is reiterated and even strengthened here in *Lumen Gentium.* The point is repeated over and over again, as a matter of fact. The idea that Vatican II in general, and this dogmatic constitution in particular, somehow downplayed the role of the pope, and ushered in a "new Church" in which the traditional understanding of the pope's supreme authority no longer obtains, is specifically excluded by the plain and repeated language of *Lumen Gentium.*

In fact, the text goes on to underline the unique powers, responsibilities, and prerogatives of the pope in other respects, for example, with regard to ecumenical councils (cf. *LG* 22). In no way is the pope's office or role in the Church diminished, as has been believed and repeated by some. On the contrary, no other Church document has laid out a stronger or more complete authoritative statement of the pope's position, function, and role in the Church than what is found here. Everything that Vatican I decreed in the matter is repeated here, often in the same words.

However, *Lumen Gentium* aimed to go farther. Just as Vatican I's dogmatic constitution *Pastor Aeternus* set forth for all time the Church's teaching on the pope and on the papacy, so Vatican II aimed to accomplish the same result for the bishops and for the episcopacy. *Lumen Gentium* expressly proposed "to proclaim publicly and enunciate clearly the doctrine concerning bishops, successors of the apostles, who together with Peter's successor, the Vicar of Christ, and the visible head of the whole Church, direct the house of the living God" (*LG* 18).

It was not only highly appropriate that Vatican II should take up the subject of the bishops in a special way; the Council was actually convened with the idea in mind that this topic would be one of its principal preoccupations. While setting forth its teaching regarding the pope and the papacy, the First Vatican Council had fully intended to do the same for the bishops and the episcopacy as well but was interrupted by the outbreak of the Franco-Prussian War in 1870. When the French troops protecting Rome and its immediate environs—what was left of the old Papal States—were rather suddenly withdrawn to join the war effort in France, the troops of the newly unified Kingdom of Italy immediately entered Rome and put an end to the temporal power that had been exercised by the popes for nearly a millennium and a half. The pope, Blessed Pius IX, henceforth became "a prisoner in the Vatican" (his characterization).

The Italian government that had taken over the city of Rome tacitly allowed the pope with his Curia to occupy St. Peter's and its immediate environs and a few other Church properties. But this new Italian government did not hesitate to take over the pope's former Quirinale Palace, for example, for the use of the head of the Italian government; and, meanwhile, the Holy See *was* henceforth hemmed in by unfriendly anticlerical Italian governments for decades to come. This situation obtained for the popes until their independence and sovereignty over Vatican City was finally recognized by the Lateran Pacts of 1929. Under such circumstances, the normal conduct of Church affairs was rather severely hampered, and so it was no surprise that Vatican I was never reconvened in the immediate years following its abrupt end. As a result, no conciliar document was ever issued covering the episcopacy in the way that *Pastor Aeternus* had covered the papacy. *Lumen Gentium*, more than ninety years later, would turn out to be the document that finally would complement and complete *Pastor Aeternus* (while reiterating its substance).

While reinforcing the teaching that Christ built his Church upon the rock of Peter and his successors in the See of Rome, as attested in the deservedly famous passage in Matthew 16:16–20, *Lumen Gentium* went on to make clear that Christ established his Church also on the other apostles and their successors, the bishops of the Catholic Church, as well as on Peter and his successors, the bishops of Rome. Indeed, Christ had explicitly promised *all* the apostles in Matthew 18:18 that whatever *they* bound or loosed on earth would be bound or loosed in heaven, just as he had made a similar promise to Peter at Caesarea Philippi, as recorded earlier in the same Gospel of Matthew.

Thus, the Catholic Church was established on the rock of Peter *and* on the other apostles. Just as Peter and his successors were given authority over the whole Church, so the other apostles and their successors were given authority over that portion of the Church, the individual dioceses, as they came to be called, that were allotted to them. The authority granted to the popes and the bishops, transmitted to them by means of sacred ordination in a direct line from Peter and the other apostles, constituted them all alike as "teachers of doctrine, ministers of sacred worship, and holders of office in government" (*LG* 20); that is, all bishops alike sanctify, teach, and rule in the Church, the pope over the whole Church, and each bishop over his own diocese. Just as Christ was priest, prophet, and king, so each ordained bishop carries out these same functions in Christ's Church in his diocese—as the pope carries them out over the Church as a whole.

The Catholic Church was thus set up with an unusual if not unique twofold authority structure: even as bishops exercise plenary authority in their own dioceses, they do so only under the general overall authority of the pope. Nevertheless, the authority bishops possess is *theirs*; it is not delegated to them by the pope: "nor are they to be regarded as vicars of the Roman pontiff," *Lumen Gentium* strongly emphasizes (*LG* 20). The pope is the Vicar of Christ, indeed, but each bishop is similarly a "vicar of Christ" in his own diocese: "They exercise the powers which they possess in their own right" (*LG* 27). This is one of the reasons, by the way, why, once installed, bishops are rarely removed, although the pope ultimately does have the authority to remove them—as Pope Pius VII once removed an entire national hierarchy, that of France, and appointed an entirely new hierarchy in its place, in connection with the restoration of the Church following the ravages of the French Revolution. As a rule, though, popes do not normally remove bishops except for the gravest of reasons; for bishops are *not* simply "managers," subject to "hiring and firing" under the pope; they are commissioned by Christ and act in his name.

At the same time, though, as *Lumen Gentium* repeatedly makes clear, the authority of a bishop cannot be exercised except in communion with the pope and with the other bishops of the Church. The bishop receives his full powers at his ordination, though he can licitly exercise them only with the consent of the pope and in communion with his fellow bishops. This idea of the necessary "communion" of the bishops with each other and with the pope is also very strongly emphasized in *Lumen Gentium*—as it has normally been in the practice of the Catholic tradition down through history. The idea can be traced back to the apostles themselves; the document specifies that Christ constituted them "in the form of a *college*, or permanent assembly, at the head of which he placed Peter, chosen from amongst them" (*LG* 19; emphasis added). In the document's own words:

> Just as, in accordance with the Lord's decree, St. Peter and the rest of the apostles constituted a unique apostolic college, so in like fashion the Roman Pontiff, Peter's successor, and the bishops, the successors of the apostles, are related with and united to one another. (*LG* 22)

And just as the original college of the apostles functioned with and under Peter, so "the college or body of bishops has . . . no authority unless united with the Roman pontiff, Peter's successor" (*LG* 22). The very notion that the bishops of the Catholic Church constitute a permanent "college," or organic body, was one of Vatican II's most heavily debated and controversial issues. The whole question was raised and debated in order to give the bishops their due and situate them properly within the Christ-established hierarchical structure of the Church—just as Vatican I had properly situated the pope at the head of Christ's Church and described his various powers and responsibilities.

But the issue remained controversial, if only because many Council Fathers feared that trying to bring out and describe what the collegiality of the bishops actually consisted of could, and perhaps inevitably would, undermine the already established and defined position of the pope in and at the head of the Church. In the light of the public contestation of the pope's authority that followed Vatican II—for example, the claim of some dissident theologians that a consensus of their opinions constitutes a kind of "magisterium" equivalent to the Christ-established Magisterium, or teaching authority, of the pope and the bishops—it can hardly be maintained that these fears of an undermining of the pope's authority were groundless.

Because of the great importance in the Church of the relationship of the Catholic bishops with the supreme bishop, the pope, and with each other, we need to examine in further detail just what it was that Vatican II decided about episcopal "collegiality," and why.

IV.

Some of the people in the postconciliar era who at various times expressed disapproval of Pope John Paul II, or even opposed him, often labeled him a "restorationist." In the eyes of such people—usually they themselves were of a decidedly "liberal" bent—John Paul II was supposedly trying to "restore" the pre–Vatican II Church and take us back to the era of what was seen as the preconciliar centralization of authority in Rome. In reality, of course, John Paul II was often *applying* what Vatican II really said when he was accused of being a "restorationist." Those who disapproved of his actions generally did not know what the Council really had said but were simply relying on a vein of liberal popular opinion about what the Council was *supposed* to have said.

Such people often seem to have interpreted Vatican II's teaching about the collegiality of the bishops as somehow diluting the supreme, central authority in the Church of the pope. For them it seems to have meant a kind of "federalism" in the Church, with the authority of the bishops now "balancing" the authority of the pope.

A correct reading of *Lumen Gentium*, however, reveals nothing of the sort: the pope's authority after Vatican II remained what it always had been. What the Council primarily wanted to do was to define and describe the *bishop's* proper authority in his own diocese—as well as the manner in which each of the Church's bishops in his own diocese also works in cooperation with the other Catholic bishops, each the head of his own diocese. Vatican II's teaching on collegiality is in no way another version of American-style federalism, although some people continue to try to interpret it that way. The Council Fathers were thus correct in their understanding that the concept had to be precisely described and defined.

Typical of the reservations concerning collegiality expressed by many of the bishops at the Council were the remarks of Archbishop

Geraldo de Proença Sigaud of Diamantina, Brazil, who warned in an intervention on October 9, 1963, that granting ultimate authority to the collegiality of the bishops, even when acting in concert with the pope—this had always been the case with ecumenical councils, of course—would establish a sort of "world parliament" within the Church, something that Jesus Christ had most assuredly not established. Another possible outcome to be feared would be the enactments of decisions by national conferences or regional councils of bishops, to which the pope might then find it practically impossible to deny his assent. "Such bodies would present very serious impediments . . . to the exercise of the supreme ordinary power by the Holy Father," the Brazilian archbishop averred, "and also *to that of the ordinary power of the individual bishop*" (emphasis added). The individual bishop might find it difficult if not impossible not to go along with decisions voted by a majority of his own particular bishops' conference.

This latter problem proved to be all too real in the postconciliar years, as a matter of fact. Most Catholic bishops evidently have found it difficult to diverge very far, if at all, from what the bishops' conference to which they belong decides. This can be a very serious defect when bishops' conferences—as has unfortunately actually sometimes been the case with the U.S. bishops' conference—decide as a practical matter on such things as trying to promote feminist inclusive language, tolerating theological dissent, allowing a seriously deficient "catechetical establishment" to monopolize the teaching of religion, turning a blind eye to serious departures from Church discipline in many religious orders, or failing to enforce canons in the Code of Canon Law such as those pertaining to universities. The same kind of thing occurred in some of the Latin American bishops' conferences with regard to the tolerance of quasi-Marxist ideas in the once very popular "theology of liberation."

An individual bishop usually finds it difficult if not impossible in practice to go against, even if only tacitly, what his colleagues have decided in some matters such as these, even, sometimes, when Church law pretty clearly stipulates otherwise.

The experience of the postconciliar years thus demonstrated how real and well-grounded were some of the fears of the bishops at the

Council who opposed emphasizing episcopal collegiality. Moreover, the typical way in which episcopal collegiality has been understood following the Council *has* tended toward undermining and downgrading the pope's position and authority, in spite of *Lumen Gentium*'s plain and strong language to the contrary. Bishops can be tempted to disregard and undermine the pope's authority *even though* he may just be calling them back to their plain duty. If they have in fact been neglecting their duty in any way, they are almost certainly going to resent being reminded of it.

This common and perhaps inevitable attitude can be verified by reference to such phenomena as the much-publicized 1996 Oxford University lecture of retired archbishop John R. Quinn of San Francisco, a former president of the U.S. bishops' conference, who in his Oxford lecture called for a "decentralization" of "Vatican authority." What really seemed to be at issue for Archbishop Quinn was perceived Roman interference concerning some of the decisions of the U.S. bishops' conference (apparently seen by him as "micromanagement"). Yet, at the time, in the 1990s, the U.S. bishops *did* sometimes seem to be dragging their feet on such things as the implementation of Pope John Paul II's apostolic constitution *Ex Corde Ecclesiae* on Catholic universities; they were still continuing to press for feminist so-called inclusive language in the liturgy in the face of a rather definite contrary judgment by the Congregation for Divine Worship and the Discipline of the Sacraments; also, openly dissenting theologians and others sometimes *were* being allowed to remain "in good standing" in the Church without correction by the hierarchy. And so on. Archbishop Quinn himself had headed an inquiry into the state of the consecrated religious life in the United States that essentially provided a whitewash covering over aberrations that had become notorious. Roman officials, including the pope himself, were simply doing their jobs when trying to correct the bishops on such matters.

True collegiality thus surely requires considerably more than just having Rome henceforth give the bishops their headship. What if they are *not* doing their jobs, as the revelations of clerical sex abuse beginning in January 2002 indicated and as the U.S. bishops' own National Review Board later confirmed?

However that may be, the issue of the collegiality of the Catholic bishops with each other, and with their head, the pope, was aired and debated much more thoroughly at the Second Vatican Council than perhaps any other single topic. Father Ralph Wiltgen, S.V.D., in his lively short history of the Council, *The Rhine Flows into the Tiber*, which we have already mentioned—the best of the histories of the Council that came out immediately after it completed its work—called it "the most important and dramatic battle that took place at the Second Vatican Council." Similarly, the pseudonymous "Xavier Rynne," who was actually an American Redemptorist priest and historian, Father Francis Xavier Murphy, in his history of the Council, *Vatican Council II*, made famous by its serial appearance in the *New Yorker* magazine during the Council, called it "the very core of Vatican Council II."

Pope Paul VI, in his opening address to the Third Session of the Council, called upon the bishops present to decide the question and declared that the Council's decision "will certainly be what distinguishes this solemn and historic synod in the memory of future ages." The pope said that he looked forward "with great expectations and confidence to this discussion which, taking for granted the dogmatic declarations of the First Vatican Council regarding the Roman Pontiff, will go on to develop the doctrine regarding the episcopate, its function, and its relationship with Peter."

The path toward this goal proved far from smooth, however. There were extensive and sometimes acrimonious debates, along with much maneuvering behind the scenes. A series of test votes taken on October 30, 1963, indicated general agreement among a majority of the Council Fathers in favor of some general propositions affirming episcopal collegiality; but then it proved that there were further disagreements on the text of the revised *schema* that had been prepared by the Theological Commission headed by Alfredo Cardinal Ottaviani, prefect of the Congregation of the Holy Office (which later, on December 7, 1965, became the Congregation for the Doctrine of the Faith).

Cardinal Ottaviani was one of the most intelligent and determined of the "conservative" bishops at the Council, and hence in the atmosphere of liberal euphoria that then reigned he regularly suffered from a very bad press at the hands of those who were anxious to see approved what they evidently considered to be a long overdue "democratization" of the Church. These kinds of people in the media tended to see the whole collegiality issue as a kind of American-style "check and balance" procedure necessary to curb or restrict the traditional papal centralization of authority in the Holy See. That was hardly what the debate was really about, of course; there were serious theological and practical issues at stake; and it was important that the Council get it right *because* a clear and definitive Church teaching on the episcopacy was long overdue.

Cardinal Ottaviani was nevertheless viewed and described as one of the principal obstacles to what the Council was trying to do. He certainly did *not* enjoy a sympathetic press and media. He generally gave as good as he got, however. A very witty man, he joked that his favorite scriptural passage on episcopal collegiality was Mark 14:50, which reads: "And they all forsook him and fled"! When informed that the German bishops, who strongly favored the approval of a teaching on collegiality, having promoted it from the first days of the Council, "wanted his head," Cardinal Ottaviani riposted that "it would be the first time they would be in possession of any brains"! The favorite joke at the Council told *about*, and at the expense of, this conservative Curia cardinal, though, had him boarding a taxi and asking to be taken to "the Council"—whereupon the taxi driver promptly headed for Trent!

It was during one of the debates on collegiality that Joseph Cardinal Frings of Cologne launched an attack on Cardinal Ottaviani's Holy Office, which, for liberal observers, was one of the high points of the Council. According to this intervention of Cardinal Frings, delivered in the *aula* of St. Peter's, the Holy Office's "methods in many cases no longer correspond to modern conditions and as a result many are scandalized. . . . No one should be judged and condemned without a hearing and without an opportunity to correct his book or his action."

This criticism was somewhat unfair, or at least exaggerated, however, since the Holy Office did have a procedure in place for persons accused of doctrinal deviations; they *were* given a hearing and an opportunity to reply. It was true, though, that in the case of already published articles or books, the Holy Office generally did simply proceed to identify and condemn errors without recourse to the author. It was considered that the damage to the faith had already been done in the case of published books and articles. This sort of rationale certainly exposed the Holy Office to almost inevitable criticism by liberals, however; but most liberals apparently did not seem to think it was important or necessary to identify and try to correct errors in any case.

The Holy Office was similarly criticized for the "secrecy" of its proceedings (as the Congregation for the Doctrine of the Faith continues to be criticized today). But who in the world would ever want allegations of error or heresy to be publicized *before* they were proven to be true? Once again, the real, operative assumption on the part of many would seem to be that errors do not need to be corrected at all.

It is ironic that the criticism of the Holy Office at the Council should have been led by Joseph Cardinal Frings, of all people. For one of this Cologne cardinal's *periti* at the Council was none other than the young theologian Father Joseph Ratzinger, who one day would turn out to be a successor to Cardinal Ottaviani as prefect of the Congregation for the Doctrine of the Faith (where he too often suffered no little criticism himself, sometimes vicious criticism, such as being called by such names as "the enforcer," "God's Rottweiler," or "*der Panzerkardinal*").

In the end, Alfredo Cardinal Ottaviani was destined to be on the losing side of the collegiality debate at the Council. It happens to be the case, after all, that the pope and the bishops are united with each other in a "college." The apostles of Christ *did* form a "college," as their successors do. Thus, once the question was raised, the Council included a strong statement on the truth of their collegiality in *Lumen Gentium.* For his part, Cardinal Ottaviani surely did not doubt that the bishops when acting in concert with the pope constituted a "college"; his misgivings had to do with spelling this out in words vulnerable to serious misinterpretation. It can hardly be said, in the aftermath of the Council, that its teachings on this subject have *not* been subject to misinterpretation, after all, sometimes serious misinterpretation.

Once the Council adopted its doctrine in the matter, however, Cardinal Ottaviani naturally went along with the final decision, since the "orthodox" doctrine in the matter for this very "orthodox" prelate was that the valid acts of an ecumenical council of the Church, duly ratified by a pope, are nothing else but—according to St. Athanasius of Alexandria speaking about the decisions of the Council of Nicaea—"the word of the Lord"!

As the debate on collegiality progressed during the Third Session, more and more bishops came around, until finally a majority came to favor the idea. Nevertheless, Pope Paul VI was still obliged to make one of his more dramatic interventions in the conciliar process in order to bring along the last holdouts to what the Council was on its way to approving by a majority. For the pope understood that it needed to be approved by more than just a majority; it needed to be approved overwhelmingly in order to maintain the credibility of the Council.

To allay the fears of those who still thought the Council was going too far too fast out into uncharted waters, then, the pope decreed that a special explanatory note, or *Nota Explicativa Praevia* (commonly known since simply as the *Nota Praevia*), had to be prefixed to the text that became chapter 3 of the dogmatic constitution on which the Council Fathers had to vote. This decision of the pope's was announced to the Council as having come from "superior authority"—thus proving by itself that the pope *did* retain his ultimate primacy even within the framework of the episcopal collegiality that was now being solemnly approved.

The *Nota Praevia* explained "the mind and sense" in which chapter 3 and its particular subject matter was to be understood. It was later added as an appendix to the final, approved text of *Lumen Gentium* itself. Basically, this *Nota Praevia* reiterates and reaffirms the Church's understanding of the primacy and infallibility of the pope, as solemnly decreed by Vatican I. With this clarification, nearly all of the Council Fathers came around and voted to approve this long-disputed chapter 3 of *Lumen Gentium*, with its doctrine of episcopal collegiality.

It is not hard to understand why this whole question of the relationship between the pope and the bishops became such a bone of contention at Vatican II. The subject had long since been raised and debated following Vatican I, when it was thought by many that the position and powers of the Catholic bishops had simply been superseded and absorbed by those of the supreme pontiff, as spelled out in the definitions of Vatican I's *Pastor Aeternus.* The German "Iron Chancellor," Otto von Bismarck, for example, took it as an established fact that the

Vatican I definitions had effectively superseded the autonomy of the German bishops; this belief was one of his motives in launching his famous *Kulturkampf* ("culture battle") of the 1870s against the Catholic Church in Germany. He thought that he needed to protect the interests of the German state against what he viewed as papal totalitarianism.

Similarly, in Britain, four-time prime minister William Ewart Gladstone thought that the Vatican I definitions necessarily undermined the loyalty of British Catholics to the British crown, and he wrote a popular pamphlet on the subject. Gladstone's contention was to be answered, memorably, by John Henry Newman in the latter's famous *Letter to the Duke of Norfolk*, in which the true meaning and import of the primacy and infallibility of the pope were masterfully explained by Newman in a way that has hardly been equaled since.

But all of this meant that it was only after more than ninety years that the Church herself finally placed the definitions of 1870 in their proper perspective and explained the relative roles and relationships of the pope and the bishops in the Church of Christ. *Lumen Gentium* brought all this out more clearly than had ever been done, or had even been attempted, before. The Catholic Church's unique twofold authority structure had existed and functioned for centuries, from the time, in fact, that Jesus Christ first commissioned Peter and the other apostles; but the system had never really been clearly laid out and described, as finally was done in chapter 3 of Vatican II's Dogmatic Constitution on the Church, *Lumen Gentium*.

V.

The third chapter of *Lumen Gentium* on the hierarchy turned out to be controversial in other ways than in its treatment of episcopal collegiality. For example, the text concluded with the Council's interesting decision "to restore the diaconate to its permanent rank of the hierarchy" (*LG* 29). Deacons, established as helpers to the apostles, as attested in the Acts of the Apostles (cf. Acts 6:1–6), had long since in the Western Church become simply an ordained rank on the way to the priesthood. The proposal to revive the diaconate as a permanent ministry, however, was hotly debated at the Council, in part because of fears that the Catholic laity would be scandalized by the prospect of *married* deacons and that priestly celibacy could thereby be undermined. This seemed to be the belief of nearly all the Italian bishops, for example. And New York's Francis J. Cardinal Spellman, during the Council's Second Session, also delivered himself of a vigorous intervention arguing against the revival of the permanent diaconate, holding that it had become "obsolete" for good reasons and that its revival could undermine vocations to the priesthood.

On the other side of the argument, however, was the undoubted fact that the diaconate had formed part of the Church's sacred hierarchy in apostolic times. The triad of "bishops, priests, and deacons" comprised that hierarchy, and, within it, there were urgent ministerial tasks that permanent deacons could carry out in a renewed Church today. The world's missionary bishops, in particular, argued strenuously for a revived diaconate, as did most of the progressive "Rhine-flows-into-the Tiber" bishops from Belgium, France, Germany, and the Netherlands. At one point during the Second Session, Cardinal Ottaviani, in a spirited intervention, reproached certain unnamed *periti*—widely understood to be the influential Jesuits Karl Rahner and Gustav Martelet, along with the cardinal's own remote future "successor," Father Joseph Ratzinger—for "lobbying" various groups of bishops in favor of a restored diaconate. This was not the role of the *periti*, the Curia cardinal averred; nor should the Council be politicized, he thought, in the way these *periti* were acting.

In the end, though, the Council Fathers did decide to revive the permanent diaconate. This decision was recorded in the final paragraph of chapter 3 of *Lumen Gentium* (*LG* 29), and thus the diaconate became again a notable and visible reality in the postconciliar Church. Yet all of this, significant as it was going to be for the ongoing life of the Church, was still not the end of the significance of this so thoroughly controverted and debated chapter 3 of *Lumen Gentium*, entitled "The Church Is Hierarchical." We still have to devote, in fact, in sections that follow, more attention to a topic that in the postconciliar era came to loom much larger in importance than almost anything else in the chapter at all. It was a topic that the Council Fathers themselves scarcely even imagined at the time; for it was treated quite routinely, with very little debate, in the chapter's numbered section 25, which laid out the degrees and levels of authority in Church teachings—and the levels and degrees of belief in and assent to those Church teachings required of the faithful by the Church.

The topic in question was *theological dissent.* What was entirely not foreseen during the Council itself was the extent to which, in the postconciliar era, widespread theological dissent would attempt to undermine the very core of what *Lumen Gentium* 25 had taken great pains to affirm. *Lumen Gentium* 25 does not even seem to have been much debated at the Council. The attitude that reigned seemed to be that of Blessed John XXIII, as expressed in his opening address to the Council, namely, that no ecumenical council was necessary merely to deal with Church doctrine. He thought Church doctrine was "well-known and familiar to all"; the cheerful pope even thought, amazingly in retrospect, that "errors vanish as quickly as they arise, like fog before the sun." The *schema De Ecclesia* that became *Lumen Gentium* thus simply described the degrees and levels of magisterial teaching, and the degrees and levels of belief in and assent to these doctrines required of the faithful.

It was certainly not the case, though, that John XXIII considered doctrine unimportant. On the contrary, in that very same opening address to the Council, he had said that "the *greatest* concern of the Ecumenical Council is this: that the sacred deposit of Christian doctrine should be guarded and *taught more efficaciously*" (emphasis added). His great emphasis was on teaching the faith "more efficaciously." For him this meant that "the substance of the ancient doctrine of the deposit of the faith is one thing, and the way in which it is presented is another." One of the implications of this formulation was that John XXIII evidently thought that the faith had *not* always been taught as efficaciously as he believed possible and necessary, and the Council was supposed to be one of the remedies for this failing. Thus, one of the main things the Council was supposed to do, precisely, was to devise ways to propagate and expand "more efficaciously" the Catholic truths that were already supposedly established, known, and accepted by the Catholic faithful, according to John XXIII, but that now needed to be effectively conveyed to a modern world badly in need of them.

During the Council itself, there was hardly any suspicion at all that, in the postconciliar era, the Church would be faced with a crisis relating to her teaching authority that would undermine the very foundation of her ability to teach truth at all. Many if not most of the Council Fathers seem to have shared John XXIII's optimism that Catholic doctrine was a fixed, known, solid, and universally accepted thing. His successor, Pope Paul VI, initially seems to have thought pretty much the same thing (although he would soon be constrained to learn better!). In his encyclical *Ecclesiam Suam* ("Paths of the Church"), issued on August 6, 1964, and thus just prior to the beginning of the Third Session of the Council that would approve *Lumen Gentium*, Paul VI asserted that "by the grace of God" there did not exist "within her today . . . any specific heresies or general disorders" (*ES* 44).

There was, nevertheless, no dearth at the Council of regular and dire warnings from some of the known "conservatives" to the effect that the Church would suffer such and such consequences if this or that language or course of action was adopted. However, not even these "prophets of doom" (whom John XXIII expressly decried in his opening address) foresaw either the nature or the extent of the actual post-conciliar doctrinal crisis in the Church that would soon come about.

And while even Blessed John XXIII admitted in his opening address that there was no "lack of fallacious teaching, opinions, and dangerous concepts to be guarded against and dissipated," these false opinions were "so obviously in contrast with the right norm of honesty," he thought, and had already "produced such lethal fruits," in his words, that false doctrine, heresy, and dissent from Church teachings were apparently no longer considered to be serious problems. There was apparently no need for them even to be discussed or debated by the Council.

In fact, there is scarcely any reference at all made to heresy or false doctrine in all of the various histories and accounts of the Council's proceedings; neither the indexes of these histories nor those of the major collections of the Council documents even have entries for some of these topics. It was as if the question of doctrinal heresy or false doctrine had somehow simply disappeared from the Catholic scene. It is true that, already during the First Session of the Council, in November 1962, fourteen cardinals sent a letter to Pope John expressing "their disquietude over false doctrines" actually being aired on the floor of the

Council, according to them. But this letter really did not cause much of a stir; it proved to be a rather isolated incident; and the concern it evidenced soon tended to get neutralized in the midst of the general euphoria. False doctrine was just not considered to be a burning issue. Basic loyalty to the Church and her teachings was taken for granted, even if some of the ideas being expressed in the Council debates *were* surprisingly frank and spirited in some instances, and not always perhaps even all that "orthodox"! Still, "openness" tended to remain the order of the day, and there were few fears that the Church's teachings could seriously be undermined or doubted.

There was yet another instance, though, during the Third Session of the Council in the fall of 1964, when England's Archbishop John Heenan (later a cardinal) complained to the assembly that the Church was being harmed by some of the opinions being openly expressed by Council *periti.* "They are few in number, but their sound has gone forth to the ends of the earth," the English prelate said. "These few specialists care nothing for the ordinary teaching authority of the bishops," he went on. "Nor, I regret to say, for that of the pope." Hardly anyone imagined at the time how prophetic these words would turn out to be.

It was not long after the end of the Council, though, that some Church leaders finally began to notice that there was a growing doctrinal problem in the Church, that what "had repeatedly been taught," in John XXIII's words, and could be "presumed to be well-known and familiar to all," was *not* necessarily so well known, or, at any rate, was no longer necessarily *believed,* especially by some professional Catholic theologians, even some of those who serving as *periti* at the Council. Increasingly, doubts concerning certain Catholic teachings were being more and more openly expressed by theologians and even by other churchmen. Some of these doubts had actually surfaced during the Council, as Cardinal Heenan had noted; but they were still pretty much on the margins of what was being noticed and reported or thought significant. Following the Council, though, those voicing doubts began to take on the dimensions of a veritable chorus of contrariness and dissent from Church teachings.

At the first meeting in Rome in 1967 of the newly constituted Synod of Bishops, for example—a permanent episcopal advisory body set up by

Pope Paul VI in response to a recommendation of the Council—the Synod Fathers addressed the issue of false doctrine, among other things, in a document that they issued on October 28, 1967. This document was entitled On Dangerous Opinions and On Atheism, the Latin title of which was *Ratione Habita* (included in the second volume of the Flannery collection of conciliar and postconciliar documents). The Synod bishops addressed these issues primarily in terms of modern atheism and irreligion generally, "by which man so exalts his earthly responsibilities that the 'vertical dimension' by which he is related to God and to supernatural salvation becomes obscure; and so man is easily led to atheism, either practical or theoretical."

Meanwhile, it was becoming quite clear that key tenets of the faith, especially those related to supernatural salvation, were becoming "obscure" also among some within the Church, particularly among professional theologians. "In some places matters have reached such a point," the Synod of Bishops document declared, "that it is no longer a question of sound and fruitful [theological] investigation, or of legitimate efforts to adapt the expression of traditional doctrine to new needs, and to the ways of modern human culture, but rather [it is a question of] *unwarranted innovations, false opinions, and even errors in the faith*" (emphasis added).

This was a far cry from Blessed John XXIII's sunny optimism of only five years earlier; yet it represented the considered opinion of an official body representing the teaching Church at close to the highest level, and it was issued only two years after the end of the Council itself. Things were moving fast. The Synod Fathers noted a number of areas where doubts were being expressed concerning established Church teachings, including questions related to our knowledge of God, to the person of Christ and his Resurrection, to the Eucharist, to original sin, and to "the enduring objectivity of the moral law, and the perpetual virginity of the Virgin Mary."

Nor were these doubts about these and other doctrines confined to theologians. The key areas of doctrinal distortions mentioned in the Synod document also corresponded to the characteristic errors, distortions, and omissions that were already beginning to appear, for example, in the "new catechetics" that emerged after the Council—

these were the very "doctrines" (or lack of them), in other words, that were typically beginning to be taught to Catholic children in religion classes in Catholic schools and CCD programs. In 1967, however, there was little doubt or hesitation among the bishops represented at the Synod of Bishops as to what stance should be adopted and what action should be taken toward the purveyors of these false doctrines. According to the Synod document, the generally positive orientation of Vatican II should not "prevent the firm exercise of authority in directing the Church of God, according to the mind of the Second Vatican Council, to the exclusion of abuses and deviations, either in doctrinal matters, or in pastoral or liturgical questions."

This was one of the first postconciliar notices by Church officialdom of the fact that there was even a problem concerning false doctrine or error within the postconciliar Church, though it was clearly a rapidly growing problem. The bishops at the 1967 Synod of Bishops quite firmly rejected the idea that this false doctrine or error should in any way be minimized or tolerated. On this point, the 1967 Synod Fathers were firm and clear: "Those who are rash or imprudent should be warned in all charity," the Synod Fathers declared. "*Those who are pertinacious should be removed from office*" (emphasis added).

Unfortunately, as would soon become clear, this kind of firmness in the face of dissenters from Church teaching was not destined to persist or to characterize the position of Church authority generally, whether that of the pastors or of the bishops—or even, often, of the Holy See itself—in the face of challenges from dissenters in the postconciliar era. Very soon, in fact, dissent and error on a large scale would characterize the views not only of many theologians but of large numbers of individual Catholics as well. By the time this occurred and became clear, though, a new Church policy of basically tolerating theological dissent had unfortunately become the reality in practice, at least as far as most Catholic bishops were concerned. It is true that the bishops of the day, like practically everybody else, did not really understand what was happening, or the scale on which it was happening, and hence preventive measures were not immediately put in place.

Eventually the Holy See would attempt a number of initiatives in order to try to counter the new trend toward toleration of dissenters and would even try to identify and condemn specific instances of error and dissent, as well as disciplining some specifically named dissenters. For the most part, however, these initiatives of the Holy See would turn out to be fairly minimal—and, for the most part too, the bishops generally acted on such matters only when specifically pressed by Rome.

The 1967 Synod of Bishops recommended two further steps in order to try to provide a remedy for the growing problems of doctrinal error that it had identified and stigmatized. These two further steps were: (1) the setting up of a Pontifical Theological Commission and (2) the drawing up of a declaration concerning correct faith. Pope Paul VI soon implemented both of these recommendations, though without notable effect in heading off the doctrinal crisis that was rapidly coming upon the Church.

Then, on June 29, 1968, on the Feast of Sts. Peter and Paul, the pope issued a new statement of the faith of the Church. This was his Credo of the People of God, which, for the most part, admirably summarized and reaffirmed the essential articles of Catholic belief. This was the declaration of true and correct faith that the Synod had asked for. Pope Paul's Credo was inspired not only by the recommendations of the Synod, though, but also by the affair of the so-called Dutch Catechism—a highly questionable and indeed heterodox "new" catechism issued in the Netherlands in 1966. Unlike traditional catechisms, this one contained no question-and-answer treatment of the articles of faith but rather consisted of a smooth and plausible narrative that provided a rather different perspective on some points of the faith than normally found in a compendium of doctrine. Indeed, it sometimes either left out, or came close to denying outright, doctrines that all along had been firmly part of the patrimony of the Catholic faith.

As a result of the issuance of the Dutch Catechism and of some other aberrations, Pope Paul VI was soon fully alerted to the doctrinal dangers that were now confronting the Church. The pope therefore declared a "Year of Faith" for the whole Church; and it was at the end of this Year of Faith, on June 29, 1968, that he issued his Credo of the People of God in order to confirm what the Church had always believed and still believed and would always believe, and to try to reaffirm this belief of the Church in a solemn and, it was hoped, effective way.

However, it proved already to be too late to head off the immediate danger. A sneering editorial in *Commonweal* magazine, for example, openly, immediately, and expressly repudiated the pope's Credo in print. Imagine: a magazine edited by Catholic laymen presuming to dispute—and reject—the supreme teaching authority of the Church! It is worthwhile quoting from this *Commonweal* editorial in order to show how far, how fast, a literal falling away from the faith—the faith that was nevertheless still proclaimed by the Church—was occurring, particularly among the Catholic intelligentsia. The editorial declared:

> There cannot be many Catholic biblical theologians left who would be willing to speak of an "original offense" committed by someone named "Adam." There cannot be many sacramental theologians left who would say that the doctrine of the real presence is "very appropriately called by the Church transubstantiation." There cannot be many liturgists around to glorify adoration of the "Blessed Host." There cannot be many ecclesiologists left who would give the biblical image of the Church as "Body of Christ" primacy over other images. There cannot be many dogmatic theologians left who would care to speak of those who refuse God's love and pity as "going to the fire that will not extinguish." In sum, there cannot be many theologians left who would be able to assent to a message and a "new Credo" whose content not only fails to reflect even Vatican II, but even more fails to admit what has happened to theology since then. (*Commonweal*, July 12, 1968)

Although this editorial seems to appeal to Vatican II as the basis for its new attitude toward certain articles of faith, in actuality it surely amounts to a plain and flat denial of the key Vatican II teaching that the Catholic Church is "the teacher of truth" (*Dignitatis Humanae* 14). We should recall that the document being criticized by *Commonweal* was an official creed of the Church, solemnly issued by the Church's highest authority, and as such binding upon the consciences of the faithful.

In fact, a growing body of Catholic theologians was rapidly coming to agree with the *Commonweal* editorial. And as for the Pontifical Theological Commission that Pope Paul VI had also set up in response to recommendations of the 1967 Synod of Bishops, while it has afforded a prestigious series of appointments for orthodox Catholic theologians—and while it has, of course, done solid and even admirable theological work—at that time it still made no visible effort to counter the growing dissent in the ranks of theologians and, indeed, has since been almost invisible as far as the Church's efforts to try to maintain the integrity of her doctrine are concerned.

And it was only one month after the proclamation of the Credo of the People of God that Pope Paul VI issued his famous encyclical *Humanae Vitae*, reaffirming the Church's traditional teaching that each and every marriage act must remain open to the transmission of life (cf. *HV* 11)—that is, reaffirming the Church's teaching that modern artificial means of birth control (or, more precisely, conception control) remain, in the eyes of the Church, immoral—as the Church had constantly taught for many centuries.

Nevertheless, the reiteration of this traditional teaching by Pope Paul VI went totally counter to the expectations of virtually the entire modern world; and it brought about a moral and theological earthquake within the Catholic Church that, in turn, unleashed a tidal wave of dissent and disbelief that has scarcely subsided up to our own day. The encyclical inaugurated what may be termed a virtual Age of Dissent in the Church. This Age of Dissent remains with us still. More than six hundred theologians in North America alone—probably a majority of all the Catholic theologians working there at the time—publicly dissented from the pope's solemn teaching as set forth in the encyclical. Nor was this public dissent from papal teaching effectively corrected by Church authority. Bland episcopal statements were issued in support of the pope, but there was generally no effective follow-up to ensure that these statements were taken seriously by Catholics generally.

Yet public dissent of this type from a papal encyclical by Catholic theologians was unprecedented, unheard of. There is scarcely any previous example in the entire history of the Church of such open and public disagreement with established Catholic magisterial teaching by Catholic theologians—who by definition are supposed to be engaged in the upholding and defending of Church teachings. Even more serious than this theological dissent, however, was the "practical dissent," and consequent disobedience, of what surely amounted to a majority of Catholic married couples, who were now being told that there was nothing wrong in resorting to the use of contraception in their married lives. For the message of the dissenting theologians very quickly had its intended effect. Henceforth contraception came to be considered acceptable by what probably amounted to a large majority of Catholics; and this logically had to mean that the Church's official teaching was *no longer accepted by them.*

Of course there were no doubt many reasons why so many of the Catholic faithful so quickly and easily abandoned a long-standing teaching of the Church that just about everybody already knew had become an especially distinctive "Catholic" thing, namely, the rejection of birth control. Some of these reasons were probably the same as those that had brought about the widespread acceptance of contraception in modern society generally. There were strong economic and social reasons, after all, why it was no longer easy, nor was it any longer thought desirable, to have a large family. People no longer typically lived on the family farm, where each additional child constituted another able hand and a net help. Women in the workplace also played a part. Social Security and other retirement plans supposedly eliminated the need for children to take care of their aging parents. Children increasingly came to be seen more as a burden and a responsibility than as an asset (or a "blessing"!). The rising cost of education alone severely limited family numbers. Contraception came upon the scene at the very time when an increasing number of people were only too ready to see it as a great new benefit.

For Catholics the Church's known strong moral teaching to the contrary no doubt continued to constitute a deterrent for some. But when Catholic theologians in good standing in Catholic institutions suddenly came upon the scene virtually dominating the public discourse with the message that contraception was not, in fact, morally wrong after all, it could scarcely be any surprise that many Catholics would seize upon this message as the justification for what they were very much tempted to do anyhow. Thus, the open theological dissent by so many in the Church's "professional" ranks played an enormous part in the undermining of the Church's moral teaching on human sexuality in the minds and hearts of so many of the Church's own erstwhile faithful. St. Paul had described the situation long ago: "From among your own selves will arise men saying perverse things, to draw away the disciples after them" (Acts 20:30).

Moreover, this open and public dissent from Catholic teaching has persisted in these same "professional" ranks. This was certainly shown by the number of Catholic theologians who again openly dissented from Pope John Paul II's 1993 encyclical *Veritatis Splendor* ("The Splendor of Truth") on the Church's moral teaching, especially her teaching that some things are "intrinsically wrong." But it was especially and quite dramatically shown when, on May 29, 1994, Pope John Paul II issued his *Ordinatio Sacerdotalis,* reiterating the traditional teaching that the Church has no power to ordain women to the sacred priesthood.

Once again, *hundreds* of Catholic theologians dissented from this motu proprio of the pope's. It was *Humanae Vitae* all over again. Large numbers of Catholics in the pews also, apparently, continue to reject the idea that the ordination issue has in any way been settled by the Holy Father's definitive teaching in the matter—when the pope plainly said that the ordination issue was settled. According to a Gallup Poll conducted in the late 1990s, though, a substantial majority of Catholics—67 percent—supported the idea of women as priests. Other polls have yielded the same kind of results. Polls have similarly shown that very high percentages of Catholics polled do not believe that the use of contraception is wrong.

Such proved to be the fruits of tolerated dissent: it quickly and perhaps inevitably becomes the *norm* to be applied to other authentic Church teachings that are found to be unpalatable in today's permissive moral climate.

VI.

The advent of a new Age of Dissent, of all things, following Vatican Council II was one of the last things that could ever have been imagined, if we were to go by the bare text of *Lumen Gentium* 25. Here is what this major conciliar document says about the levels and degrees of authority of the teachings of the Church's Magisterium (the pope and the bishops in their teaching role):

> Bishops who teach in communion with the Roman Pontiff are to be revered by all as witnesses of divine and Catholic truth; and the faithful, for their part, are obliged to *submit* to their bishops' decision, made in the name of Christ, in matters of faith and morals, and to adhere to it with a ready and respectful allegiance of mind. This loyal submission of the will and intellect *must be given* in a special way to the authentic teaching authority of the Roman Pontiff, even when he does not speak *ex cathedra*, in such wise, indeed, that his supreme teaching authority be acknowledged with respect, and sincere assent be given to decisions made by him, conformably with his manifest mind and intention. (*LG* 25; emphasis added)

Thus, "loyal submission of the will and intellect," that is, *assent*, is to be given to the authentic teaching of the pope, even his *ordinary* teaching (that is, even when he is *not* speaking *ex cathedra*, or "from the chair," as the Council's document expresses it in the Church's traditional language). Here it is especially to be noted that this paragraph *requiring* assent—and therefore logically *excluding* dissent—does not refer to the infallible teaching of the pope; it refers to his ordinary teaching—the teachings in his encyclicals, for example, or even in his weekly audiences.

Much has been made of the whole question of papal infallibility, ever since Vatican Council I solemnly defined that the pope, when speaking *ex cathedra* in order to instruct the faithful on matters of faith and morals, "enjoys the infallibility with which the divine Redeemer wished to endow his Church." Vatican II, of course, reaffirmed this Vatican I teaching in these very same words right here in *Lumen Gentium* 25. Vatican II even went on to teach that the unanimous teaching of the Catholic bishops of the world, teaching in union with the pope, can also be infallible. It is not just the pope who is infallible, in other words; it is the Church. It is worthwhile quoting what *Lumen Gentium* said on this subject as well:

> This infallibility . . . with which the divine Redeemer wished to endow his Church in defining doctrine pertaining to faith and morals, is co-extensive with the deposit of revelation, which must be religiously guarded and loyally and courageously expounded. The Roman Pontiff, head of the college of bishops, enjoys this

> infallibility in virtue of his office, when as supreme pastor and teacher of all the faithful—who confirms his brethren in the faith (cf. Lk 22:32)—he proclaims in an absolute decision a doctrine pertaining to faith or morals. For that reason his definitions are rightly said to be irreformable by their very nature and not by reason of the assent of the Church, inasmuch as they were made with the assistance of the Holy Spirit promised to him in the person of blessed Peter. (*LG* 25)

All this seems pretty clear and straightforward—as it is eminently traditional. Nor, following the Council, did anyone directly dispute this particular teaching. The tactic of the postconciliar dissenters, following their initial dramatic public dissent from the encyclical *Humanae Vitae*, was to declare that the teachings with which they disagreed and which they dissented from, principally the teaching against the use of contraception, were not *infallible* teachings. The Church's infallibility presumably remained intact even for most of them, though not for all of them. Swiss theologian and prominent Council *peritus* Father Hans Küng, for example, disagreed just as vehemently with the teaching of *Humanae Vitae* as did the six-hundred-plus publicly dissenting North American theologians; but he moved in a different direction to justify his dissent. For his part, he believed that the Church's traditional teaching condemning the use of contraception *had* to be considered an infallible teaching on account of the virtual historical unanimity of the Church's hierarchy in teaching it for so many centuries.

But since for Father Küng the teaching was also so patently *wrong*, it followed that the Church could therefore *not* be infallible in her teaching, despite what both Vatican I and Vatican II taught. In 1968, after the Council, Father Küng published a much-discussed book on the subject entitled, in its English translation, *Infallibility: An Inquiry*. In this book Father Küng argued the case that the Church was *indefectible*, rather than infallible, and thus could be relied on not to depart significantly from her historical faith, even though she might not always be right in detail. For since in the case of *Humanae Vitae*, in the view of Father Küng, the Church had proved to be so palpably mistaken in judging contraception to be morally wrong, the idea that she was infallible in her teaching could no longer be credibly maintained. Many Catholics grasped this logic almost instantly in the *Humanae Vitae* affair: how could the Church be considered infallible if she was so wrong about this?

In 1979, Father Küng was judged, after a lengthy investigation by the Congregation for the Doctrine of the Faith, to be no longer a Catholic theologian. This had really been obvious for some time, but it took no less than a dozen years for Rome to come to that conclusion in what should have been an immediate recognition of a clear-cut case of plain, old-fashioned *heresy*.

Most of the theological dissenters from *Humanae Vitae*, however, did not follow Father Küng's approach. They avoided outright heresy by skirting around the infallibility question. They did so by the simple expedient of claiming that the teachings with which they disagreed were not *infallible* teachings. This was how they avoided the charge of heresy—a word that was almost never uttered any longer by anybody. It was as if there was not any such thing as heresy any longer in the postconciliar era! Theological dissent, the dissenters expressly argued, was *not* heresy, which is a pertinacious denial of *defined* teaching. But they held that simple dissent had to be permitted at least from *noninfallible* teachings, which, by definition, might possibly be changed, since they were not irreformable. Infallible teachings, meanwhile, were presumably still binding upon the faithful. Thus, no dissent could presumably be permitted from *them*, only from noninfallible teachings.

Thus, *Humanae Vitae*'s specific teaching that any artificial interruption of the human generative process, before, during, or following marital intercourse, was intrinsically evil was effectively contradicted for all practical purposes. Yet all the while, the theologians who disagreed with the teaching earnestly disclaimed holding to any heresy. They simply happened to dissent from a "noninfallible" teaching. But they were not heretics. Oh, no! Unfortunately, their disclaimer was quite widely and uncritically credited and accepted by many, even at least tacitly by many members of the hierarchy. Hardly anyone in modern society, after all, could imagine any longer that contraception might possibly *be* morally wrong. It was the Church that was believed to be plainly wrong in continuing to teach such a thing.

Following the massive public dissent registered against the pope's encyclical, however, serious arguments were nevertheless made by theologians loyal to the Church's Magisterium, which held that the teaching was nevertheless true and even infallible. Pope Paul VI himself never made this latter claim. Indeed, his theological spokesman at the time the encyclical *Humanae Vitae* was issued, Archbishop Fernando Lambruschini, specifically told the press that the encyclical was *not* infallible. To have mentioned infallibility at all in this connection, however, proved to have been a catastrophic mistake for the credibility of the Church's Magisterium.

Still, as even a Hans Küng realized, a highly persuasive argument could be made on the basis of the virtual unanimity with which the popes and the bishops had always undeviatingly maintained down through the centuries that contraception was an evil. Surely this was an infallible teaching if anything was. *All* Christian bodies had once maintained it, in fact; it was a universal teaching among all Christians for centuries. This was the case up until the Church of England first broke ranks on the matter at its Lambeth Conference in 1930, after which there was a very rapid, indeed a precipitous, collapse in the upholding of the teaching on the part of virtually all non-Catholic communions.

The great encyclical *Casti Connubii* issued by Pope Pius XI on the last day of the year 1930, for example, which powerfully reaffirmed the teaching, speaking as it did of the Church "standing erect amid the moral ruin which surrounds her," was surely issued as a reaction to the Anglican moral cave-in that very same year. But birth control was rapidly becoming morally acceptable nearly everywhere anyway.

Nevertheless, the argument that the anti–birth control teaching was infallible by virtue of the unanimity with which it had always been taught by the Church's hierarchy was later brilliantly made by two American moral theologians, Father John Ford, S.J., who had been one among the number of those advising Pope Paul VI on the subject, and a layman, Professor Germain Grisez. These two men published an article entitled "Contraception and the Infallibility of the Ordinary Magisterium" in the June 1978 issue of the journal *Theological Studies*, which has never been satisfactorily answered. Other writers have held the encyclical to be infallible on yet other grounds.

Such arguments in favor of the Magisterium proved unavailing, however. The argument that *Humanae Vitae* was noninfallible and therefore could licitly be dissented from—and could be ignored in practice by Catholics—more or less carried the day, as it very largely continues to do so up to the present time. A Gallup Poll in the late 1990s, for example, found that some 80 percent of U.S. Catholics disagreed with the statement: "Using artificial means of birth control is wrong." A poll taken in England in 2002 found nearly half of all working Catholic priests still disagreeing with the encyclical's teaching. More recent polls have verified these high percentages.

Even the Catholic bishops of the United States, in practice, have largely failed to insist very effectively that the teaching was binding upon the consciences of the faithful. It is not easy to see, of course, how they could have effectively insisted on this in the face of such massive dissent. Nobody really knew how to counter such a dramatic turn away from the Church's teaching. The bishops might indeed have simply succeeded in driving more people out of the Church if they had tried to insist on the teaching. For, as a matter of fact, many people *did* leave the Church as a result of the pope's decision to reaffirm the teaching against birth control, and many today continue to fault the Church for the same reason.

But the American bishops hardly helped matters when they collectively decided that the theological dissent from the teaching that had manifested itself could, under certain circumstances, be allowed within the Church. Nor was it just tacitly that they decided this. No: in November 1968, in a pastoral letter entitled "Human Life in Our Day," the U.S. bishops included a category covering what they styled "licit dissent." They first defined "dissent" simply as mere academic-style doubt or disagreement by theologians concerning some Church teaching or other; and then, provided this disagreement was well-founded and respectfully stated and provided that the Church's official teaching was correctly stated and taught alongside the theologian's expressed doubts—the bishops conceded that such theological dissent might well be classed as "licit."

Of course, the type of dissent the bishops were faced with on the part of publicly dissenting theologians was not just any abstruse academic-style doubt or disagreement that remained more or less within the groves of academe. Rather, it was an open and public contestation and denial of what the Church was solemnly trying to teach; it was a declaration that in this matter, in effect, the Church was quite simply wrong. Nobody was stating the Church's teaching "alongside" expressions of dissent or doubt; the Church's position was stated only in order to be attacked. Established theologians delivered public lectures, wrote books and articles, and even appeared on television in order to do precisely this. It was an open revolt against the teaching authority of the Church, consciously designed to persuade the faithful to question the latter. It therefore had enormous and, indeed, catastrophic consequences for the integrity of the faith and for the living out of the authentic Christian life for huge numbers of Catholics.

None of these considerations seems to have registered very strongly with the American bishops back in 1968, however; they seemed to be more concerned at the time with concluding a truce with their rebellious theologians than with how the new sexual permissiveness was now affecting the marriages of the members of their flocks and, indeed, allowing the idea that sexual relations outside marriage might not always be immoral as had long been taught. When challenged, few of the bishops of that time were apparently capable of defending the Church's teaching against contraception.

Faced with massive disagreement on the subject on the part of both their theologians and their faithful, then, most of the bishops simply opted not to attempt to defend the teaching. Henceforth the subject of contraception—along with the pope's nevertheless continuing well-known, if not universally known, negative judgment concerning it—for a long while would mostly be passed over in silence by the Church in America, whether by the bishops in their teaching role or by pastors and priests in their pulpits and confessionals. It was as if the question were really not all that important. To great extent, this way of dealing with the problem has persisted up to the present day.

As time has passed, however, more and more people have been coming around to see the evil of contraception once again. For one thing, the use of contraception has hardly increased marital happiness generally, as was supposed to have happened. The near universal use of contraception today, in fact, coincides with the highest divorce rates ever in society at large—not to speak of even more serious phenomena such as the meteoric rise of cohabitation and other indications that marriage is no longer even considered necessary for the use of sexual faculties that the availability of contraception has supposedly freed up.

For another thing, the acceptance and legalization of abortion in our society quickly followed upon the widespread acceptance of contraception. As Pope John Paul II would later point out in his 1995 encyclical *Evangelium Vitae* on the Gospel of Life, a "contraceptive mentality," the idea that human beings are in control of the transmission of new life without reference to the law of God, soon leads almost inevitably to the conclusion that the actual killing of a human life conceived but not yet born is also acceptable in order to make that control effective. This is exactly what has happened in our society today. The ravages of legalized abortion nearly everywhere today have gradually helped more people to realize that the Church was right all along in insisting that the use of human sexuality and the transmission of life must be governed by the moral law of God as formulated and articulated in the teaching of the Church.

Then there were the series of teachings of Pope John Paul II in his weekly audiences in the early 1980s, now collectively known as "the theology of the body," in which the pontiff, among other things, showed how the use of contraceptives amounts to a form of falsehood contradicting the truth of the marital union, where the spouses are failing to give themselves to each other precisely because they are holding back the complete gift of themselves by using contraception. Such a new understanding of the meaning and purpose of the marital union, along with an increasing realization of the evil effects generally of "the contraceptive revolution," have helped many to relearn the wisdom of the Church's teaching. The wisdom of the Church's teaching seems a lot more compelling, in fact, as the depopulation of formerly Christian Europe now finds the birth rates of most European countries below replacement levels.

A number of such factors have converged to bring about a realization that the moral law of God as proclaimed by the Church remains more valid across the board in sexual matters than many people have been willing to credit up to now. Moreover, a new generation of American bishops is rediscovering both the ability to reaffirm the

Church's authentic moral teachings and the conviction that this needs to be done. At their annual meeting in November 2006, for example, the American bishops actually issued a document reaffirming the Church's traditional teaching against contraception and calling upon married couples to conform their lives and behavior to it. Entitled "Married Love and the Gift of Life," the document passed with 95 percent of the bishops voting for it and no debate on the floor. A story in the secular press reported that "the bishops were as unified behind their teaching on contraception as their flock and the dominant culture are against it. The expression 'countercultural' came up repeatedly in conversations with bishops."

Anyone truly familiar with the history and teachings of the Catholic Church would have to have known all along that no teaching solemnly set forth in papal encyclicals, as the teaching against contraception was set forth in both Paul VI's *Humanae Vitae* and Pius XI's *Casti Connubii*, was ever going to be repudiated by the Church. Teachings at that level and with that authority simply do not get dropped—because they are guaranteed to be true! The Catholic Church is the *teacher of truth*, after all (cf. Vatican II, *Dignitatis Humanae* 14).

Thus, the once widespread idea that *Humanae Vitae* would have to be dropped because of the near universal public rejection of it was never anything but a mistaken idea. The Catholic Church does not operate that way. It is just that, in our very permissive secular culture, it has simply taken a good long while for the Church's authentic teaching to reassert itself again. It may take an even greater amount of time for the teaching to regain the acceptance of a majority of the Catholic faithful, but there cannot be any doubt that, in the perspective of the long history of the Church, the authentic teaching of the Church will become normative again for Catholics. Recent developments in this regard may be no more than the beginning of a return to what has remained the Church's authentic teaching all along, but they very definitely *are* a beginning.

VII.

Following the widespread theological dissent from the encyclical *Humanae Vitae* in 1968, there should have been a greater realization of the dangers inherent in tolerating anything like "licit dissent" from established Catholic teaching. Focused on other problems, the incumbent U.S. bishops in 1968 failed to see these dangers and thus also in this very important sense at least failed the test of the collegiality that Vatican II had so specifically assigned to them in the governance of the Church. It was effectively left to the Holy See to attempt to deal with the consequences of theological dissent.

The fact is, though, that the Holy See too failed at first to see the dangers inherent in what the U.S. bishops were allowing. Rome too was slow to react to what should have been immediately seen as an unprecedented situation in the Church created by a deliberate and concerted revolt against the authority of Church teaching by many of those holding positions in the Church's official structures. Initially, the dissenters were able to carry off this revolt successfully: when the first smoke of the public explosion of dissent against *Humanae Vitae* cleared away, most of the dissenters were found to be still in possession of their Church positions, whether on university or seminary faculties or in diocesan or parish assignments. At the same time, of course, as has been explained, the dissenters quite consciously and carefully considered themselves as having stopped short of espousing what was commonly understood to be actual heresy. The perception that actual heresy was involved might have triggered a more immediate and vigorous response from Church authority; but by and large it was accepted that dissent was not heresy, and hence the dissenters effectively won their initial battle to define their status within the Church and remain in place while rejecting a key teaching of the Church.

But as things developed, what was at stake was not immediately all that clear to many. The *Humanae Vitae* dissenters strenuously maintained, and not without at least some plausibility, that there was no heresy involved in their position. They claimed to abhor heresy as much as anyone. The traditional definition of heresy as a pertinacious denial of a truth proposed by the Church as *revealed by God* also served to help the dissenters make their case, since the teaching against contraception was surely not something revealed by God, at least not directly and in so many words, but was rather, evidently, only a deduction from other revealed Church teachings.

Dissent *was not* heresy, in other words—so it was stoutly maintained by the leaders of the dissenters: heresy was the denial only of revealed teaching; the dissenters were contesting only a "noninfallible" teaching. As a practical matter, this argument gained acceptance almost in the degree that hardly any dissenters were ever actually formally disciplined as a result of their dissent.

Nevertheless, the acids of skepticism inherent in the dissenters' position, once it got accepted and condoned, continued to corrode the faith of Catholics, and this was true on other issues besides just the immorality of contraception. This was inevitable, in fact, because if the Church could be so wrong about contraception, as was now being asserted and believed, she could be equally wrong about some of her other teachings as well. It took awhile for the logic of this to work itself out, however, and for the results of it to become manifest in the life of the Church.

It was not until more than ten years after the first public dissent from *Humanae Vitae* that the Congregation for the Doctrine of the Faith finally got around to initiating an investigation of one of the most prominent and acknowledged leaders of the dissent in North America, Father Charles E. Curran. Father Curran was a moral theologian and a member of the faculty of the Catholic University of America. He received a letter dated July 13, 1979, from Franjo Cardinal Seper, then prefect of the Congregation for the Doctrine of the Faith, informing him that his theological writings were under investigation, enclosing a number of CDF written "Observations" on those same writings, and inviting a response from him.

In the course of the long "Curran affair" that followed, Father Curran complained with some justice that he was being singled out for "persecution," in view of the large number of theologians and other Catholics who were also publicly known to dissent from the teaching of *Humanae Vitae*. Why was he alone being chosen for an investigation by the CDF? Why were only his writings and his opinions being questioned, when they coincided with the writings and opinions of so many others?

In point of fact, Father Curran was no lonely victim or martyr, however. He was actually a tenacious and even a vociferous defender of what he called "faithful dissent" from Catholic teaching. He had played a prominent part in leading and orchestrating the public dissent of the six-hundred-plus theologians and other specialists in the sacred sciences who had publicly come out against the papal encyclical. In the process, he had shown himself to possess a kind of genius in the manipulation of public opinion through the mass media. The only surprise about the choice of Father Curran as the subject of an investigation by the CDF was the amount of time it had taken for the CDF to get around to initiating an investigation of him.

And the CDF investigation in question occupied yet another "biblical" seven years. There were visits and appeals to Rome in his favor, not only by Father Curran himself but by notable members of the Church's theological establishment, including even some bishops. The Catholic Theological Society of America consistently and vigorously championed him. Meanwhile, the kind of dissent that Father Curran himself so belligerently defended had become both widespread and fashionable in many quarters; it had long since even come to be considered almost respectable, in fact. Thus, Father Curran himself continued to be a prominent member of the existing "theological establishment" whom nobody wanted to see disciplined.

In the end, however, Father Curran's responses to the Congregation's questions concerning his writings were judged unacceptable. In a letter dated July 26, 1986—the eighteenth anniversary of the issuance of the encyclical *Humanae Vitae*—Joseph Cardinal Ratzinger, by then the CDF prefect, officially informed Father Curran that he was no longer "suitable nor eligible to exercise the function of a Professor of Catholic Theology."

Yet more time would elapse before this priest-theologian would finally be removed from his position in a Church institution. The Catholic University of America would still have to defend itself against a lawsuit filed by Father Curran, claiming a right to continue as a tenured professor. The civil court would eventually find that the Church did have a right to dismiss teachers unwilling to teach authentic Catholic doctrine. On the whole, though, all this represented a pretty hollow "victory," especially considering all the effort that had been expended by the CDF in the matter. But at least the theological dissenters were now on notice that their dissent was *not* licit, in spite of what had been allowed to go on up to then. The Curran case had forced Rome to examine the phenomenon of theological dissent more carefully.

Thus, some four years later, on July 5, 1990, the CDF issued its Instruction on the Ecclesial Vocation of the Theologian, *Donum Veritatis*, in which the Church at long last officially declared that theological dissent, even from ordinary, noninfallible teachings, was *not* licit and could not be permitted.

The CDF instruction *Donum Veritatis* reviewed and reestablished the required levels of assent for all Church teachings. In the words of the instruction: "When the magisterium of the Church makes an infallible pronouncement and solemnly declares that a teaching is found in revelation, the assent called for is that of theological faith" (*DV* 23). Similarly, "when the magisterium proposes 'in a definitive way' truths concerning faith and morals, which even if not divinely revealed are nevertheless strictly and intimately connected with revelation, these must be firmly accepted and held" (ibid.). Here the CDF was introducing a new category describing Church teachings, namely, *definitive* teachings. The Congregation's careful examination of the dissenters' claim that dissent from noninfallible teachings was permissible proved to be more complicated than just a question of whether a teaching was infallible or not. Some teachings, even if not divinely revealed, could nevertheless be so intimately and centrally connected to core revealed teachings—as they were often necessary to guard and explain those same revealed teachings—that any change or alteration in them had to be considered an impossibility; they were therefore "definitive" teachings. Even if they were not declared to be infallible by the Church (because not considered to be actually revealed), they were effectively "infallible" as a practical matter; that is, they were irreformable. Some teachings that had eventually been *defined*, as the primacy and infallibility of the pope was defined at Vatican I in 1870, would have been considered "definitive" before they finally were defined, according to this nomenclature.

Finally, in addition to infallible and definitive teachings, the instruction specified that "when the magisterium, *not* intending to act 'definitively,' teaches a doctrine to aid in a better understanding of revelation and make explicit its contents, or to recall how some teaching is in conformity with the truths of faith, or, finally, to guard against ideas that are incompatible with these truths, the response called for is that of the *religious submission of mind and will*" (ibid.; emphasis added). This third level of assent to those teachings requiring the "loyal submission of the will and intellect," even in the case of noninfallible and nondefinitive teachings of the Magisterium, was, as we have seen, required all along by *Lumen Gentium* 25. This was what the theological dissenters mainly disputed and denied, of course. In their view, noninfallible and nondefinitive teachings, *since* they were noninfallible and nondefinitive, could be *wrong*; if they could be wrong, they could be dissented from.

In the view of these dissenters, *Humanae Vitae*'s teaching that the use of artificial contraception was intrinsically evil and hence morally prohibited was wrong and therefore served as Exhibit A in the case they were trying to make. They considered the teaching to be erroneous on its face. At first the dissenters did not state this quite so baldly; they simply held that Catholics "in conscience" could disagree with it and act accordingly (that is, could use contraception). Later on, however, Father Charles Curran, among others, quite forthrightly claimed that the teaching was simply wrong and therefore that the Church's Magisterium had erred in teaching it.

And if the Magisterium could err in the case of a teaching such as this—which had been undeviatingly and unanimously taught by the popes and bishops from the earliest days of the Church down to the present day—in what other ways might the Magisterium also err? It soon came to be considered established truth by some that the Magisterium *could* err, and hence dissent logically had to be permitted (so that theologians could correct the mistakes of the Magisterium where necessary). But if dissent was permitted from any given teaching on the basis of individual private judgment, why not from any other teaching? Once dissent is admitted, there is no limiting of it.

The CDF instruction *Donum Veritatis*, though, had a very different "take" on the supposed "mistakes" of the Magisterium. The instruction stated forthrightly:

> When it comes to the question of interventions in the prudential order, it could happen that some magisterial documents might not be free of all deficiencies. Bishops and their advisers have not always

> taken into immediate consideration every aspect or the entire complexity of a question. But it would be contrary to the truth if, proceeding from some particular cases, one were to conclude that the Church's magisterium can be habitually mistaken in its prudential judgments or that *it does not enjoy divine assistance in the integral exercise of its mission.* (*DV* 24; emphasis added)

This last point, whether or not the Church enjoys "divine assistance in the integral exercise of its mission," became a key point for the CDF in deciding that dissent from the noninfallible and nondefinitive teachings of the Magisterium could never be licit or permitted. After all, Christ established the Church to help and guide the faithful on the road to their sanctification and salvation; the Church Christ established, therefore, has to be able to guide the faithful *correctly*, even on matters that may not have been directly revealed but that are nevertheless essential for right belief and for the proper living out of the Christian life. But the manner in which Christians live out their married lives surely is one of those essentials, and, throughout her history, the Church has not hesitated to teach quite specifically in this area.

Nor has her teaching been limited to what has expressly been revealed by Christ concerning Christian marriage, namely, that a validly contracted and consummated Christian marriage is *indissoluble*, as the Church insists. The Church has always gone farther. She has always taught also, for example, as Pope Paul VI expressed it in *Humanae Vitae*, that "each and every marriage act [*quilibet matrimonii usus*] must remain open to the transmission of life" (*HV* 11).

When the Church delivers herself of such a teaching, however, it is essential that it be true. Vatican II's Declaration on Religious Liberty, *Dignitatis Humanae*, literally describes the Church as "the teacher of truth" and goes on to say that "it is her duty to proclaim and teach with authority, the truth which is Christ, and, at the same time, to declare and confirm by her moral authority the principles of the moral order which spring from human nature itself" (*DH* 14). And it is not just those principles of the moral order that come from revelation about which the Church teaches truly but those that "spring from human nature itself" as well. The proper interpretation of the natural law falls within the competence of the Church's Magisterium.

If the Church is the teacher of truth, in other words, she must be able to teach truly—and not just in her infallible teachings. If she can be wrong in something as important as her teaching regarding the transmission of life, then she is evidently not the teacher of truth that Vatican II taught that she was. This is the ineluctable conclusion that follows from the premise that dissent from noninfallible teachings can be licit. Nor were the theological dissenters slow in drawing this conclusion—though few of the dissenters have ever had the honesty to admit that their position *logically entails a denial of Vatican II*! Yes: *Lumen Gentium* 25 forbids dissent; if you think dissent is licit, you are effectively denying the Council's firm teaching.

The Congregation for the Doctrine of the Faith was thus strictly obliged to issue its Instruction on the Ecclesial Vocation of the Theologian, *Donum Veritatis.* The only real question is why it took more than twenty years after the public challenge to the Church's Magisterium before the CDF finally got around to eliminating officially the category of "licit dissent" that the U.S. bishops, in their 1968 pastoral letter "Human Life in Our Day" had so mistakenly and unwisely decided to allow.

Given the clear conciliar teaching that the Church is the teacher of truth, there should never have been the slightest question of allowing anything resembling "licit dissent" from what the Church teaches. The Church of Christ either teaches truly on matters of faith and morals or she does not. *Lumen Gentium* 25 clearly states that "religious submission of mind and will"—a phrase taken up again and repeated in *Donum Veritatis*—is owed even to noninfallible teachings of the Magisterium. The instruction took this language directly from *Lumen Gentium* 25, in fact, while adding its own new distinction regarding teachings that are neither infallible nor noninfallible but definitive.

We should note well here how this particular language requires what is termed religious *submission* to the Church's noninfallible and nondefinitive teachings. This term was carefully chosen in order to express the mind of the Church correctly. We should recall that *Lumen Gentium* 25 requires of the faithful *theological faith* in revealed, infallible teachings (*de fide credenda*), while teachings judged definitive (*de fide tenenda*) must be *firmly accepted and held* by them. By contrast, authentic Church teachings that are declared to be neither infallible nor definitive require, precisely, religious *submission of mind and will.*

This means, in one important sense, that acceptance of the Church's teaching *because* it is the Church's teaching is necessary, whether or not one understands it or agrees with it. The Church, for her part, dares to require this of her faithful *because* she is confident that she enjoys "divine assistance in the integral exercise of [her] mission."

Now, if at the very least this "religious submission of will and intellect" is *required* of *all* Church teachings, as *Lumen Gentium*, in fact, makes very plain, then theological dissent is logically *excluded* thereby. Vatican II forbade all along, in other words, the theological dissent that arose in the postconciliar years and was believed by many to be one of the results of the Council (good or bad, depending upon your point of view). No: this kind of dissent was excluded all along by the clear language of the Council itself and should never have been allowed the freedom of the Church, as unfortunately became the case for a while. As Pope John Paul II, during his 1987 pastoral visit to the United States, reminded the U.S. bishops:

> It is sometimes reported today that large numbers of Catholics do not adhere to the teachings of the Church on a number of questions, notably sexual and conjugal morality, divorce and remarriage. Some are reported as not accepting the Church's clear position on abortion. It has been noted that there is a tendency on the part of some Catholics to be selective in their adherence to the Church's moral teachings. It is sometimes claimed that dissent from the magisterium is totally compatible with being a "good Catholic," and imposes no obstacle to the reception of the sacraments. This is a *grave error* that challenges the teaching office of the bishops of the United States and elsewhere.
>
> I wish to encourage you in the love of Christ to address this situation courageously in your pastoral ministry, relying on the power of God's truth to attract assent and on the power of the Holy Spirit which is given both to those who proclaim the message and those to whom it is addressed. (John Paul II, Address to the U.S. Bishops, September 16, 1987; emphasis added)

Pope John Paul II went farther than just speaking out against dissent. In 1998, he moved to make binding and permanent in canon law the threefold levels of teaching described in the instruction *Donum Veritatis*, along with the degree of certitude or belief required of the faithful by the Church at each level, namely: (1) theological faith in a divinely revealed truth; (2) firm acceptance of a teaching proposed by the Church "in a definitive way"; and (3) "religious submission of will and intellect" to a teaching proposed by the ordinary teaching authority of the Church. The first and third of these categories were already contained in *Lumen Gentium*, as well as in canon law. In his *Ad Tuendam Fidem* of June 29, 1998, the pope added to the code as incumbent upon the faithful the second of these two categories, namely, that pertaining to doctrines to be definitively held (*de fide tenenda*).

John Paul II's action in *Ad Tuendam Fidem* was pretty obviously motivated by the Church's experience with theological dissent in the postconciliar era. Once this dissent arose and unfortunately found such a prominent place in the thinking and acts of theologians and the faithful, it became necessary for Church authority to spell out correctly not only how and why divinely revealed and infallibly defined doctrines had to be believed but also why the same thing was true of those doctrines that logically follow from or buttress the divinely revealed teachings, as well as those that the Church teaches generally in order to round out the fullness of her teaching. The whole fabric of the truth of the Catholic faith is, in fact, a seamless garment.

If dissent were to be permitted from any teaching at all, it would logically have to be permitted from any *other* given teaching—and thus from virtually *all* teachings in the end, at the option of the dissenter. It is thus simply not possible to draw the line that the dissenters attempted to draw between infallible and noninfallible teachings. Instead, it has proved necessary to identify explicitly the category of teachings designated as "definitive." This was strictly necessary, because, as was pointed out when *Ad Tuendam Fidem* was issued, a teaching found to be definitive today might well be defined as infallible tomorrow by the living Magisterium of the Church.

This was the case, for example, with the dogma of the Immaculate Conception, defined in 1854, and that of the Assumption of the

Blessed Virgin Mary, defined in 1950. Before these dogmas were defined, they were considered ordinary teachings. Was it "licit" to dissent from them? They were, in fact, "definitive" teachings destined to be proclaimed as infallible teachings. At the very least, dissent from them would have evidenced a profoundly un-Catholic, and perhaps even an anti-Catholic, way of thinking. (Some might immediately point out that St. Thomas Aquinas, for example, did not subscribe to the doctrine of the Immaculate Conception. But is it really necessary, or in any way profitable, to have to point out that the way St. Thomas approached theology and doctrine bears no resemblance whatsoever to the modern enterprise of today's theological dissenters?)

When we reflect on these kinds of questions, we see that theological dissent is not a simple question of someone just happening to disagree with "nonessential" Church teachings. First of all, there are *no* "nonessential" Church teachings: the faith as it was delivered to us by Christ, and as it has been handed down and developed in the Church in the course of her long history, is an organic whole that hangs together as such—or in the end, does not hang together but rather quickly disintegrates, as the experience of the last nearly forty years since *Humanae Vitae* has amply shown, when teachings of the Church are rejected.

Dissent, if allowed, will inevitably undermine the faith generally. If the Church does not teach truly on faith and morals across the board, why should she be believed on *any* particular point? The average man in the pews understands this perfectly and has not been slow to draw out the practical consequences of it, as the polls on the current state of Catholic belief and practice now regularly attest. The toleration of theological dissent in the postconciliar era has thus been very costly and has done enormous damage to the teaching authority of the Church, as well as to the integrity of the faith generally.

Even the Holy See only tardily realized the seriousness of the problem of theological dissent, and only with this late realization did it move to try to counter it. Although the Congregation for the Doctrine of the Faith has, characteristically, provided an admirable solution in theory for the whole problem, with its Instruction on the Ecclesial Vocation of the Theologian, *Donum Veritatis*, the problem is still far from finding any complete resolution in practice. More than fifteen years after the issuance of *Donum Veritatis*, in fact, the document is still not being completely enforced, and it is still far from having found widespread acceptance (although this may be, and probably is, slowly changing). Still, in today's Age of Dissent, too many theological dissenters have simply dissented from the Roman document forbidding dissent!

Yet, all along, the authentic Church teaching was right there in *Lumen Gentium* 25. Vatican II was right all along about this. If theologians so often prone to invoke "the spirit of Vatican II" had been willing to pay attention to the Council's actual teaching in the matter, they could certainly never have come up with anything like Father Curran's idea of "faithful dissent." All along, the authentic teaching contained in *Lumen Gentium*—which plainly excludes theological dissent—needed to be brought out and put into practice, both by theologians and by the faithful generally.

VIII.

Given how things went following the Council, *Lumen Gentium* 25 turned out to be one of the most important single statements in all of the Council's sixteen documents: it provides the contemporary doctrinal basis for rejecting the idea that we can lay aside and treat as non-teachings those Church teachings that go contrary to many modern preconceptions. Yet this single numbered section of the Council's great Dogmatic Constitution on the Church hardly outweighed or eclipsed the importance of the document as a whole. We must now look at the remaining, also very important, chapters of *Lumen Gentium*.

After speaking of the mystery of the Church and of the People of God in its first two chapters, and continuing in its third chapter with its definitive treatment of the Church as hierarchical—all of which topics we have now considered at some length—*Lumen Gentium* goes on in its fourth chapter to speak of the laity.

It should not have to be said that the Catholic laity are *not* the equivalent of the People of God, by the way, although there has been some confusion about this in the years since the Council, as we have noted. The Council did, however, wish to treat the laity as a distinct component within the People of God, and this marked the first time the topic of the laity was ever treated as such by an ecumenical council. It may seem strange that the Catholic Church should have waited for almost two thousand years before addressing the topic of her laity in this manner. Once when asked by his bishop, "Who are the laity, anyway?" the future cardinal John Henry Newman, then still an Oratorian priest, ventured the memorable rejoinder that "the Church would look pretty silly without them"! The overwhelming majority of the Church's members are lay people.

Just as its chapter on the People of God aimed to place our understanding of the Church in a new perspective, so *Lumen Gentium*'s treatment of the laity in a separate chapter was intended to focus our attention on this hitherto neglected component of the Church of Christ. And just as the Council in this dogmatic constitution treated the hierarchy in general, only to go on to issue separate documents on both bishops and priests later, so the Council also later issued a separate decree on laity, the Decree on the Apostolate of Lay People, *Apostolicam Actuositatem.*

Interestingly, the Church had never defined the term "laity" prior to Vatican II, and even here in *Lumen Gentium* the Council Fathers found themselves hard pressed to offer anything but a "negative" definition: "The term 'laity,'" they said, "is here understood to mean all the faithful except those in Holy Orders and those who belong to a religious state approved by the Church" (*LG* 31). This admittedly "negative" view of what constitutes the laity was deplored during the Council's Second Session, in an intervention delivered in October 1963, by the then bishop of Pittsburgh, John J. Wright (later Cardinal Wright, and prefect of the Congregation for the Clergy). Bishop Wright, considered one of the "intellectuals" among the American bishops of the day, did not like the idea of a layman being defined as "neither a cleric nor a religious." "The faithful have been waiting for four hundred years," he declared, "for a positive conciliar statement on the place, dignity, and vocation of the layman." As it turned out, though, the Council did not succeed in crafting a definition beyond that of describing the laity as neither clergy nor religious but rather as "everybody else."

But the text does immediately then go on to say many positive things about the laity, emphasizing that they are incorporated into Christ by baptism and hence "share the priestly, prophetic, and kingly office of Christ" (ibid.). Indeed, *Lumen Gentium* becomes quite eloquent about what it means to belong to the Catholic laity:

> By reason of their special vocation, it belongs to the laity to seek the kingdom of Christ by engaging in temporal affairs and directing them according to God's will. They live in the world, that is, they are engaged in each and every work and business of the earth and in the ordinary circumstances of society and family life which, as it were, constitute their very existence. There they are called by God that, being led by the spirit of the Gospel, they may contribute to the sanctification of the world, as from within like a leaven, by fulfilling their own particular duties. Thus, especially by the witness of their life, resplendent in faith, hope, and charity, they must manifest Christ to others. (*LG* 31)

In other words, the laity, as baptized into Christ in the Church, are in the world for *more* than just the salvation of their own souls (although that primary aim should never be forgotten or downplayed, as has sometimes happened in the postconciliar years). They are "called by God" to do nothing less than "manifest Christ to others" and to "contribute to the sanctification of the world," and to do this "by fulfilling their own particular duties." A little farther on, the same text declares that "the apostolate of the laity is a sharing in the salvific mission of the Church. By baptism and confirmation all are appointed to the apostolate by Christ himself. . . . The laity . . . are given this special vocation: to make the Church present and fruitful in those places and circumstances where it is only through them that she becomes the salt of the earth" (*LG* 33). The laity are out there in the world, in other words, in a way that the clergy and religious *cannot be*, and it therefore behooves them in a special way to be conscious that the world will judge Christians and the Church by *them*. "Even by their secular activity," the Council teaches, "they must aid one another to greater holiness of life so that the world may be filled with the spirit of Christ and may the more effectively attain its destiny in justice, love, and peace" (*LG* 36).

This emphasis on communicating and spreading the faith to others—evangelization—is one of the major themes of this chapter of *Lumen Gentium*, as it was of the Second Vatican Council generally. In one important sense, evangelization was indeed the primary theme and purpose of the Council. The Council saw that, in the modern world, the faith could no longer be taken for granted. Christendom, like the Christian state, or even any semblance of a Christian society, has been less and less a reality with every passing year. Indeed, in the United States at least, as well as especially in Europe, the dominant society has become increasingly *hostile* to Christianity and to the Church. And even if active persecution of Christians, as this was encountered in the ancient world and as was also common in the modern Communist and Nazi totalitarian empires, is not yet a daily reality in former Christendom, there are nevertheless increasing signs that such a thing could actually come about and perhaps is not as remote as we fondly imagine.

The Council saw this and said, in effect: We must *evangelize*, or reevangelize, a world that is at the very least ignorant of Christ, where it has not actively and consciously rejected him. Most of the deliberations and acts of the Council took place within the framework of precisely this realization and were intended to orient the Church more effectively toward greater efforts to evangelize. Evangelization is what Christianity and the Church have always been about in one sense, of course; but the need for evangelization, and, especially, the reevangelization of our former Christian society, had become much more obvious, insistent, and urgent by the mid-twentieth century at the time of the Council and is more marked today. And *Lumen Gentium* places a heavy responsibility in this regard on the Catholic laity: "The Lord desires that his kingdom should be spread by the lay faithful" (*LG* 36). Or again: "Each individual layman must be a witness before the world to the resurrection and life of the Lord Jesus" (*LG* 38).

Setting forth what the Christian laity ought to be vis-à-vis the world, namely, constant witnesses to the reality of Jesus Christ in their lives, this fourth chapter of *Lumen Gentium* does not fail to make clear the role of the laity within the Church herself. There has been no little confusion about this in the postconciliar era, of course, especially following such occurrences as the clerical sex abuse scandals of 2002. Some laity saw this kind of failure of "the system" as a call for the laity to step in to remedy the sins and errors of some priests and bishops and even to take over some of the "management" of the Church, which had evidently been so badly mismanaged in the case of these scandals. Even the bishops themselves, by setting up their clergy sex abuse review boards everywhere, have sometimes seemed confused about the nature of the authority they have from Christ.

Lumen Gentium makes abundantly clear, however, what the role and position of the bishop should be. And it was Christ himself who established the Church on a sacerdotal and hierarchical basis, as we have now verified at some length in our review of the document's chapter 3. The remedy for erring bishops and sinning priests in Christ's Church is the same as it has always been, namely, for the erring bishops and sinning priests in question to "repent and believe the Gospel" (Mk 1:15). As the successor of the head apostle, Peter, the pope has an indispensable oversight role in this regard. So do other priests and bishops; they have serious responsibilities generally to admonish and correct erring and sinning brothers in the ordained ministry, responsibilities that have rarely been properly carried out in the postconciliar era, especially given the kind of "culture" that has grown up in the bishops' conferences, for example, where virtually never does one bishop criticize any other bishop—in this respect, today's bishops seem to have imbibed a generous portion of today's "no-fault," "nonjudgmental" culture.

But since the Church is hierarchical, the laity are *not* called to leadership in the Church as such. On the contrary, "the laity should promptly accept in Christian obedience what is decided by the pastors who, as teachers and rulers of the Church, represent Christ" (*LG* 37). While this may seem to be a hard saying for some, especially today, it nevertheless belongs to the nature of the Church as set up by Christ. On the other hand, human nature being what it is, even under grace, the danger of clericalism on the part of those granted the unique powers Christ wished those ordained to his service to have has also almost always been present in the Church and must constantly be guarded against. We saw this dramatically in the clerical sex abuse scandals. Among the most disconcerting aspects of these scandals were the revelations of Church pastors and bishops totally unwilling to hear or take in complaints from the faithful—and often, apparently, *unconcerned* about justice for the victims of clerical sex abuse. Such attitudes were especially shocking when juxtaposed with the frequent leniency and even indulgence shown to many clerical offenders. Too often bishops were shown to have acted as if they belonged to some exclusive club consisting of the ordained, to which the Catholic faithful simply did not belong. This was clericalism in an extreme form, and unfortunately it proved to be only too alive and well in the Church in 2002.

Such clericalism, however, was hardly in accord with either the letter or the spirit of Vatican II. Rather, in *Lumen Gentium*, the Council Fathers urged pastors "to recognize and promote the dignity and responsibility of the laity in the Church" (*LG* 37). More than that, they confirmed that

> [l]ike all Christians, the laity have the right to receive in abundance the help of the spiritual goods of the Church, especially that of the word of God and sacraments from the pastors. To the latter the laity should disclose their needs and desires with that liberty and confidence which befits children of God and brothers of Christ. By reason of the knowledge, competence, or pre-eminence which they may have, the laity are empowered—indeed sometimes obliged—to manifest their opinion on those things which pertain to the good of the Church. (*LG* 37)

Like many of the other provisions of Vatican II, however, it cannot be said that this particular vision of the relationship between the pastors and the lay members of their flocks has been very widely realized or fulfilled. Indeed, scarcely any attempt at all has been made in the postconciliar era to establish actual channels or mechanisms by which the "needs and desires" of the laity might be conveyed to the pastors with some hope of getting any kind of a hearing. As most of those who have ever tried to register complaints with Church authorities about such things as liturgical abuses, defective catechetics, and the graphic, morality-free sex education that soon became widespread and characteristic features of the postconciliar Church can readily attest, the bishops and pastors have rarely deigned to hear any complaints on such subjects. Mostly, such complainers have been stigmatized as themselves "the problem"—an all-too-common form of blaming the messenger for the bad news.

Nor have the opinions of the laity "on those things which pertain to the good of the Church" generally been welcomed by the pastors or the bishops. On the contrary, clerical and episcopal reactions to opinions expressed by the laity are still too often dismissive if not downright discourteous. Some of the revelations concerning the scandals of 2002 certainly brought out examples of how the pastors and bishops were sometimes unwilling to deal with the laity at all. Since the Church, of course, is not a democracy, and since bishops and pastors are hardly installed in office by any popular process or vote, they almost never demonstrate the kinds of attitudes that are common, for example, among congressmen, city councilmen, or other elected officials. The latter are often almost pathetically eager to please, and even to pander to, the "demands," even outrageous demands, of their constituents. The same thing is true of their staffs, who tend to be instantly attentive and, where possible, accommodating to anybody who calls, writes, e-mails, or comes in from the "home district"—unlike the staffs of the average diocesan chancery, who tend to take on the aloofness, and even sometimes the unfortunate inaccessibility, of their bishop-ordinaries.

It is really too bad that, in this respect, the contemporary secular world tends to outperform the Church in responding to the "needs and desires" of average people. It is doubly unfortunate when we consider the teaching of *Lumen Gentium* on the subject. Here again, we surely have one more area where the proper implementation of Vatican II has not yet occurred and is therefore still urgently called for.

IX.

Just as it specifically treats of bishops, priests, and the laity, so *Lumen Gentium* treats specifically of consecrated religious as well. Yet perhaps oddly enough, the chapter on the religious does not follow directly upon that on the laity. Rather, chapter 5 of the document is entitled "The Call to Holiness." Only later in chapter 6 are questions of religious and the religious life as such treated.

Chapter 5 on the call to holiness, though, is deservedly one of the best known and most quoted parts of *Lumen Gentium* and, indeed, of the Vatican II documents as a whole. It is deservedly prominent because of the admittedly all too common idea before Vatican II that "holiness" was somehow the exclusive possession and prerogative of vowed religious and ordained priests. This is an idea that, for centuries, tended to get reinforced by the disproportionately large number of priests and religious formally canonized by the Church. To a great extent, this is still the case, although, especially during the pontificate of Pope John Paul II, the Church made a serious effort to approve canonizations more representative of the People of God as a whole, not just of vowed religious or ordained priests. Vatican II, of course, decided, and rightly, that "*all* Christians, in any state or walk or life are called to the fullness of Christian life and to the perfection of love" (*LG* 39; emphasis added).

Lumen Gentium's chapter 5 carefully passes in review the principal components of what the document styles "the holy People of God," which, of course, constitutes the Church. These components include "the shepherds of Christ's flock," that is, the bishops, as well as priests, ministers of lesser rank, Christian married couples, widows, single people, "those who engage in human work," and "those who are weighed down by poverty, infirmity, and other hardships"—all of these, whatever their state in life, *Lumen Gentium* says, are obliged to seek Christian perfection by hearing the word of God in the teaching of the Church; by doing God's will with the help of grace; by frequently partaking of the sacraments, "especially the Eucharist"; and by practicing "prayer, self-denial, active brotherly service, and the practice of all virtues" (*LG* 41–42).

The paragraph that concludes *Lumen Gentium*'s chapter on the call to holiness is quite often quoted—and, as we have noted, this is well deserved—and so it is worth quoting again here:

> Therefore all the faithful are invited and obliged to holiness and the perfection of their own state of life. Accordingly, let all of them see that they direct their affections rightly, lest they be hindered in their pursuit of perfect love by the use of worldly things and by an adherence to riches which is contrary to the spirit of evangelical poverty, following the apostle's advice. Let those who use this world not fix their abode in it, for the form of this world is passing away. (*LG* 42)

The emphasis, then, is on "*all* the faithful." All are called to holiness; none is excluded or excepted or granted the indulgence of being merely a mediocre Christian. Experience teaches that not all will respond to this call of God's to holiness in equal measure. All of us, in fact, fall short. This remains as true since Vatican II as it was before. Still, the Council was no doubt correct in issuing the call as a salutary reminder of the call that was first issued when Jesus Christ began to preach in Galilee. The original proclamation by Jesus is something that has to be repeated in every place and in every generation. Vatican II's version came in the form of its "universal call to holiness": this "call" is surely one of the Council's most important and permanent legacies, and one that has attracted a fair amount of attention. But the important thing, of course, is that Christians *answer* the call to holiness!

In passing in review the principal components of the holy People of God, *Lumen Gentium*'s chapter 5 does not neglect vowed and consecrated religious. Indeed, it speaks in this connection of those that the Church has always, and especially, honored, namely, the *martyrs*. "Some Christians have been called from the beginning, and will always be called, to give this greatest testimony of love to all, especially to persecutors. Martyrdom makes the disciple like the master, who willingly accepted death for the salvation of the world" (*LG* 42).

But not all Christians are called to be martyrs (although Pope John Paul II never tired of repeating that there have been more Christian martyrs in the course of the bloody twentieth century than in all of the previous centuries of Christianity combined!). More common than martyrs who shed their blood, however, are those "who devoted themselves to God alone . . . with an undivided heart in virginity or celibacy" (ibid.). These are the vowed and consecrated *religious*, to which *Lumen Gentium* devotes its chapter 6. The placement of this chapter on consecrated religious becomes more intelligible when we see how it follows from the discussion of the Council's universal call to holiness generally; for the life pursued by vowed religious actualizes in a special way a "love for the kingdom of heaven which has always been held in high esteem by the Church" (ibid.). The religious life is based, first of all, on "a love for the kingdom of heaven."

Lumen Gentium's chapter 6, devoted to the religious life, focuses mainly on the vows, or evangelical counsels, of poverty, chastity, and obedience, which in the history of the Church have traditionally characterized those who wish to serve God more completely and draw closer to Christ by embracing a consecrated religious life. This life, *Lumen Gentium* pertinently notes, "is the kind of poor and virginal life which Christ the Lord chose for himself, and which his Virgin Mother embraced also" (*LG* 46). This is a very important statement about the nature of any life truly consecrated to God, since in our contemporary debates and discussions about the celibacy of the clergy, for example—as in the much rarer discussions about the poverty, chastity, and obedience characteristic of the religious life—the fact is rarely adverted to that Jesus Christ himself chose to live such a chaste celibate and, indeed, virginal life—not to speak of the poverty of the life he led everywhere attested to in the Gospels, nor of the obedience which he expressly and consistently gave to the will of his Father!

No less than three times in the course of two chapters in the Gospel of John, Jesus declares that he has not *come* to do his own will "but the will of him who sent me" (Jn 4:34; 5:3; 6:38). In the Letter to the Hebrews he plainly says: "I have *come* to do thy will, O God!" (Heb 10:6; emphasis added). When we speak or think of an "imitation of Christ," then, we should never forget that among the salient things about him that need to be imitated are his poverty, chastity, and obedience, as consecrated religious vow to do.

And, as *Lumen Gentium* reminds us, the same thing is true of his Blessed Mother Mary! As Pope Paul VI was later to say in his 1974 apostolic exhortation *Marialis Cultus*, For the Right Ordering and Development of Devotion to the Blessed Virgin Mary:

> [T]he Virgin Mary has always been proposed to the faithful by the Church as an example to be imitated, not precisely in the type of life she led, and much less for the socio-cultural background in which she lived and which today scarcely exists anywhere. She is held up as an example to the faithful, rather, for the way in which, in her life, she fully and responsibly accepted the will of God (cf. Lk 1:38), because she heard the word of God and acted upon it, and because charity and a spirit of service were the driving force of her actions. She is worthy of imitation because she was the first and most perfect of Christ's disciples. All of this has a permanent and universal exemplary value (*MC* 35).

What, then, could be *more* appropriate in the seeking of perfection than to adopt the Church's traditional three vows, or evangelical counsels, of poverty, chastity, and obedience, as religious do? The document further recognizes, moreover, that,

> while the profession of the evangelical counsels involves the renunciation of goods that undoubtedly deserve to be highly valued, it does not constitute an obstacle to the true development of the human person, but by its nature is supremely beneficial to that development. For the counsels, when willingly embraced in accordance with each one's personal vocation, contribute in no small degree to the purification of the heart and to spiritual freedom (ibid.).

Those who live out the religious life, the Council believes, enable the Church to "truly show forth Christ through them" (ibid.). "All members of the Church should unflaggingly fulfill the duties of their Christian calling," the Council teaches. The religious life, though, enables those committed to it to realize their Christian calling more perfectly. Moreover, it serves as a shining example to all Christians:

> The profession of the evangelical counsels shines before them as a sign which can and should inspire them to do so. For the People of God has here no lasting city but seeks the city which is to come, and the religious state of life, in bestowing greater freedom from the cares of earthly existence on those who follow it, simultaneously reveals more clearly to all believers the heavenly goods which are already present in this age, witnessing to the new and eternal life which we have acquired through the redemptive work of Christ (*LG* 44).

Emphasizing the good produced by the religious life for the whole Church, then, and not just for those actually engaged in it, *Lumen Gentium* emphatically denies "that their consecrated life alienates religious from other men or makes them useless for human society" (*LG* 46). The regular prayers and sacrifices of those engaged in the religious life are, on the contrary, eminently beneficial for human society, not only in the good works performed by religious brothers and sisters themselves but also in the very fact itself that they are vowed to live out the life of Christ more fully: Christ is thereby that much more present in the world.

Lumen Gentium further notes that "it is for the hierarchy to make wise laws for the regulation of the practice whereby the perfect love of God and of our neighbor is fostered in a unique way" (*LG* 45). The religious life is very much an ecclesial pursuit, in other words, one which is inseparable from the life and holiness of the Church; and so members of religious orders, in their turn, must show respect and obedience to their religious superiors and to the Church hierarchy (cf. *LG* 45).

In its final Fourth Session, Vatican II would go on to issue a separate document, the Decree on the Up-to-Date Renewal of the Religious Life, *Perfectae Caritatis*. It is eminently worth reading as a description of how the religious life should be carried on in its proper place. Short as it is, though, this sixth chapter of *Lumen Gentium* on the religious life also covers the essential points about this particular kind of life, helping us to understand how this special and consecrated calling fits into the life of the Church and thereby serves both God and the People of God. Vowed religious, then, whether they are solitary or living in community, represent an integral part of the life of the Church; and their consecrated religious life, consistently practiced in the Church since ancient times, is very strongly explained and affirmed in *Lumen Gentium*'s chapter 6.

X.

Chapter 7 of *Lumen Gentium*, entitled "The Pilgrim Church," is the principal place in the documents of Vatican II where the whole question of *eschatology* comes up. Eschatology is the branch of theology that treats what have traditionally been called the Four Last Things: death, judgment, heaven, and hell. It must be said at the outset, however, that eschatology was evidently not the Second Vatican Council's major forte. Focused as it was so strongly on this world and upon the Church's life and problems and prospects within this world, the Council tended to neglect the Four Last Things somewhat, at least relatively speaking. Not that what the Council says about them is in any way wrong or false—what is said about them is right and true—but it is perhaps a case of "once over lightly" for these elements of the Church's life that, while they could not be entirely neglected, were not really at the heart of the Council's main concerns and preoccupations either. In this respect, chapter 7 of *Lumen Gentium* on "the pilgrim Church" does not quite measure up to the rest of the document in importance.

However, the Christian message is simply not complete if the eschatological dimension is downplayed or truncated. As the Canadian media guru Marshall McLuhan once remarked: "Even the good news of the Gospel can be sold only by hellfire. Vatican II made a bad mistake in this, as in other matters."

The chapter does deal, however, at least to some extent, with those things traditionally associated with our eternal destiny and with life after death, including such characteristic Catholic beliefs and practices as heaven, purgatory, prayers for the dead, veneration of the saints, angels, the Second Coming, and so on. Although these traditional Catholic elements are treated or at least touched upon and affirmed in this text, they are for the most part not enumerated, carefully defined, or discussed as distinct topics in the manner of more traditionally styled treatises. Rather, the style is discursive, and some things are mentioned almost as if only in passing. The narrative is at times both beautiful and inspiring, but it also sometimes leaves some of the elements of Catholic belief and practice related to its topic somewhat indistinct.

It is not that the narrative consciously downgrades or denies any aspect of traditional Catholic belief or practices. On the contrary, these beliefs and practices are mostly strongly and sometimes even eloquently affirmed; but they are affirmed in such a way that suggests the Council Fathers aimed at getting them set down as quickly as possible and then put out of the way so that the Fathers could get on to things that interested them more at the time; these elements could not be ignored, but they did not, it seems, have to be dwelt upon at great length either.

It is a rather patent fact that Vatican II, generally, was more interested in what used to be called "the Church Militant," the Church here and now, than in "the Church Suffering" (purgatory) or "the Church Triumphant" (heaven). Significantly, these traditional expressions are not even used in this text, and purgatory, in particular, is only briefly described.

It is to be noted too that the Four Last Things themselves are not treated in the traditional way in chapter 7 of *Lumen Gentium* nor, for the most part, are they treated anywhere else in the sixteen documents of Vatican II, apart from occasional references—and apart from a brief but very fine text on the "mystery of death" in the Pastoral Constitution on the Church in the Modern World, *Gaudium et Spes* (cf. *GS* 18). Vatican Council II very definitely gave less attention to eschatology than to most other branches of theology.

Both the brevity and reticence of this kind of treatment did not pass without notice during the Council itself, however; and, indeed, this part of the *schema De Ecclesia*, which eventually became the dogmatic constitution, was specifically criticized in the *aula* of St. Peter's by some of the Council Fathers. Among others, Ernesto Cardinal Ruffini, archbishop of Palermo, Sicily, and one of the more vigorous and active "conservative" prelates at the Council, criticized the draft of this chapter quite severely and even recommended that it not be approved. In an intervention delivered in September 1964, Cardinal Ruffini complained about the lack of coherence and order in the discussion of the last things; in particular, he deplored the fact that purgatory and the condemnation of those dying in mortal sin were being passed over in virtual silence.

Purgatory does seem to have been given some added attention in the final draft, perhaps as a result of the cardinal's criticisms; but there are still only scattered references to the damned in the final approved test. As for hell, the word itself is not mentioned as such. Like the word "heresy," the word "hell" was almost never heard during the conciliar debates, and it is not to be found listed in the indexes of the major histories of the Council or in those of the collections of the Council's documents either. Nor do I recall seeing the word anywhere else in the Council documents. The words "devil" and "Evil One" *are* mentioned several times (e.g., in *LG* 48 and 16).

This nonmention of hell persisted in spite of specific requests of Council Fathers that it be mentioned. These requests came in addition to the remarks of Cardinal Ruffini just noted. During the debate on the *schema*, for example, Archbishop Alberto Gori, the Latin-rite archbishop of Jerusalem, strongly objected to the fact that the draft contained no explicit references to "the existence of hell, the eternity of hell," or to the possibility of "personal damnation" ("damnation" being another word that does not appear in those indexes, although *Lumen Gentium* 14, for example, refers several times to those who are "not saved"). The truths about the existence and eternity of hell had been explicitly revealed, Archbishop Gori said, and the Council should not be silent about them, as so many contemporary priests, he thought, had already become relatively silent about them in their preaching. There can be no doubt that the archbishop was on the mark in what he said about many modern priests; but the spirit of the times seemed to militate against undue emphasis on hell and damnation in the conciliar texts.

In the end, the text was somewhat strengthened with regard to the Four Last Things, though perhaps not as much as the critics had wished. The way the approved text treats the unpleasant subjects of death, judgment, and hell—the text goes on about heaven *at length*!—is by *quoting Scripture* on these topics. Thus, there are very clear scriptural references to "the wiles of the devil" (Eph 6:11), to "the eternal fire prepared for the devil and his angels" (Mt 25:41), and to "the resurrection of judgment" (Jn 5:29). The text with equal clarity, and without beating around the bush, quotes St. Paul to the effect that "we must all appear before the judgment seat of Christ, so that each one may receive good or evil, according to what he has done in the body" (2 Cor 5:10). So the Council certainly did not deny or downgrade any of these doctrines, although it certainly could have treated them more fully.

Similarly, as we saw earlier when dealing with the question of those who belong to the Church, and in what degree, *Lumen Gentium* very plainly recognizes the possibility of some *not being saved*. While the text prefers this formulation to speaking about "damnation" or "the damned," it does not evade or avoid the question (e.g., cf. *LG* 14 and 16). Still, death, judgment, and hell are hardly emphasized in the chapter. Both its tone and its content attempt to remain determinedly "positive." This "positive" tendency, and the avoidance of mentioning hell by name, continued to be carried over into the postconciliar period in some of the Church's other teaching documents. Pope Paul VI, for example, in his 1968 Credo of the People of God, issued mainly in response to challenges by revisionists to important Church doctrines, similarly speaks of those who have rejected God "going to the fire that is not extinguished"; but the pontiff does not employ the word "hell" as such.

Of course, not every Council necessarily has to deal with every Church doctrine, but the absence of the word "hell," like that of the word "heresy," from the Vatican II documents is surely a significant lack. Given the stark emphasis of Jesus himself in not a few of his sayings—"Fear him who can destroy both soul and body in hell" (Mt 10:28); "It is better for you to enter life maimed than with two hands to go to hell" (Mk 9:42); "Fear him, who after he has killed, has power to cast into hell" (Lk 12:5)—*Lumen Gentium* surely failed to include the proper *emphasis* on truths that the Church has not ceased to teach, namely, that death comes to all, judgment is certain, and the irreparable loss of one's soul is possible.

The Latin-rite patriarch of Jerusalem at the Council was correct in saying that modern priests today dislike dwelling upon these realities in their preaching. This has been even more true since the end of the Council; often, if not regularly, today, the impression is given that everyone is really going to go to heaven anyway; many people now simply assume this as a matter of course. And the "new catechetics," of course, introduced this emphasis into Catholic classrooms with a vengeance. One of the worst of the defects that afflicted religious education in the postconciliar era, and to some extent still does, has been a downgrading of the supernatural generally; but it is especially marked where the possible loss of one's soul and eternal punishment are concerned. This surely represents an injustice to those whose souls possibly are in jeopardy.

Some of the responsibility for this deemphasis of these particular immutable Church teachings must be laid at the door of Vatican II itself. This is unfortunately true of chapter 7 of *Lumen Gentium* on "the pilgrim Church." While the document for the most part is a great one, this is unfortunately not true of this particular chapter. And while it is usually salutary to take a positive approach, if only in order to attract people to the Christian message, this cannot be legitimately done—and should not be done—at the expense of neglecting or downgrading essential teachings of the faith.

It was the *Catechism of the Catholic Church*—which in some ways we may consider a long-delayed catechism of Vatican Council II—that finally came along and definitely righted the balance in Church eschatological teaching in the way the *Catechism* treated both judgment and hell (see esp. *CCC* 1033–41). This was a necessary correction in emphasis. And just as the Fathers of Vatican II failed to anticipate the crisis of authority in Church teaching that arose out of the tolerated theological dissent that came in the aftermath of the encyclical *Humanae Vitae*, so they failed to reckon with the watering down of the faith that would come as a result of the fact that the Council dwelt so heavily on the necessities of earth and the joys of heaven that it gave only minimal attention to the pains of hell.

In defense of the Council Fathers, however, it must be added that they did explicitly affirm the truth and necessity of the Church's authentic tradition in this whole area. They did not fail to state, for example:

> This sacred council accepts loyally the venerable faith of our ancestors in the living communion which exists between us and our brothers who are in the glory of heaven or who are being purified after their death; and it proposes again the decrees of the Second Council of Nicaea, of the Council of Florence, and of the Council of Trent. (*LG* 51)

It is good to know that the teachings of these venerable councils were not forgotten. At the same time, though, the text of *Lumen Gentium* did not go on to state, as without doubt it should have stated, the equally authentic tradition of the Fourth Lateran Council of 1215:

> [Christ] shall come at the end of time to judge the living and the dead and to render to each one according to his works, to the reprobate [*reprobis*] as well as to the elect. All of them will rise again with their own bodies which they now bear, to receive according to their works, whether these have been good or evil, the ones *perpetual punishment with the devil* and the others everlasting glory with Christ. (Symbol of Lateran IV; emphasis added)

It has often, and aptly, been said of the Catholic faith, for instance by the late theologian Father John A. Hardon, S.J., that it almost always has to include the word "and": God is transcendent *and* within us; Christ is human *and* divine; revealed truth is found in Scripture *and* Tradition; we are saved by grace *and* the faith and good works Christ inspires in us—and so on with regard to so many of the manifold truths of the faith (grace *and* nature, body *and* soul, etc.). In their desire to frame the positive message of Jesus in a way that would appeal to the modern world—as Blessed John XXIII had expressly wished—perhaps the Council Fathers neglected somewhat to give proper emphasis to one of the "ands" without which no statement of the faith can be complete, namely, that even though Christ has saved us from sin, and heaven is our proper destination, hell is nevertheless real and is a place to which the reprobate can be liable, if those same reprobates do not finally repent and believe in the Gospel (cf. Mk 1:15).

XI.

The eighth and final chapter of *Lumen Gentium* is devoted to Our Lady. The question of how to deal with Catholic belief in and devotion to the Blessed Virgin Mary was, perhaps oddly—or perhaps understandably—one of the most hotly debated topics at the Council. The mostly progressive bishops of the European Alliance were very interested in ecumenism and did not want to alienate Protestant observers, with whom it was hoped there could be fruitful ecumenical dialogue following the Council. As a result, they did not wish the Council to overemphasize the kind of Marian belief and practice in the Catholic Church at which Protestants tended, and tend, to look askance.

On the other hand, the fact that Marian belief and practice *are* very strongly rooted in the Catholic Church—not to speak of the Orthodox Churches of the East, with which it was also hoped, of course, that fruitful ecumenical dialogue could be carried on—meant that Our Lady had many ardent advocates at the Council, not only among some of the religious orders and some of the *periti*, but also among not a few of the Council Fathers themselves. Some of these advocates were eager to promote the Marian cause and perhaps even add new titles to her name, such as Mediatrix and Coredemptrix—not to speak of the new title that *would* be added to her name before the end of the Council, namely, "Mother of the Church."

The debate at the Council developed first along the lines of whether there should be a special *schema* on the Blessed Virgin or whether the Church's teaching concerning her should form part of another *schema*. Few or none doubted that the Council had to treat the subject; it was a question of where and how it should be done. The pro-Marian people by and large wanted a separate *schema* devoted to her; the others wanted to deal with Marian doctrine in connection with some other, broader *schema*. Following the end of the First Session, the Council's Coordinating Commission ruled that the subject was to be treated independently. Consequently, a separate Marian *schema* was prepared and distributed in anticipation of the debate to come in the Second Session in 1963.

When the German, Austrian, and German-Swiss bishops received copies of this draft Marian *schema*, they asked Jesuit father Karl Rahner, whom many considered to be the most accomplished and outstanding of all of the theologians and other *periti* at the Council, to prepare a paper on it that the German-speaking bishops could consider at a conference they planned to hold at Fulda in August 1963, in advance of the opening of the Second Session. Father Rahner's paper judged that "unimaginable harm would result from an ecumenical point of view in relation to both Orientals and Protestants" if the draft Marian *schema* were adopted as written. (Around that same time, in 1962, the German Evangelical Church had stated that the Catholic Church's teaching on Mary was one of the major impediments to reunion.)

Father Rahner also thought that the draft Marian *schema* contained statements that, theologically, were "not sufficiently developed"; he particularly objected to the use of the title "Mediatrix of All Graces" and thought that if the idea of mediation was to be used at all in connection with Mary, it must be clearly defined. He also thought that the whole subject could best be handled by merging the Marian *schema* with the *schema* on the Church. The German-speaking bishops adopted Father Rahner's basic approach. They also promptly enlisted the Scandinavian bishops on their side. This was a frequent occurrence at the Council, by the way, where the northern European, "Rhine-flows-into-the Tiber" bishops would approach upcoming issues with papers well prepared in advance by well-known theologians such as Father Rahner and with many bishops already lined up in support of their favored positions. In this particular case, by the time the Second Session began, there was already a solid group of more than sixty bishops who wanted the draft Marian *schema* combined with the *schema De Ecclesia* on the Church.

Cologne's Joseph Cardinal Frings proposed this solution to the full Council when the debate on Mary took place in September 1963.

The pro-Marian bishops were not as solidly organized. Very soon, most of the English and French bishops also lined up behind the German bishops, as did a number of Latin American bishops, following the lead of Chilean cardinal Raul Silva Henríquez, who told the Council that devotion to the Blessed Virgin Mary sometimes went beyond the bounds of what authentic Christian devotion required. This was a somewhat surprising development since, generally speaking, the strongest support for a separate Marian *schema* had tended to come from countries with a Latin tradition, where Marian devotion had always been especially strong.

Thus, it was Benjamin Cardinal de Arriba y Castro of Tarragona, Spain, who spoke for many bishops in support of a separate Marian *schema* along the lines of the existing draft. He was strongly seconded by Rufino Cardinal Santos of Manila, the Philippines. Similar support came from areas as diverse as Eastern Europe and Brazil and also from entities such as some of the religious orders and the Eastern Catholic Churches. New York's Francis Cardinal Spellman was probably typical of most of the American bishops of the day in favoring a "devotional" approach and hence a separate Marian *schema.* Most of the contemporary reporting on the debate, however, favored the combined *schema* idea, although the Italian- and Spanish-speaking press favored the contrary view.

In the end, a vote was taken on whether or not the draft Marian *schema* should become part of the *schema* on the Church. The vote was close: 1,114 in favor of combining the two *schemata*, and 1,097 opposed—a difference of only seventeen votes out of a total of 2,211. Nevertheless, this outcome was taken to be yet another "victory" for the European Alliance. Both the careful preparation and the consistent networking of the European Alliance accounted for its success much of the time.

Yet it should not have been in the least surprising that the pro-Marian viewpoint had also shown considerable strength. Authentic Catholic faith and practice have always been strongly Marian, as the pontificate of Pope John Paul II has since abundantly verified. Perhaps the true surprise should have been that so many Catholic bishops were apparently prepared to appear "moderate" and thus deemphasize some of the Church's notably Marian features in the interests of the wholly theoretical possible future ecumenical benefits (not to speak of the fact that the ecumenical task would actually be rendered *more difficult* in the eyes of the Eastern Catholic Churches if Marian beliefs and practices were deemphasized or downgraded).

In the end, the text as we find it now in chapter 8 of *Lumen Gentium* in no way deemphasized or watered down the position and importance of the Mother of God in the divine plan of redemption. The debate itself ensured that. When the debate resumed on a by then much revised text during the Third Session in 1964, there were a number of strong interventions from the floor, which resulted in a further strengthening of the text. Notably, there was an intervention by Stefan Cardinal Wyszynski of Warsaw, Poland, calling attention to the absolutely fundamental importance of the Blessed Virgin Mary in the life of the Church. Cardinal Wyszynski revealed that the Polish bishops had actually called upon Pope Paul VI to declare formally that Mary was "the Mother of the Church."

Another strong pro-Marian intervention, perhaps surprisingly, came from the Belgian cardinal Léon-Joseph Suenens of Mechelen-Brussels, one of the principal movers and shakers at the Council and surely a "charter member" of the progressive European Alliance if there ever was one. However, coming from Marian-oriented (at least *then*!) Belgium, Cardinal Suenens frankly said that he wanted to see emphasized the spiritual maternity "which Mary continues to exercise in the Church today." As a result of the debate that included such interventions as these, the text was both strengthened and lengthened by about one-third—so much so that the well-known Protestant theologian Professor Oscar Cullmann, one of the Protestant observers at the Council, complained, "Mariology at this Council has been intensified to a degree which is not in keeping with the ecumenical tendencies of Protestantism . . . and with a return to the Bible. Our expectations in this connection have not been fulfilled."

But if the Marian element is as important an element of authentic Catholic faith and practice as both history and theology attest, then it was surely inevitable that a general council of the Catholic Church would end up by strongly affirming that element. In a discourse delivered on the same day that *Lumen Gentium* was approved, November 21, 1964, Pope Paul VI declared that "knowledge of the true Catholic doctrine regarding the Blessed Virgin Mary will always be a key to the exact understanding of the mystery of Christ and the Church." And so it proved.

What kind of a text was it, then, that actually emerged enhanced and strengthened as a result of not a few efforts and even machinations at the Council aiming to deemphasize it? That had been one of the main intentions, after all, of combining the *schema* with the Constitution on the Church rather than issuing it as a separate Council document. But the answer to the question is that the final text constitutes a concise though essentially complete treatise on the true place of Mary in the economy of salvation. The text states that it does not "intend to give a complete doctrine on Mary, nor does it wish to decide those questions which the work of theologians has not yet fully clarified" (*LG* 54).

Nevertheless, it deals quite amply with Mary as she is understood and venerated in the Catholic tradition. In his apostolic letter on the Rosary, *Rosarium Virginis Mariae*, issued on October 16, 2002, Pope John Paul II describes this eighth and final chapter of *Lumen Gentium* as "a chapter which discusses the wondrous presence of the Mother of God in the mystery of Christ and the Church" and adds that "the Rosary is, in some sense, a prayer-commentary on th[is] final chapter of the Vatican II Constitution on the Church, *Lumen Gentium*."

The idea of the Rosary as a "prayer-commentary" on chapter 8 of *Lumen Gentium*, though perhaps an unexpected idea, is not really such a strange idea when we think about it. As the pope points out in this same *Rosarium Virginis Mariae*, "against the background of the words *Ave Maria*, the principal events in the life of Jesus Christ pass before the eyes of the soul. They take shape in the complete series of joyful, sorrowful, and glorious mysteries"—and, of course, it was precisely by means of this same apostolic letter that John Paul II *added* a set of "luminous mysteries" to the recitation of the Rosary in order to fill out the "principal events in the life of Jesus Christ." "They put us in living communion with Jesus," the pope said, "through—we might say—the heart of the mother" (*RVM* 2).

This, of course, was precisely what the pro-Marian Council Fathers were aiming to do with their recommendations for the Marian *schema*; they wanted to put the faithful in closer touch with Jesus through the heart of his mother. The final approved text measured up to the challenge.

Lumen Gentium's chapter 8 on Mary, then, has proved to be quite adequate to the task of bringing out the indispensable place of Mary in the economy of salvation. As the text itself states:

> The Virgin Mary, who at the message of an angel received the Word of God in her heart and in her body and gave life to the world, is acknowledged and honored as being truly the Mother of God and of the Redeemer. Redeemed in a more exalted fashion, by reason of the merits of her Son and united to him by a close and indissoluble tie, she is endowed with the high office and dignity of Mother of the Son of God, and therefore she is also the beloved daughter of the Father and the temple of the Holy Spirit. Because of this gift of sublime grace, she far surpasses all creatures, both in heaven and on earth. But, being of the race of Adam, she is at the same time united to all those who are to be saved; indeed [quoting St. Augustine *De S. Virginitate* 6] "she is clearly the mother of the members of Christ . . . since she has by her charity joined in bringing about the birth of believers in the Church, who are members of its head" (*LG* 53).

The text goes on to spell out further the function of the Blessed Virgin in God's plan of salvation, as well as her role in the Church. The text is at pains to quote what, as it happens, is the essential scriptural passage in this regard, to the effect that "there is but one God and one mediator of God and men, the man Christ Jesus, who gave himself as a ransom for all" (1 Tim 2:5–6). Mary's function "in no way obscures or diminishes this unique mediation of Christ," the text goes on to say, "but rather shows its power" (*LG* 60).

The text gets around the possibly sticky theological problems inherent in the concepts of Mary being an Advocate, Helper, Benefactress, and Mediatrix by simply recording that she is "invoked in the Church under the[se] titles" (*LG* 62). The controversial term "Coredemptrix" was not included in this listing, by the way.

The text also deals with what is styled (more in the European than in the American vocabulary) "the cult of the Blessed Virgin Mary." The text points out that this "cult" of (or, as we Americans might prefer to say, "devotion" to) the Blessed Virgin Mary is eminently traditional in the Church, as it is also very ancient: "Following the Council of Ephesus" (A.D. 431), *Lumen Gentium* declares, "there was a remarkable growth in the cult of the People of God towards Mary, in veneration and love, in invocation and imitation, according to her own prophetic words: 'All generations shall call me blessed because he that is mighty has done great things to me' (Lk 1:48). This cult, as it has always existed in the Church, for all its uniqueness, differs essentially from the cult of adoration, which is offered uniquely to the Incarnate Word and to the Father, and the Holy Spirit" (*LG* 66).

The text goes on to urge that this "cult, especially the liturgical cult, of the Blessed Virgin, be generously fostered, and that the practices and exercises of devotion toward her, recommended by the teaching authority of the Church in the course of centuries, be highly esteemed and . . . religiously observed" (ibid.).

In brief, there was no deemphasis or downgrading of Mary at Vatican II. More than that, the completion of this text set the stage for the subsequent action by which Pope Paul VI declared Mary to be "the Mother of the Church" (as the Polish bishops, among others, had requested and, as we have seen, St. Augustine too so prophetically foresaw, in the passage from *Lumen Gentium* quoted above, in which the bishop of Hippo recognized her as "the mother of the members of Christ . . . since she has by her charity joined in bringing about the birth of believers"). The title "Mother of the Church" had actually been included in the draft text, and some of the Fathers complained when it did not appear in the final draft that was voted upon and approved.

Pope Paul VI moved to remedy this omission at the end of the Third Session, even before the final approval of the text. In an action that illustrated the way in which the collegiality so strongly insisted upon by *Lumen Gentium* can sometimes operate, the pope, on November 18, 1964, acting on his own authority but reflecting the wishes of many bishops, declared that "we shall close this session of the Ecumenical Council . . . by joyfully bestowing on Our Lady, the title due to her, Mother of the Church."

In his concluding address to the Council's Third Session, Pope Paul VI said that the relationship between Mary and the Church, "so clearly established in today's conciliar Constitution," caused him to believe that this was "the most solemn and appropriate moment" to fulfill what "very many Council Fathers" also wished: "Therefore, for the glory of the Virgin Mary, and for our own consolation," he said, "we proclaim the Most Holy Mary as the Mother of the Church, that is to say, of all the People of God, of the faithful as well as the pastors, who call her their most loving Mother."

This proclamation was greeted by a standing ovation from the assembled Council Fathers. Yet this was hardly the end of the story as far as Vatican II's Marian message was concerned. We have already cited Pope John Paul II's description of this chapter of *Lumen Gentium* in his 2002 apostolic letter *Rosarium Virginis Mariae*, and this was only one of a number of postconciliar documents in part inspired by and carrying on with the Council's emphasis on the Marian dimension of the Catholic faith. Pope Paul VI, for example, on February 2, 1974, issued an apostolic exhortation entitled For the Right Ordering and Development of Devotion to the Blessed Virgin Mary, *Marialis Cultus*, in which he pointed out how "the Church's reflection on the mystery of Christ and on her own nature has led her to find at the root of the former and as a culmination of the latter the same figure of a woman: the Virgin Mary, the Mother of Christ and the Mother of the Church."

As its subtitle in English indicated, *Marialis Cultus* aimed at the "right ordering" and renewal of Marian devotion in the light of the Council's reaffirmation of such devotion's importance in the overall scheme of Catholic worship of the divine Majesty. Among other things, Pope Paul VI described in this exhortation the improved ways in which Mary is now celebrated in the restored Roman Calendar; he was also critical of those post–Vatican II churchmen who, in his words, "scorn, *a priori*, devotions of piety which, in their correct forms, have been recommended by the magisterium. . . . They forget," the pontiff went on, "that the Council said that devotions of piety should harmonize with the liturgy, not be suppressed" (*MC* 30). This was a pertinent and timely admonition to those whose postconciliar reforming zeal had too often led them to try to abolish such devotions as the Rosary and the Angelus (both of which Paul VI expressly and warmly commended to the faithful).

Similarly, Pope John Paul II, already known to the whole world for his markedly "Marian" pontificate, was specifically inspired by the eighth chapter of *Lumen Gentium* in a number of his initiatives—as we have already seen with his *Rosarium Virginis Mariae*. In his encyclical *Redemptoris Mater* ("Mother of the Redeemer"), On the Blessed Virgin Mary in the Life of the Pilgrim Church, issued on March 25, 1987, the Polish pope has provided us with what is practically an extended commentary on the Vatican II text:

> The Second Vatican Council, by presenting Mary in the mystery of Christ, also finds the path to a deeper understanding of the mystery of the Church. Mary, as the Mother of Christ, *is in a particular way united with the Church*, "which the Lord established as his own body" (*LG* 52). It is significant that the conciliar text places this truth about the Church as the Body of Christ (according to the teaching of the Pauline Letters) in close proximity to the truth that the Son of God "through the power of the Holy Spirit was born of the Virgin Mary." The reality of the Incarnation finds a sort of extension *in the mystery of the Church—the Body of Christ*. And one cannot think of the reality of the Incarnation without referring to Mary, the Mother of the Incarnate Word. (*RM* 5; emphasis in the original)

The encyclical *Redemptoris Mater* as a whole is framed within what the pope calls "the pilgrimage of faith" in which " 'the Blessed Virgin advanced,' faithfully preserving her union with Christ" (*LG* 58; *RM* 5). The encyclical is rich in references to the Council. For example, *Lumen Gentium* 59 sees a correspondence between Mary at the Annunciation and the apostles at prayer with her in the upper room on the day of Pentecost. Pope John Paul II extends this idea by writing that

> there is a unique correspondence between the moment of the Incarnation of the Word and the moment of the birth of the Church. The person who links these two moments is Mary: *Mary at Nazareth* and *Mary in the Upper Room at Jerusalem*. In both cases

> her discreet yet essential presence indicates the path of "birth from the Holy Spirit." Thus, she who is present in the mystery of Christ as Mother becomes—by the will of the Son and the power of the Holy Spirit—present at the mystery of the Church. (*RM* 24)

There are other and similar insights in the encyclical. Nowhere is there a better description of and justification for designating Mary as the Mother of the Church (cf. *RM* 24) than here. John Paul II, in line with his strong ecumenical interest, also laid great emphasis on how the Eastern Churches venerate Mary (cf. *RM* 31–32). At the conclusion of his encyclical, he proclaimed a Marian year to extend from Pentecost in 1987 through the Feast of the Assumption in 1988 (cf. *RM* 48). About few things in his pontificate was Pope John Paul II more definite than about the place of Mary within the whole framework of the Catholic faith.

And yet the encyclical *Redemptoris Mater* is only one of the Marian initiatives of this eminently Marian pope that can be said to derive at least in part from *Lumen Gentium*'s treatment of Mary. There are others. In his excellent and authoritative *Witness to Hope*, for example, the biographer of John Paul II, George Weigel, pointed out how, in an address to the Roman Curia on December 22, 1987, in the middle of the Marian Year, the Polish pope established what Weigel calls the Marian "profile" of the Church as fundamental:

> Mary, he suggested, was the first disciple, for her assent to the angel's message made possible the incarnation of the Son of God. The incarnation had been "extended" in history through the Church, the mystical Body of Christ. Mary's assumption into heaven prefigured the glorification of all who will be saved. Thus, Mary provides a "profile" of what the Church is, of how the people of the Church should live, and of what the destiny of the disciples will be.
>
> This understanding of the relationship between Mary and the Church challenged the way many Catholic leaders had come to think of themselves and their powers. The "Marian profile" of the Church is, John Paul suggested, even "more fundamental" than the "Petrine profile." Without being divided from it, the "Marian Church"—the Church of disciples—preceded and made possible the "Petrine Church"—the Church of office and authority. Indeed,

> office in the Church has no other purpose "except to form the Church in line with the ideal of sanctity already programmed and prefigured in Mary . . . the Marian profile is pre-eminent."

George Weigel concludes from this that John Paul II is saying that "discipleship came before authority in the Church and sanctity came before power, even the apostolically transmitted priestly power to 'bind and loose' sins. This was not Mariology in the service of traditionalism," Weigel goes on to say. "This was Mariology demolishing the last vestiges of the Church-as-absolute-monarchy."

Nor was John Paul II the only one in the postconciliar years to emphasize the importance of Mary as presented in the final chapter of *Lumen Gentium.* In a chapter entitled "The Ecclesiology of the Second Vatican Council" included in his 1988 book *Church, Ecumenism, and Politics,* Joseph Cardinal Ratzinger observed that

> [t]he Council's Constitution on the Church ends with the chapter on the Mother of God. The question whether a separate document should be devoted to her was, as is known, the subject of vigorous debate. I think it was nevertheless a good arrangement for the question of Mary to enter directly into the doctrine of the Church. In this way the point that we started out from becomes visible once again: the Church is not some piece of machinery, is not just an institution, is not even one of the usual sociological entities. It is a person. It is a woman. It is a mother. It is living. The Marian understanding of the Church is the most decisive contrast to a purely organizational or bureaucratic conception of the Church. We cannot make the Church: we have to be it. And it is only to the extent that faith moulds our being beyond any question of making that we are the Church, that the Church is in us. It is only in being Marian that we become the Church. In its origins the Church was not made but was born. It was born when the intention, "Let it be to me according to your word," awoke in the soul of Mary. That the Church should awaken in our souls is the deepest desire of the Council. Mary shows us the way.

We have already noted in our examination of chapter 3 of *Lumen Gentium* how much at pains the Fathers of the Council were to emphasize that, although the hierarchical nature of the Church is both Christ-established and absolutely indispensable to the mission confided to the Church by Christ, the hierarchy is nevertheless not "the Church." *Lumen Gentium*'s chapter 2 on the People of God aimed to make the same point. Pope John Paul II's thinking, as well as Cardinal Ratzinger's, on the "Marian Church" is thus very much in line with the thought and aims of the Council generally, but it seems particularly appropriate that their thought should correspond so closely with this eighth and final chapter of *Lumen Gentium* on Our Lady. In retrospect, it seems both providential and prophetic that Vatican II's great Dogmatic Constitution on the Church should have concluded with this treatment of Mary, the Mother of the Church.

It was at the end of the Third Session of the Council in 1964, then, that *Lumen Gentium* as a whole was approved and added to the Church's permanent patrimony of truth.

XII.

At the beginning of this chapter, it was stated that *Lumen Gentium* is "the most important single statement that the Catholic Church has ever made about herself in the nearly two thousand years of her life on this earth." Now that we have reviewed in some detail the eight separate chapters of this document, along with some of the postconciliar Church documents and actions that grew out of it, it should be easier for us to see how it is that this dogmatic constitution is indeed of the highest importance and, moreover, to see why this is so.

The early councils of the Church formulated and developed the very precise creedal statements that we profess today expressing the Church's belief concerning who and what this Jesus Christ was and is, "who was born of the Virgin Mary, suffered under Pontius Pilate, was crucified, died, and was buried, and on the third day, rose again from the dead." Later councils defined and spelled out the Church's belief concerning the myriad of topics that form the whole fabric of our faith. A look at the table of contents of such collections of Church teachings as the very useful volume edited by the Jesuit fathers Neuner and Dupuis entitled *The Christian Faith in the Doctrinal Documents of the Catholic Church* records numerous papal and conciliar decisions on such topics as revelation and faith, Scripture and Tradition, the Triune God, original sin and the Fall, the Savior, the Mother of the Savior, worship and the saints, grace, the Eucharist and the other sacraments, the Christian moral life, and so on.

The entries shown for "the Church" in this collection, however, mostly deal only with discreet and specific questions such as papal authority or the necessity of the Church for salvation; they do not deal with the Church as a whole. This is true even of the First Vatican Council's 1870 Dogmatic Constitution on the Church of Christ, *Pastor Aeternus,* which scarcely got beyond defining the primacy and infallibility of the pope. This was the case even though the original intention had been to define and describe the nature of the Church more broadly. Unfortunately, however, as we have noted, Vatican I was obliged to adjourn on account of the outbreak of the Franco-Prussian war; and it turned out that this adjournment was destined to be *sine die.*

Lumen Gentium is different. Drawing upon the entire tradition of the Church, this Vatican II dogmatic constitution draws out for the instruction and understanding both of ourselves and of future generations the rich and manifold nature of the Church herself as mystery, as People of God, as pilgrim Church, and as a visible sacerdotal and hierarchical organization; it describes clergy, laity, and religious as essential components of this same Church; it issues its memorable and permanently valid universal call to holiness (which is nothing else but a renewal of the first proclamation of the Gospel by Jesus); and, finally, it situates Our Lady in relation to Christ's Church so that Pope Paul VI was able legitimately to declare her to be the Mother of the Church.

If Vatican Council II had issued no other document at all in addition to *Lumen Gentium,* it would still rank as one of the most important ecumenical councils in the history of the Church on the basis of this document alone. This dogmatic cconstitution thus represents a permanent achievement in the long development of the Church's self-understanding. Even though it was not the only document issued by Vatican II, we will find that the groundwork for the understanding of almost all of the other documents of Vatican II has already been solidly laid for us by our consideration here of *Lumen Gentium.*

Nevertheless, as has already been brought out in more ways than one, *Lumen Gentium* has been subjected to much misunderstanding and misinterpretation in the postconciliar years. We need think, for example, only of the constant misuse of the concept of "the People of God." As we have seen, this does not mean what so many have regularly taken it to mean, namely, that "the people," in some presumably "democratic" sense, are "the Church." Some Church authorities, including especially the Holy See, early became aware of the misuse to which this, among other key ideas of Vatican II, was being put. As a consequence, on June 24, 1973, the Congregation for the Doctrine of the Faith issued its Declaration in Defense of the Catholic Doctrine of the Church against Some Present-Day Errors. With the Latin title, *Mysterium Ecclesiae*, this declaration attempted to correct some of the errors and misconceptions about the Church that already, within less than a decade after the end of the Council, had become manifest and, in some cases, quite widespread.

Noting that Vatican II had "shed fresh light . . . on the mystery of the Church," as we ourselves have also now seen, the declaration went on to say that, nevertheless, some interpretations of the Council, "through the use of ambiguous or even erroneous language, have obscured Catholic doctrine, have at times gone so far as to be opposed to Catholic faith, even in fundamental matters." *Mysterium Ecclesiae* therefore addressed some of the errors that had followed the Council, and it did so under five general headings: (1) the oneness of Christ's Church; (2) the infallibility of the Church's Magisterium; (3) the Church's gift of infallibility not to be diminished; (4) the notion of the Church's infallibility not to be falsified; and, finally, (5) the Church as associated with the priesthood of Christ.

With regard to the oneness of Christ's Church, the declaration made clear that, although the Catholic faithful, following the Council, should respect the truly Christian endowments of our separated brethren, nevertheless "the followers of Christ are not permitted to imagine that Christ's Church is nothing more than a collection (divided but still possessing a certain unity) of Churches and ecclesial communities. Nor are they free to hold that Christ's Church nowhere really exists today, and that it is to be considered only as an end which all Churches and ecclesial communities must strive to reach."

This latter idea was not uncommon in the immediate postconciliar years among some with a rather uncritical enthusiasm for ecumenism.

In the first flush of the permitted ecumenical dialogue following the Council's approval in principle that such dialogue was indeed to be fostered, some enthusiasts rushed heedlessly forward, regardless of still-existing and never-resolved differences. The Council itself, however, had specified that ecumenical dialogue, if it was to be fruitful, could be conducted only according to the rules laid down by the Church. The faithful also had to be warned that they must continue to accept the teaching of the hierarchy, "given in Christ's name, with an assent that is proportionate to the authority" declared by that same hierarchy. This particular dictum thus appeared in *Mysterium Ecclesiae* more than a quarter of century before the 1990 CDF instruction forbidding theological dissent, *Donum Veritatis.* It is evident that the Congregation was beginning to be concerned about the downplaying of doctrinal questions in the midst of the ecumenical euphoria that followed the Council.

With regard to the infallibility of the Church's Magisterium, again anticipating the 1990 instruction *Donum Veritatis,* already back in 1973 the CDF was also reminding the faithful that "the pastors of the Church enjoy the assistance of the Holy Spirit" in a very special way and that, moreover, "the infallibility of the magisterium extends not only to the deposit of faith, but also to those matters without which that deposit cannot be preserved and expounded." The Magisterium does not teach truly *only* regarding revealed truth, in other words; it teaches truly regarding those things that are necessary to the integrity of the faith. With *Mysterium Ecclesiae,* the Congregation for the Doctrine of the Faith was thus already on the job formally reiterating this truth quite early in the development of the postconciliar Age of Dissent.

As for Father Hans Küng's erroneous idea that the Church was indefectible rather than infallible, *Mysterium Ecclesiae* expressly contradicted this position more than six years before Father Küng himself was forbidden by the Congregation for the Doctrine of the Faith to continue to function as a Catholic theologian. "The faithful are in no way permitted to see in the Church merely a fundamental permanence in truth," the CDF declaration stated under its third general heading, "which, as some assert, could be reconciled with errors contained here and there in propositions that the Church's magisterium teaches to be held irrevocably." No: as the declaration went on to make clear under its fourth heading,

> it sometimes happens that some dogmatic truth is first expressed incompletely (but not falsely), and at a later date, when considered in a broader context of faith or human knowledge, it receives a fuller and more perfect expression. In addition, when the Church makes new pronouncements, she intends to confirm or clarify what is in some way contained in Sacred Scripture or in previous expressions of Tradition; but at the same time she usually has intentions of solving certain questions or removing certain errors. All these things have to be taken into account in order that these pronouncements may be properly interpreted.

Moreover, *Mysterium Ecclesiae* goes on very clearly and firmly to declare that "it must be stated that the dogmatic formulas of the Church's Magisterium were from the very beginning suitable for communicating revealed truth, and that as they are they remain forever suitable for communicating this truth to those who interpret them correctly." In other words, the many doctrines and judgments of the Church's Magisterium delivered in the course of her long history do not have to be—indeed, cannot be—modified today simply because some may have declared them "outmoded" or "historically conditioned." These magisterial teachings were valid then and are valid now.

Under its fifth and final heading, the CDF Declaration in Defense of the Catholic Doctrine on the Church against Some Present-Day Errors, *Mysterium Ecclesiae*, affirms the distinction made in *Lumen Gentium* 10 concerning the essential difference between the ministerial priesthood and the common priesthood of all the faithful. This distinction, of course, not only would be affirmed and elaborated upon in the Council's later two documents on the priesthood itself, *Optatam Totius*, On the Training of Priests, and *Presbyterorum Ordinis*, On the Ministry and Life of Priests, but would inspire yet another postconciliar document specifically on the subject of the ministerial priesthood, issued by the Synod of Bishops on November 30, 1967, entitled *Ultimis Temporibus* (again contained in the Austin Flannery volume that brings together a number of these important postconciliar documents).

Mysterium Ecclesiae itself, however, affirms, against the theologians who were now saying that the development of the ministerial priesthood only came later in the history of the Church, that "the ministerial priesthood . . . can be shown to have been invariably conferred from apostolic times by a sacred rite." Moreover, "this rite conferred upon priests not only an increase of grace for carrying out ecclesiastical duties in a holy way, but was also a permanent designation by Christ, or character, by virtue of which they are equipped for their work and endowed with the necessary power that is derived from the supreme power of Christ."

Like baptism and confirmation, in other words, holy orders not only confers grace but—as used to be commonly said—impresses an indelible mark or seal upon the soul of the recipient. The objective, or *ex opere operato*, character of all the sacraments of the Church cannot be too strongly emphasized in an era as strongly tempted as our own to deny sacramental, and indeed all supernatural, realities.

What are we to make of a document such as *Mysterium Ecclesiae*, issued within a few brief years after the end of the Council, in order to correct some of the specific errors concerning the Catholic doctrine of the Church that were already rife? We might have thought that the possibility of such errors would have been eliminated by the very firm and clear teaching of *Lumen Gentium* itself. Instead, it was almost as if this same firm and clear teaching was itself somehow the signal for some to begin entertaining various other and novel doctrines concerning the nature of Christ's Church! Considering the proneness to error on the part of certain modern theologians that was so soon to become manifest, it was surely fortunate that the living Magisterium of the Church continued to function effectively in the midst of the vast confusion that descended upon the Church shortly after the end of the Council.

Mysterium Ecclesiae demonstrates that the Church's Magisterium did not fail to function in this instance. At a time when even "the gates of hell" can seem to be prevailing because some of the very ones responsible for expounding the Church's doctrine have themselves mysteriously gone astray, the promise of Christ to the Church nevertheless continues to be borne out. The "spirit of truth" (Jn 14:17) remains in the Church after all, in this instance through the instrumentality of the

Congregation for the Doctrine of the Faith in Rome. The faithful are not left without proper guidance, if only they will look for it in its proper place, namely, in the decisions and judgments of the Church's living Magisterium.

This is true par excellence of the teachings of the Second Vatican Council. In particular, *Lumen Gentium*, the Council's Dogmatic Constitution on the Church, is preeminently an example of how, twenty centuries after Christ announced and promised it, the Holy Spirit in the Church continues to "teach you all things, and bring to you remembrance all that I have said to you" (Jn 14:26).

CHAPTER THREE

Gaudium et Spes

I.

NO SUBJECT was given more attention at the Second Vatican Council than the subject that became the title of the Council's longest and most varied document, the Pastoral Constitution on the Church in the Modern World, *Gaudium et Spes* ("Joy and Hope"). In one very important sense, of course, Blessed Pope John XXIII's main purpose in convoking the Council in the first place was to equip the Church to deal better with the modern world and the changed conditions of the present day. On September 11, 1962, one month before the opening of the Council, Pope John delivered a radio-television address in which he laid out his hopes and plans for the Council. He stood by a large globe of the earth, four feet in diameter, which he used as a stage prop. He wrote out four Latin words, summarizing the content of his address: *Ecclesia Christi lumen gentium* ("The Church of Christ is the light of the nations"). The task of the Church was to bring Christ's light to the world, and the Council was to study and develop ways and means of doing this more effectively.

Unfortunately, this vivid image of a world in need of Christ's light responding to the ministrations of the Church did not last. It quickly became displaced in people's minds with the misleading image of Pope John opening up the windows of the Church to let in the putative fresh air of the modern world. But it was supposed to have been the other way around. The windows of the Church were supposed to have been opened to let the light of Christ *out*!

In spite of the fact that Blessed John XXIII hoped and intended to set in motion a process by which the Church would impact more effectively on the world—and he very clearly expressed his hopes and intentions in this regard prior to and at the Council—none of the preparatory *schemata* for the Council specifically addressed or built upon these specific hopes and intentions of the pope. It was only in the course of the protracted debate during the First Session on the *schema* entitled *De Ecclesia*, which became the Dogmatic Constitution on the Church, *Lumen Gentium*, that a proposal was made that resulted in another, separate *schema* being drafted that would specifically address the issues of the modern world. The occasion was the key speech delivered by Léon-Joseph Cardinal Suenens on December 4, 1962, when the Belgian prelate outlined his idea that the Council's work should be divided up between the *ad intra*, or internal concerns of the Church, and the *ad extra* issues, that is, those external to the Church but of vital concern to her. Cardinal Suenens enumerated some of his own examples of the latter kinds of issues; they included civil society, social justice, war and peace, population, poverty, hunger, marriage, evangelization of peoples, science and technology, and so on.

This address of Cardinal Suenens was well received and vigorously applauded. It was seconded by a number of bishops, notably by the two Italian cardinal-archbishops considered at the time to be perhaps the two leading *papabili*, or candidates for the papacy, to succeed John XXIII. They were Giacomo Lercaro of Bologna and Giovanni Battista Montini of Milan (who within less than a year would be elected and would occupy the papal chair as Pope Paul VI). Cardinal Montini's intervention, which marked only the second time he addressed the Council as a participating bishop, was considered especially significant because it was believed by many that he spoke *for* Pope John XXIII.

The immediate result of the Suenens proposal and the endorsements it quickly garnered was the creation, by the pope, of a conciliar Coordinating Commission "to coordinate and direct the work of the Council." This Coordinating Commission had Amleto Cardinal Cicognani, the papal secretary of state, as its president. Its other members consisted of cardinals Achille Liénart (Lille), Julius Döpfner (Munich), Carlo Confalonieri (Curia), Francis Spellman (New York), Giovanni Urbani (Venice), and Léon-Joseph Suenens himself (Malines-Brussels). Fairly soon this new body began to impose some order on all of the topics and *schemata* under consideration by the Council.

As regards the new *schema*, which the Coordinating Commission initially identified as "the effective presence of the Church in the world today," it was decided that it would have six chapters: on the vocation of man; on man in society; on marriage and the family; on culture; on economics and the social order; and on the community of nations and peace. A joint commission consisting of all the members of the Theological Commission and of the Commission on the Apostolate of the Laity was formed to draft the new *schema*, under the copresidency of Alfredo Cardinal Ottaviani and Fernando Cardinal Cento, heads of the two commissions combined for the task. As work progressed, other bishops and *periti* were brought in at various stages, and additional subcommissions and working groups were formed to deal with the extensive and sometimes complex and difficult subject matter being considered.

The *schema* itself went through various drafts and was to be subjected to longer and more thorough debates in the Third and Fourth Sessions. Americans will be interested to know that the bishop of Pittsburgh, John J. Wright (later the cardinal-prefect of the Congregation for the Clergy), performed significant work on this *schema* and ended up as chairman of the subcommission on the human person, which produced chapter 1 of part 1 of this long and involved document. Similarly, Archbishop Patrick A. O'Boyle of Washington (later a cardinal), in the course of the debate on the draft during the Third Session, in October 1964, delivered a memorable address in the name of all the American bishops, in which he called for the insertion of a statement condemning "all forms of racial discrimination on the grounds that all men are equal and brethren because they are sons of God." He called racial discrimination "one of the most deplorable and repugnant crimes of mankind today." Such a statement was, in fact, included in the completed text (see *GS* 29).

On a less happy note, the secretary of the joint commission that operated throughout the long and involved drafting and approval process was the German Redemptorist priest Father Bernard Häring, C.Ss.R. During the Council, Father Häring was considered one of the foremost moral theologians in the world and one of the most outstanding *periti* at the Council. After the Council, however, he became an open and aggressive dissenter from magisterial teaching; among other roles, he was a teacher and mentor of the American dissenter Father Charles E. Curran. During the Council, Father Häring was already taking the position that the use of contraception could be morally licit—or that, at any rate, married couples could decide on its use "in conscience." As we shall see, however, he and others of his way of thinking were prevented in a rather dramatic way by the pope from getting their erroneous views incorporated into the Council's finished document.

The *schema* that eventually became *Gaudium et Spes* was not considered at all during the Second Session in 1963. It was extensively if not exhaustively debated, however, in both 1964 and 1965. "Xavier Rynne," in his book of collected *New Yorker* articles reporting on the Council entitled *Vatican Council II*, devotes nearly one hundred pages of close print to these debates. Other Council historians similarly devote considerable space to them. We need not cover these debates in such great detail, however. For one thing, they are quite repetitive, as was typical of debates at the Council, with one bishop after another making similar—or opposing—points. We see how it all comes out only when we examine the completed documents.

In the meantime, though, it is important that we take note of a few of the highlights, notably some of the interventions concerning whether the Council should have been dealing with the modern world at all, and, if so, in what kind of document. Also, we need to single out for special attention some of the discussions, and we shall do so on those dealing with the subjects of atheism and marriage and the family. Giving special attention to these two topics will illustrate how the debates went generally. These examples, besides being important in themselves, will give us a pretty good idea of how the Council produced its longest, and some believe its most important, document.

The first extended debate on the *schema*—which, by this time, had come to be identified as *Schema* 13—opened on October 20, 1964, after a couple of earlier postponements had aroused suspicions as to whether it was really going to be debated at all. Such was the climate toward the end of the Third Session, which ended, in fact, with what came to be known as "Black Week," an appellation bestowed by the Dutch, owing to Pope Paul VI's decisions to insist on having the now well-known *Nota Praevia* appended to the text of *Lumen Gentium* and to require that a number of amendments be made in the text of *Unitatis Redintegratio*, the Decree on Ecumenism.

Especially troubling during the same week to a large number of bishops, including especially the American bishops, who practically mounted a minirevolt over the issue, was the postponement to the Fourth Session of action on the draft dealing with religious liberty. Then there was the dissatisfaction expressed by some other bishops when Pope Paul VI during the very same week designated Mary as the Mother of the Church without consulting the Council Fathers.

As regards *Schema* 13 itself, however, the debates were extensive and spirited. In the way that had by then become familiar, many of the principal members or allies of the progressive European Alliance lined up to urge the approval of this *schema* on the modern world. They included Cardinals Bea, Döpfner, Léger, Lercaro, Liénart, and Silva Henríquez. On this occasion they were joined by the American cardinals Meyer and Spellman and the Peruvian cardinal Juan Landázuri Ricketts. All of these prelates approved both of the Council taking up the question of the Church in the modern world and of the draft they had before them. Cardinal Lercaro noted in his intervention, though, that "it seems well nigh impossible for a new revision of the *schema* and its final approval to take place during this session." But this was all right with the proponents of the document, since there was much they wished to see added to it. Many Council Fathers lined up to speak, pro and con, but mostly pro.

A discordant note in the debate did come, however, with the intervention of Archbishop John Heenan of Westminster (later a cardinal), who referred to the draft as "a set of platitudes" and characterized it as "unworthy of a general council." It was on this same occasion that the English prelate, as we noted earlier, offered his prescient criticism of the Council's theologians, who, according to him, cared "nothing for the ordinary teaching of the bishops—nor, I regret to say, for that of the pope." He thought that many of these same theologians had what he called "a childlike trust in the opinions of men in the world." He feared that the Council could become a "laughing-stock in the eyes of the world if it now rushed breathlessly through a debate on world hunger, nuclear war, and family life." Archbishop William Conway of Armagh, Ireland, echoed this same criticism, noting that *Schema* 13 contained "only a fraction of what the Church has to say to the modern world." He thought that people might ask: "Do you have nothing else to tell us? Is this all?"

Such criticisms definitely represented a minority viewpoint, however. Archbishop Heenan's criticisms were directly answered by Father Benedict Reetz, O.S.B., abbot of a monastery in Germany, who lauded those who had "labored and sweat over the *schema*, [and who] need not be feared but loved and praised," he thought. Bishop André Charue of Namur, Belgium, while admitting that the *schema* was probably still "premature," maintained that the joint commission in charge of the draft had employed "excellent experts." If others were added, "the results would be good." He declared that the whole world was waiting for the Council's word on the modern world.

There was in fact no serious doubt that the Council would move forward in its plan to relate the Church more systematically to the world. In the second major debate that took place on a by then much revised *Schema* 13 on September 21, 1965, during the Fourth Session, Archbishop Gabriel Garrone of Toulouse, France (later a cardinal), in his *relatio* introducing the new draft, announced that the document on the Church in the modern world would be called a "pastoral constitution." This represented a new type of Church document, but the archbishop explained that this new designation had the approval of the Council's Coordinating Commission. Nevertheless, the designation was opposed anyway by some of the bishops. Archbishop Casimiro Morcillo Gonzáles of Madrid objected to "constitution" because this designation was normally reserved for documents on faith addressed to the faithful, whereas this document covered a myriad of topics and was to be addressed to "the whole of humanity" (*GS* 2). He preferred the term "declaration" or even "dialogue." A number of bishops agreed, but it seemed that some of the opposition to the title was really opposition to the document itself and indicated a desire to lessen or downgrade its importance. Others thought the term "pastoral" should be eliminated since it led to confusion regarding the status of the document.

Nevertheless, the title was confirmed in the course of the final revisions that were made following the second debate. By then *Schema* 13 was clearly laid out with a part 1 and a part 2, the first part containing doctrine and the second part applying that doctrine to certain areas of modern life. It was a new type of teaching document! Hence the joint commission decided to append a note to the finished product explaining what it was, along with a brief rationale for its unique form. It is of interest that one of the members who had by then been added to the joint commission was Archbishop Karol Wojtyla of Kraków, Poland, the future Pope John Paul II. He urged both the retention of the designation "pastoral" and the inclusion of a note explaining the nature of the document. We shall record later how important the approved pastoral constitution *Gaudium et Spes* would turn out to be in the life and pontificate of the Polish pope. During the joint commission's deliberations on the final revisions of the text, Archbishop Wojtyla declared:

> A Note is definitely necessary. The document is really a "Constitution" but one that is "Pastoral." The latter term should be carefully explained. It is much more concerned with life than with doctrine. Moreover, I think that Part I is also very pastoral in places, especially where it discusses the human person. Both parts must be seen in a pastoral light.

All this was agreed to by the members of the joint commission, and what the note in question finally said is of very great interest. The following is what the note appended to the pastoral constitution said in full:

> Although it consists of two parts, the Pastoral Constitution, "The Church in the World Today," constitutes an organic unity.
>
> The Constitution is called "pastoral" because, while resting on doctrinal principles, it seeks to set forth the relations of the Church to the world and to the men of today. In Part I, therefore, the pastoral emphasis is not overlooked, nor is the doctrinal emphasis overlooked in Part II.
>
> In Part I, the Church develops her teaching on man, the world he inhabits, and her relationship to him. Part II treats at length of various aspects of life today and human society and in particular deals with those questions and problems which seem to have a greater urgency in our day. The result is that in Part II, the subject matter, which is viewed in the light of doctrinal principles, consists of elements, some of which are permanent, and some of which are contingent.
>
> The Constitution is to be interpreted according to the general norms of theological interpretation, while taking into account, especially in part II, the changing circumstances which the subject matter, by its very nature, involves. (*GS*, Preface)

Thus, the Council consciously and proudly affirmed its intention of issuing a new kind of Church teaching document—one that, it was hoped, would have a special impact upon the modern world to which it was basically addressed. How it would fare following the Council, and what impact it would in fact have, would be a question for the future to decide. At the time, however, most of the Council Fathers were confident that they were breaking new and important ground. Dozens of bishops lined up to speak in the course of the second lengthy debate during the Fourth Session. In spite of the general atmosphere, many of these interventions proved to be criticisms.

However, this time, most of the criticisms were being made with a view to improving the *schema* rather than trying to prevent its issuance. Franz Cardinal König of Vienna, for example, thought that the document, although expressly concerned with the world, as it assuredly was, was nevertheless itself much too "worldly." He wanted such things as "sin, the truth of the cross, the need for repentance, and the hope of resurrection with Christ" included in the document or more strongly emphasized. Only then, he thought, could the error be avoided of "promising a paradise on earth and a solution to all problems, something that cannot be realized save in the world to come."

Bishop Joseph Höffner of Münster, Germany, representing eighty German bishops, similarly thought that the text was too "optimistic." Goodwill and sincere cooperation among men were hardly the only requisites for social justice. "Social injustice," he thought, "will disappear only when sin disappears." The charge of undue optimism was nevertheless one that would later be leveled at the finished document. Another criticism of *Gaudium et Spes* that would frequently be made in the postconciliar years, namely, that its part 2, with all the practical applications, was considerably weaker than its part 1 on doctrine, was already being voiced at the Council, notably by Bishop Alexandre Renard of Versailles, France. He thought that the emphasis on basic human values sometimes gave the impression that these values were not implicated in original sin. "The self-sufficiency of these values is a danger," he said. "They are seen too much as stepping stones to grace and not enough as possible obstacles."

Coadjutor Archbishop Simon Lourdusamy of Bangalore, India, speaking in the name of sixty-two Indian bishops, thought that the description of man in the document focused too heavily on man in the developed world. "What about the greater part of humanity in Africa, Asia, and Latin America?" he wondered. After some seven years in Bangalore, Archbishop Lourdusamy later had a distinguished career in the Roman Curia, first as secretary of the Congregation for the Evangelization of Peoples (1973–1985), and then as prefect of the Congregation for Oriental Churches (1985–1991).

Bishop Mariano Gaviola, of Cabanatuan, the Philippines, criticized the draft's apparently uncritical acceptance of the threat of so-called overpopulation, widely believed at the time to be a looming danger for the world. In an intervention in which he deplored the evil being done in the world by those promoting illicit methods of birth control, he declared that the so-called overpopulation problem was "something not even probable." Campaigns to fight alleged overpopulation, he thought, would lead believers to "question the wisdom of God in creation or cast doubt on divine Providence, as if God, who gave man the power to multiply life, were failing to provide the means for preserving life." He noted that decreases in population, in any case, also had adverse effects on a country's economy. Forty years later, in a world now facing depopulation, especially in Europe, his view seems to have been vindicated far more than the alarmist views about overpopulation that prevailed in the world around the time of the Council. (It is of interest, by the way, that the approved text of *Gaudium et Spes* speaks consistently of "population expansion" and never of "overpopulation.")

In the course of the second debate, in 1965, on the *schema* on the modern world, Bishop John Abasolo y Lecue of Vijayapuram, India, expressed sincere astonishment that in the draft's section on human dignity, nothing was said about the immortality of the human soul—a deficiency that was eventually remedied in the completed document (see *GS* 14). Following the most extensive debates witnessed by the Council, not a few such deficiencies were corrected in what had begun as a much criticized *schema*. Here, however, as we mentioned, we can only follow in any detail two of the major topics that were debated: namely, atheism and marriage and the family.

II.

In the course of the two major debates on *Schema* 13, in both the Third and the Fourth Sessions, a great variety of subject matter was covered. One of the major issues debated was the subject of atheism. Interestingly, because of Pope John XXIII's desire for the Council to be positive, and because of St. Paul's exhortation to "overcome evil with good" (Rom 12:21)—as well as because of Pope Paul VI's emphasis on "dialogue" in his contemporaneous encyclical *Ecclesiam Suam*—the Council did not find it easy to deal with the subject of atheism. Initially, "the absence of God" was simply one of "the signs of the times" that the Church was being called to interpret "in the light of the Gospel" (*GS* 4). Later, however, as we shall see when we come to examine the approved document, atheism came to be treated in some detail as one of the characteristic modern phenomena with which the Church had to contend.

Another difficulty was that the Russian Orthodox observers at the Council had agreed to attend only after being given assurances that no public condemnation of atheistic Communism by the Council was contemplated. Nevertheless, many bishops felt strongly not only about atheism but about Communism as such. The famous Iron Curtain dividing the Communist bloc from the "Free World" was still up in those days and was seemingly indestructible. Entire national churches found themselves behind the Iron Curtain and therefore subject to ongoing oppression in various degrees. Not a few bishops considered Communism to be the Church's principal enemy, and some of them insisted on speaking out accordingly. The tone of some of the conciliar interventions on the subject sometimes caused the Russian Orthodox observers, among others, to wonder if indeed the Council would abide by Blessed John XXIII's wish that the Council should eschew harsh condemnations. It is not without significance that the Council was, in the end, willing to "condemn" some things anyway, for example, racism and discrimination, not to speak of abortion and infanticide!

Atheistic Communism seemed to many to be a valid target at a time when what President Ronald Reagan would later call the "evil empire" was at its height. In the end, though, the Council substantially did maintain a noncondemnatory stance as regards Communism. How the anti-Communist convictions of what turned out to be a large number of bishops were managed, however, proved to be one more example of how Paul VI knew how to fashion compromises that resulted in the Council documents being approved by large majorities.

Many of the most vehement speeches on atheism and Communism came from Eastern-rite bishops, some of them with émigré congregations. American Byzantine-rite archbishop Nicholas T. Elko of Pittsburgh, for example, on September 29, 1965, told his fellow bishops that "atheism brings about the ruin of the social order. It is a terrible sign of our times; it is a pestilence. It must be condemned; otherwise future centuries will accuse us of cowardice." Similarly, Ukrainian-rite auxiliary bishop Michael Rusnak of Toronto said that "it would be scandalous if a twentieth-century council did not deal with Communism. We must publicly denounce its errors and lies." He spoke feelingly of bishops being imprisoned and priests being forced to do manual labor behind the Iron Curtain.

Nor was it any great surprise when Archbishop Paul Yu Pin of Nanking, China, speaking in the name of seventy other bishops in

October 1964, insisted that the Council must not fail to "deal with atheistic Communism" because it was "one of the greatest, most evident, and most unfortunate of modern phenomena." It had to be treated because people expected it, "especially those who groan under the yoke of Communism."

Interestingly enough, though, some bishops from countries under Communist rule were sometimes a good deal more circumspect. Archbishop Karol Wojtyla of Kraków, Poland, opined during the debate in the Fourth Session that "atheism can be taken up here only with difficulty because the question is so complex." Franjo Cardinal Seper, archbishop of Zagreb, Croatia (then Yugoslavia), probably exhibited as balanced a view as anyone could when he affirmed that it was

> obligatory that the schema treat atheism. But let us speak about it in terms of the atheistic mind. . . . Let us try to understand this psychology. Many of our contemporaries were born atheists. It is therefore not their fault. . . . We must admit that Christians who defended the established social order and the unchangeableness of social structures too stubbornly, wrongly appealing to God's authority, are partly responsible for modern atheism. We must declare that the notion atheists have of God is false.

The idea that modern atheism arose because Christians too often failed to live their faith was echoed by number of speakers.

Nevertheless, the conviction that Communism needed to be condemned persisted with a large number of bishops. The conservative Coetus Internationalis Patrum, or International Group of Fathers, had presented petitions to Pope Paul VI as early as the Second Session calling for a *schema* in which "Catholic social doctrine would be set forth with great clarity, and the errors of Marxism, Socialism, and Communism would be refuted on philosophical, sociological, and economic grounds." Following the debates and the various revisions of the modern world *schema*, however, this had still not been done to the satisfaction of the Coetus. One of the leaders of the group, Bishop Luigi Carli, of Segni, Italy, drew up a letter outlining ten reasons why silence by the Council on the subject of Communism would serve to disavow all that the popes had said up to then in their previous condemnations of Communism. Brazilian archbishop Geraldo de Proença Sigaud and French archbishop Marcel Lefebvre were also involved in this effort and helped distribute the Carli letter among the bishops. Four hundred and fifty bishops actually endorsed this letter—a large number that would have seriously compromised the moral credibility of *Gaudium et Spes* if anywhere near that number declined to approve the document in the end.

Bishop Carli's letter with its ten reasons was submitted as a set of *modi*, or amendments, to the General Secretariat in the name of 450 signatories, in accordance with established procedures, but a curial official, Monsignor Achille Glorieux, a priest of the diocese of Lille, France—and hence a putative ally of the progressive European Alliance—failed to transmit the letter to the members of the joint commission for consideration by them. When a further revision of the *schema* was issued containing no reference either to Communism or to the *modi* submitted in the name of the 450 Council Fathers, Bishop Carli naturally protested to the Council presidency. In October and November 1965, the issue quickly became the subject of a number of rather sensationalized press stories critical of the Council's management. The official explanation that the holding back of the proposed *modi* of the Coetus had come about because the issue had already been considered in connection with other *modi* was embarrassingly weak, and Archbishop Gabriel Garrone was eventually obliged in the name of the joint commission to make a public admission of negligence.

Meanwhile, Pope Paul VI was inevitably made aware of the embarrassment that the whole affair was causing for the Council. The day after the pope himself had delivered an address critical of what he called "Marxist atheism," in which he deplored the claim of this ideology that "violent revolution [was] the only means for solving problems," the Italian press was running stories recounting how a conciliar official was sidelining *modi* critical of Communism. Enemies of the Council who deemed it "soft on Communism" were having a field day. Paul VI therefore did not hesitate to intervene and to direct that the following sentence be added to the text of the *schema*:

> The Church, as given over to the service of both God and men, cannot cease from reproving with sorrow yet with utmost firmness, as she has done in the past, those harmful teachings and ways of acting which are in conflict with reason and with common human experience, and which cast man down from the noble state to which he is born. (*GS* 21)

A footnote referring to the phrase "as she has done in the past" was also added, listing references to the encyclicals of Pope Pius XI, Pope Pius XII, and Pope John XXIII in which Communism *had been* duly condemned. Thus, Vatican II did not issue any *new* condemnation of Communism—as Blessed John XXIII's agents had assured the Russian Orthodox observers that it would not. Instead, Pope Paul VI saw to it that the Council would simply make clear references to the condemnations of Communism already issued by the Church.

Although looking back, we may think that this seems today to be a rather artificial solution, this way of proceeding actually turned out to be a rather successful compromise on the whole difficult subject. Certainly it swayed some of the bishops. The Coetus Internationalis Patrum still remained dissatisfied, though, and the group's Archbishop Sigaud spoke disparagingly of Paul VI's "footnote solution," noting that there was "a difference between carrying a hat in your pocket and wearing it on your head." The Coetus really objected to a number of things in the document, however, notably some passages relating to marriage and to war and peace, in addition to the document's relatively bland treatment of atheism and Communism. The group therefore urged its members and sympathizers to oppose the *schema* and to vote against it.

Yet in the end only 75 bishops actually did so. Meanwhile 2,309 of them approved of the final draft of this constitution—which for the first time in the history of the Church was styled "pastoral"! Paul VI's "footnote solution" on this and on some other issues turned out to be a remarkably effective compromise, considering all of the conflicts and controversies that had accompanied this document throughout its entire drafting and approval process. Some of these conflicts have not ceased up to the present day. Followers of French archbishop Marcel Lefebvre, who eventually organized a schismatic-type movement and was excommunicated after he illicitly ordained four bishops in 1988, for example, continue to reproach the Council for, among other things, not having condemned Communism by name.

Forty years later, however, after the fall of Communism in 1989 and the breakup of the Soviet Union in 1991—due in no small measure to the continued vitality of the Catholic Church behind the once seemingly impregnable Iron Curtain and also, as many contemporary observers agree, to the election of a pope from behind the Iron Curtain in 1979—the sometimes fevered emotions aroused by the subject of Communism at the time of the Council can today seem to be a bit overwrought. However, we should not forget the evil and the error that the Communism of the Soviet Union did inflict upon the world for a period of some seventy-five years. The Catholic bishops who were concerned about this at the time were not wrong. At the same time, the Council's refusal to magnify the problem of Communism, or consider it to be the major obstacle faced by the Church in the modern world, turned out to be a wise and prudent long-term choice—for which perhaps even the Holy Spirit deserves some credit.

III.

Pope Paul VI surely deserved great credit for his wise guidance of the Council through what were assuredly some very treacherous waters as far as the contentious subjects of atheism and Communism were concerned. The same thing proved to be true of his handling of the issues of marriage and the family when these important subjects came to be debated at the Council. Once again, against his own natural bent and his well-known personal opinions, whenever the pope realized that he would have to intervene in the proceedings of the Council in order to safeguard the integrity of Catholic teaching, he did not hesitate.

As most people were fully aware at the time, Pope Paul VI was actually a rather "liberal" pope—he had been a willing member of the European Alliance during the First Session—but then later he was not just any bishop; he was the *pope*! And when he saw that it was a question of authentic Catholic teaching, he was able to put every other consideration aside, including especially his own personal preferences. He would certainly prove this before history and before the whole world when he issued his encyclical *Humanae Vitae* in 1968. But he exhibited an equally unerring sense of what had to be done to keep the Council itself on the track of sound Catholic doctrine. His actions at the Council in this regard were much less well publicized than was his stance at the time of *Humanae Vitae*, but they were no less important. Moreover, intervening in the Council as he did, he was often obliged to face down his own friends and allies in the European Alliance, not to speak of a hostile liberal press and media, in order to preserve the integrity of the Church's teaching on marriage and on the transmission of life in marriage.

For when we go back and read over the conciliar drafts and debates on the subjects of marriage and the family, it seems pretty clear that a majority of the bishops at the Council, perhaps a large majority, were apparently prepared to follow the way of the world and to countenance a relaxation of the Church's traditional teaching prohibiting any artificial interference in the marriage act intended to prevent the conception of new life. The pressures for relaxing the constant teaching of the Church prohibiting artificial birth control were all the greater because by then pretty much the whole world except for the Catholic Church had already gone over to the acceptance of it. Birth control had become accepted not only as morally licit but as a positive and desirable human good. It was considered one of those famous ideas whose time had come.

Few ideas in history, in fact, have won such universal approbation and acceptance as contraception enjoys today. To oppose it is simply incomprehensible to our contemporaries; it is like opposing automobile travel or air-conditioning. In opposing it, the Church automatically assumes a countercultural stance—as the American bishops understood in 2006 when they issued their very countercultural statement rejecting the use of contraception in marriage. At the time of the Council in the mid-1960s, though, large and increasing numbers of Catholics no longer understood why the Church opposed and had always opposed contraception; how she could possibly go on continuing to oppose it was literally unthinkable for many people. This was probably true even of some of the Council Fathers. They, after all, were primarily engaged in trying to reach out to the world, not erect further barriers or reinforce existing ones.

It should also be recalled, though, that around the very same time that the Council was deliberating about all this, a majority of the cardinals, bishops, *periti*, and other experts serving on the Papal Birth Control Commission, as it was popularly called (the official name was the Pontifical Commission for the Study of Problems Relating to Population, Family, and Birth), were themselves about to decide in favor of advising the pope to relax the Church's traditional prohibition of the use of contraception—the defense of the Church's traditional position in the matter being left to a "minority report" authored by several theologians on the same commission.

This Papal Birth Control Commission had originally been constituted by Pope John XXIII as a "pill commission" to examine whether or not the then new oral contraceptives fell under what was still understood to be the Church's total ban on the use of artificial contraceptives. Such was the climate of the times, however, that the commission soon expanded its field of inquiry to include not just oral contraceptives but contraception generally. It then went on to decide and recommend to Paul VI that contraception *could* be employed by Catholic married couples in specific instances, so long as their marriage generally remained "open" to the prospect of new life.

Essentially, this was the same kind of "hard case" justification that the Church of England—the first Christian communion to sanction birth control—had adopted in 1930. But the unmistakable logic of it was that if artificial contraception was licit in some circumstances, then why would it not be equally licit in *every* circumstance? People were not slow to grasp this logic as far as their own practice was concerned. Within a decade or two, Protestant communions had come almost universally not only to accept but to praise and promote birth control. Pope Pius XI issued his 1930 encyclical *Casti Connubii* on Christian marriage in response to the Church of England's break with the Christian tradition; in it he reaffirmed the teaching of the Catholic Church in the strongest language and severely condemned the idea that contraception could ever be licit. In the moral climate that had already come to prevail, however, his words failed to convince many Catholics in the long run. It was this same kind of "hard case" justification employed by the Church of England in 1930 that some thirty-odd years later in the 1960s also proved persuasive to a majority of the members of the Papal Birth Control Commission. They arrived at their conclusions around the same time that the Council too was debating the questions of marriage and the family (although the conclusions of the Papal Birth Control Commission were not made public until several years later, when they were leaked to the liberal *National Catholic Reporter*, which published them in the form of a "majority report" and a "minority report" in April 1967).

At the Council itself, however, most bishops were not yet speaking in terms of the possible moral licitness of using contraceptives but rather in terms of a new understanding of marriage that had or would elevate the mutual love of the spouses in marriage to a level of importance equal to or greater than that of "the procreation and education of children." This latter phrase had up to then always figured in Catholic teaching as the *primary end* or purpose of marriage. What was rather quaintly styled "the mutual aid of the spouses and a remedy for concupiscence" was the *secondary end* of marriage, according to the traditional formulation of the teaching. Many Council Fathers, attuned to contemporary theological thinking, however, wanted to put these two "ends" of marriage on the same level, or perhaps eliminate them entirely as components of the Church's teaching on marriage. Hence they saw a need for a reexamination and a possible reformulation of the teaching that, among other things, would surely entail looking at what was delicately called the "regulation" (or "spacing") of births.

Of course, the bishops at the Council were not supposed to be discussing birth control at all. It had been made very clear from the start, and it was strongly reiterated later, that the pope had reserved this subject to himself and to the deliberations of the Papal Birth Control Commission. Such, again, was the atmosphere of the times, however, that not a few of the conciliar interventions on the subject of marriage and the family kept sliding over into the subject of birth regulation anyway, in spite of the pope's ban. The subject was in the air and could hardly be ignored. In the debate on the chapter on marriage and the family in *Schema* 13 that began on October 29, 1964, during the Third Session, Paul-Émile Cardinal Léger of Montreal cited the opinion of various theologians that the duty of fecundity in a marriage should be predicated of the marriage as a whole rather than being linked to individual acts. "We should concentrate less on the teleology of each sexual act," he said, "and more on the totality of married life." This approach, it was thought by many, might smooth the way to acceptance by the Church of some form of birth control. It was exactly the same argument, of course, that was prevailing in the course of the deliberations of the Papal Birth Control Commission, eventually leading a majority of the commission's members also to accept the erroneous view that each and every marriage act need *not* necessarily be open to the transmission of life.

That the pope, and hence the Church, could not accept this way of thinking would be made manifest only several years later when the encyclical *Humanae Vitae* was issued, and the conflict that has not been settled yet would then be aroused in the minds of most Catholics. Perceptive observers perhaps *should* have noticed which way Pope Paul VI was tending, but few did, and many theologians and bishops therefore continued to think that they were pursuing a permissible line of thought that could result in a legitimate "development of doctrine." They were wrong about this, as it turned out: acceptance of contraception would have meant the destruction, not the development, of the traditional Catholic doctrine on the subject. But this was not seen by many in the climate of the times.

In the course of the conciliar debate on marriage and the family, Cardinal Suenens, in a major address, pursued a line of thought similar to that adopted by Cardinal Léger. He asked whether the traditional teaching resulted in an adequate balance between the two ends of marriage, primary and secondary. He asked, rhetorically: "Hasn't there been too much emphasis on the passage from Genesis, 'increase and multiply,' and not enough on another phrase, 'and they shall be two in one flesh'?" He wanted a commission appointed to study the question (not adverting to the fact that the Papal Birth Control Commission was already doing exactly that!). He ended his long and elaborate speech by crying out: "I beg you, Fathers, not to repeat the trial of Galileo! One is enough for the Church!"

The aptness of this reference to Galileo was not entirely clear, but the bishops in the *aula* surely got the drift that the Church ought to try to avoid the kind of public embarrassment that the wrong decision in the Galileo case had brought upon her. Certainly the press and media got the drift, and they gave maximum play to the Belgian cardinal's intervention. The implication was that just as the Church had been wrong in putting Galileo on trial, so she was equally wrong now in insisting upon a teaching on birth control abandoned by the whole world. It was hard to see how Cardinal Suenens could have meant anything else.

A couple of weeks later, however, the Belgian cardinal found himself obliged to interrupt the debate on the missions in order to give a public response to what he called "certain reactions of public opinion interpreting my intervention on the ethics of marriage as though I had said that the doctrine and discipline of the Church had been changed." He denied having said any such thing, contending that he had "merely suggested that a study be done on this subject, not to revise what has been authentically and definitively proclaimed by the magisterium of the Church."

Cardinal Suenens thought it prudent to add: "It is evident that the conclusions of the commissions should be submitted to the sovereign pontiff, who will pass judgment on them in the capacity of his supreme authority." It seemed obvious that the Belgian prelate was not merely reacting to "public opinion" in offering this extraordinary clarification of what he had supposedly really meant by his earlier intervention. Many thought at the time, and Father Ralph Wiltgen reported it as fact in his history of the Council, that Pope Paul VI had called the popular Belgian cardinal on the carpet and insisted on a public clarification if not an outright retraction. It is hard to imagine, in fact, who else would have dared to approach the high-flying Belgian cardinal in this manner. What the cardinal felt obliged to say in his follow-up remarks was certainly not couched in his usual breathless style. It was not customary to hear phrases such as "authentically and definitively proclaimed by the magisterium" from the likes of Cardinal Suenens.

However that may be, the original intervention of Cardinal Suenens was not the only instance where a bishop delivered a speech in the *aula* that both disregarded the pope's ruling that the birth control question was not open to debate by the Council and suggested that the teaching of the Church against birth control might and possibly should be changed. Interventions by Bernard Cardinal Alfrink of Utrecht and Bishop Joseph Reuss of Mainz—both of whom turned out to be frank procontraceptionists in the postconciliar years—vigorously supported the views of Cardinals Léger and Suenens. Cardinal Alfrink pointedly asked whether "complete or periodic continence [was] the only efficacious solution for the conflicts of married life," and Bishop Reuss anticipated the *Humanae Vitae* dissenters by asserting that "human sexuality should not be considered only from a biological point of view." Bishop Reuss did counsel prudence, however, because, he said, "*for the moment* we cannot go much farther" (emphasis added).

It was probably predictable, though, that the most blunt and open intervention favoring a change in the Church's teaching should have come from the eighty-seven-year-old maverick Melchite patriarch Maximos IV Saigh. The Eastern prelate pulled no punches and pressed aggressively forward:

> I call your attention to the problem of birth control. If we are truly pastoral, the love of Christ and men urges us to confront this issue directly.
>
> Birth control poses an enormous and urgent problem. There is today a crisis in the Christian conscience on this point. This crisis is evidenced by a split between the official doctrine of the Church and the contrary practice of large numbers of the faithful. Some of them are forced to break with the Church, others live in a state of perpetual anguish because they cannot reconcile a normal conjugal life with the demands of their conscience. . . .
>
> On the other hand, there is a considerable demographic increase, and in some countries there is no hope of raising the standard of living to match the population growth. Consequently, whole peoples live in misery and without hope.
>
> Does God will such an anti-natural impasse? With confidence in the resurrected Christ and full awareness of the crisis, let us examine the problem directly, unflinchingly, and courageously. . . .
>
> The question, then, is this: should the official positions of the Church be reviewed in the light of modern sciences and discoveries? Personal fulfillment and procreation form a whole. Neither can be

> neglected. We cannot distinguish between what are called the "primary" and "secondary" ends of marriage. We must consider the whole of conjugal life.

So much for Pope Paul VI's plan that the birth control question should not be debated on the Council floor! French journalist Henri Fesquet reported in *Le Monde* of Paris at the time that "the interventions by Maximos IV, and Cardinals Léger, Suenens, and Alfrink represent such a break with what is called traditional doctrine on birth control that they mark a radical change of attitude." Much or most of their arguments and observations could have been written today, as a matter of fact, so little have the terms of the discussion changed since the whole birth control question got thrown open for public discussion in the 1960s.

But an observer at the Council could well have asked—and as we must still ask today—what if the Church is *right* about birth control after all? Regardless of what the modern world has come to believe and practice with regard to birth control—the record of the modern world in matters of sexual behavior and morality is hardly very reassuring, after all!—what if the Church's teaching is nevertheless *true*? In that case, the observations and arguments of these revisionist prelates were no more valid then than the same observations and arguments are valid when they are offered today.

Even the conservative bishops at the Council found themselves obliged to violate the pope's ban on discussion and deal openly with the subject of birth control, if only to answer some of the points being made. Some of these points could not have had any other effect except to undermine the credibility of the Church's teaching. They therefore needed to be answered. Ernesto Cardinal Ruffini of Palermo, for example, reminded the bishops that the authentic Catholic doctrine was "very clearly defined in Pius XI's encyclical *Casti Connubii* and Pius XII's 'Allocution to Midwives.'" He urged that the *schema* be revised to include and reflect this teaching clearly. Irish cardinal Michael Browne of the Roman Curia similarly offered a very cogent and able defense of the traditional teaching. Cardinal Ottaviani spoke out as well: "Are we to think," he asked, referring to the Suenens intervention, "that the precept 'increase and multiply' is contradicted by the precept 'they shall be two in one flesh'?" The command to "increase and multiply" was the very first command God ever gave to the human race, after all. In a more personal vein, Cardinal Ottaviani added: "The priest who speaks to you is the eleventh of twelve children, whose father was a laborer in a bakery. I purposely say laborer, not the owner of the bakery. My parents never doubted Providence. Their motto was 'Look to the birds of the air and the lilies of the field.' "

All this took place during the debate at the Third Session in 1964. The debate that took place in the following year on the rerevised *schema*, beginning on September 29, 1965, was almost an anticlimax by comparison. Some of the same speakers reappeared bearing the same messages: Cardinal Léger insisted that "marriage is not merely a means of procreation, but likewise a community of life and love"; Cardinal Suenens once again called for more "scientific research in the domain of sexual life." Cardinal Ruffini thought that the statement on "the fecundity of marriage" in the latest draft was still "obscure"; Cardinal Browne deplored the absence in the draft of any reference to the "primary" and "secondary" ends of marriage.

What was clear from this second debate, if it had not been clear already, was that the birth control cat was very much out of the bag in spite of Paul VI's clearly expressed intention to reserve the question to himself and to the Papal Birth Control Commission. What would happen when *Humanae Vitae* was released should have been foreseen. Recognizing this reality, Auxiliary Bishop Kasimierz Majdanski of Wloclawek, Poland, speaking in the name of all the Polish bishops, believed that the Council needed to formulate "a clear doctrine on birth control because of the confusion so widespread in the world today." Obviously, he needed to look no farther than the Council itself to verify the fact of this confusion. Yet Bishop Majdanski's speech was prophetic also in that he clearly foresaw the evil of legalized abortion that would be visited upon the world of former Christendom very soon in the postconciliar years. "This scourge is as serious as the atomic bomb," he declared. He could not have spoken truer words.

IV.

Pope Paul VI was well aware of the growing pro–birth control sentiment developing within the Council. He seems to have had a growing awareness, three years before the crisis of *Humanae Vitae*, of the deleterious consequences of allowing this sentiment to go on developing unchecked. For it was in connection with this issue that he decided upon what proved to be his most fateful and significant intervention in the conciliar process. The pontiff, often described as "Hamlet-like," who vacillated and supposedly could never decide anything, as Vaticanologists often believed and wrote, suddenly proved quite capable of deciding both firmly and definitely and without looking back.

On November 25, 1965—this was only a couple of weeks before the end of the Council—Paul VI sent through his secretary of state to the joint commission responsible for drafting *Schema* 13 a letter transmitting four *modi*, or amendments, which he said were to be added to the text at the behest of "higher authority." Within the joint commission there was consternation at this turn of events on the part of some of the members. There was even overt resistance. None other than the Canadian cardinal Léger was one of those who protested. He read out a strong statement deploring the tenor of the amendments and stated that their forced adoption would damage the reputation of the Holy See "irreparably." Nor, apparently, was he the only member of the joint commission who felt that way. The members had to be reminded by another follow-up letter delivered the next day that the amendments were indeed mandatory; the joint commission was not free to reject them but only to decide their exact phrasing and location in the text. Following the receipt of this second letter, "Xavier Rynne" reported that "Cardinal Léger was seen to fold a paper he had in his hand and slump back in his chair."

The first of these *modi* from "higher authority" called for the insertion of a phrase, *artes anti-conceptionales* ("anticonceptional arts," i.e., contraceptive practices) into a list of things already included that marred the excellence of marriage, such as polygamy, divorce, and hedonism. The joint commission did not like the phrase *artes anti-conceptionales* but actually improved upon it by adopting another phrase, "illicit practices against human generation" (*illicitis usibus contra generationem*). This is how it is translated in the Abbott translation of the conciliar documents; the Flannery translation, however, reads "unlawful contraceptive practices." Thus, the final approved text, including the papal *modus*, became:

> [T]he happy picture of the dignity of these [marriage] partnerships is not reflected everywhere, but is overshadowed by polygamy, divorce, so-called free love, and similar blemishes; furthermore, married love is too often dishonored by selfishness, hedonism, and *unlawful contraceptive practices.* (*GS* 47; emphasis added)

At a distance of forty years after the Council—with the so-called sexual revolution having occurred in the meantime—we can only wonder how the joint commission imagined that a list of the things marring the excellence of marriage could be complete without mentioning contraceptives. Pope Paul VI clearly saved the joint commission from itself when he insisted on adding this reference, whether the commission members appreciated it at the time or not (most of them apparently did not appreciate it).

The second amendment forwarded by the pope to be inserted into the conciliar text involved a full sentence to be added, while a single word was to be deleted. The full sentence read: "Children are the supreme gift of marriage and greatly contribute to the good of the parents themselves." This sentence was to be inserted following another sentence already in the text that read: "Marriage and married love are by nature ordered to the procreation and education of children." This latter sentence already in the text thus included the phrase that had long been used to describe the traditional *primary end* of marriage, that is, "the procreation and education of children." It was in the text but without being identified there as the "primary end." This omission was both conscious and calculated on the part of those who wished to do away with the idea of primary and secondary ends of marriage. By employing the phrase "the *supreme* gift of marriage"—a superlative—the sentence added by the pope in effect restored the status of "the procreation and education of children" as the primary end of marriage, without stating this in so many words.

This restoration was strengthened a few sentences later where the original text had stated that cooperation with the Creator in procreation was *also* (*etiam*) an end of marriage—as if this were the *secondary* end! The striking of this word "also" thus restored the balance to the whole passage. The drafters had known exactly what they wanted to say when they drafted the text in a way that would have eliminated the idea of primary and secondary ends (or would have actually relegated the primary end of procreating and educating children to secondary status). But Paul VI knew equally what he wanted to say, and he managed it in a characteristically subtle "Pauline" way. Having thus maintained the continuity of Catholic teaching on the matter by insisting on these two changes, the pontiff acquiesced in the joint commission's idea of adding yet another phrase of its own to another sentence establishing that married love is "directed" toward "cooperation" with the Creator; this added phrase stated that it was not the intention of the Council "to underestimate the other ends of marriage" besides the procreation and education of children. So however it was stated, we were definitely back to the idea that there *were* "ends" of marriage. The completed text goes on later to state explicitly, however, that marriage is not merely for the procreation of children; it was important to many bishops that this point should be made unambiguously too. The finished product reads:

> Marriage and married love are by nature ordered to the procreation and education of children. Indeed children are the supreme gift of marriage and greatly contribute to the good of the parents themselves. God himself said: "It is not good that man should be alone" (Gen 2:18) and "from the beginning [he] made them male and female" (Mt 19:4); wishing to associate them in a special way with his own creative work, God blessed man and woman with the words: "Be fruitful and multiply" (Gen 1:28). Without intending to underestimate the other ends of marriage, it must be said that true married love and the whole structure of family life which results from it is directed to disposing the spouses to cooperate valiantly with the love of the Creator and Savior, who through them will increase and enrich his family from day to day. (*GS* 50)

The third papal *modus* to be added referred to a sentence in the original text stating that "sons of the Church *should not* use methods which have been or may be found blameworthy by the teaching authority of the Church." This was carefully worded in a way that would have remained valid *if* the Church were ever to modify in any way her condemnation of all forms of contraception. But Paul VI's amendment directed that the sentence had to be changed to say that it was not "lawful" for Catholics to employ methods condemned by the Church. After some discussion within the joint commission, the sentence ended up reading as follows: "In questions of birth regulation, the sons of the Church . . . are forbidden to use methods disapproved of by the teaching authority of the Church in its interpretation of the divine law" (*GS* 57).

To this last sentence Paul VI directed that there should be appended another footnote making precise references to the pages in Pius XI's 1930 encyclical *Casti Connubii* and Pius XII's 1951 "Allocution to Midwives" where contraception is explicitly condemned in so many words. Paul VI thus once again found a "footnote solution" to be a useful compromise. Although the footnote he specified was duly added in accordance with his instructions, the members of the joint commission succeeded in weakening its force somewhat by also including another reference to a 1964 allocution of Paul VI himself, in which he had explained why he was reserving the question to himself and to the Papal Birth Control Commission. The suggestion was that the teaching might still somehow get changed as a result of the recommendations produced by the latter body—no doubt some of the members of the joint commission were very well aware of how the sentiment was going in that body in favor of a relaxation of the prohibition of the use of contraceptives. And yet again, in the printing of the final text, somebody on the joint commission failed to include the exact references for the papal condemnations of contraception—somebody evidently just did not want them pointed to or stressed! The pope's office had to remind the bishops before the final vote on the *schema* that these condemnations of contraception formed an integral part of the final document that the Council was voting to approve. Paul VI knew what he wanted—and what was needed.

The fourth and last amendment required by the pope to be added to this conciliar document was the addition of the words: "If spouses are to overcome their difficulties, it is altogether necessary for them to practice the virtue of conjugal chastity." After discussion it was decided that this sentence should be added to a passage stating that "objective criteria" (not subjective feelings) must govern the behavior and acts of married people. With this addition, the complete passage then read:

> When it is a question of harmonizing married love with the responsible transmission of life, it is not enough to take only the good intention and the evaluation of motives into account: the objective criteria must be used, criteria drawn from the nature of the human person and human action, criteria which respect the total meaning of mutual self-giving and human procreation in the context of true love; all this is possible only if the virtue of married chastity is seriously practiced. (*GS* 51)

Pope Paul VI's proactive intervention in shaping the final text of the treatment of marriage and the family in *Gaudium et Spes* was crucial. Apart from his intervention, the body of bishops may have been well on its way toward condoning, if not actually teaching, moral error—and moral error in a vital area of modern life at that. The pope was strongly criticized, and in some quarters even vilified, for doing what he did. He intervened in the face of terrific opposition to the very idea that a pope should have been "interfering" in any way with the operations of an ecumenical council, much less on a subject such as birth control.

However, looking back with the benefit of hindsight at the tsunami that was shortly to devastate the Church over birth control following the issuance of *Humanae Vitae* three years after the Council, we might well argue today that the pope should have intervened even more forcefully than he did. Adding footnotes, however pertinent, is scarcely equivalent to a summons to heroic virtue! Still, the pope's intervention did ensure the essential, namely, that the integrity of Catholic teaching in a crucial area was maintained. Moreover, it is not without significance that it was the *pope* who ensured this outcome. The Catholic bishops at the Council did not, unfortunately, perform very well on this, one of the first great tests of the Vatican II doctrine of episcopal collegiality.

Also, we should remind ourselves how much worse things could have been if the pope had not intervened. As it is, dissenters in the Church regularly try to invoke the Council in general and *Gaudium et Spes* in particular to justify their dissent. Pope Paul VI made it impossible for them to do so credibly as far as the issue of birth control was concerned; and he did so in the face of almost overwhelming contrary pressures. In this case, Pope Paul VI saw to it that a major conciliar document remained in essential continuity with the Church's traditional teaching. He may have done too little or done it too late in other ways and in connection with this and other issues. We have no guarantee to be spared that prospect in what our leaders do or fail to do. But if it is true that the Holy Spirit indeed guarantees the truth of the formal teachings of a general council of the Catholic Church, then in the case of this chapter of *Gaudium et Spes*, we can see the Holy Spirit at work in the hand of Pope Paul VI!

It was of special importance that *Gaudium et Spes*, of all the documents of Vatican II, should not go wrong, especially on the subject of marriage and the family. The Council Fathers had some inkling, but only an inkling, of what was shortly to come in this central area of human life. It was actually to be *après nous, le déluge* with a vengeance! What was to come is what we have today, mostly stemming from the sexual revolution, which was just getting under way in earnest while the Council was deliberating. Since then we have had, on top of the plague of clerical sex abuse in the Church herself, in society at large the concurrent plagues of no-fault divorce, so-called open marriage, so-called same-sex marriage, cohabitation, single-parent families, "hooking up," condoms in the classrooms, morning-after pills over the counter, legalized abortion, legalized sodomy, pornography, population control, and radical gender feminism aimed at leveling out all distinctions—not to speak of in vitro fertilization and the Brave New World horrors of embryonic stem-cell research and cloning that have followed upon the highly artificial and unnatural IVF process. Merely to list such phenomena is to indicate the magnitude of the contemporary crisis surrounding marriage and the family. If the twentieth century was so largely the century of political totalitarianism, the twenty-first already seems to be shaping up as the century of biotechnological totalitarianism engaged in the manipulation of human life.

In the midst of this moral shambles, Catholics at least have a guidepost pointing back to the real truths about marriage and the family. Not infrequently the Church has been able to provide sound moral guidance and leadership in this area. This has been made possible, at least in part, because her basic modern "charter" on marriage and the family, chapter 1 of part 2 of *Gaudium et Spes*, remains sound. There is much of great value in this chapter—just as there is much in *Gaudium et Spes* as a whole. It is not a perfect document by any means, nor has it entirely lived up to the Council's probably exaggerated ambitions and hopes for it. Nevertheless, we do need to look at the document as a whole as it finally issued from the Council on its next-to-last day.

V.

What kind of document, then, on the whole, did *Gaudium et Spes* turn out to be? Because of both its length and the number and variety of the topics covered in it, we can indicate only a few highlights, just as we have been able to trace in any detail only its development of the two themes of atheism and marriage and the family. It remains true now more than forty years after the Council that the Pastoral Constitution on the Church in the Modern World needs to be read and studied in its own right by serious Catholics. In describing it, we should begin by taking note of what it is not. It is not, as it has sometimes been thought to be, any kind of license or mandate to take the modern world as the standard by which the Church and her teachings must henceforth now be judged. The best known and, undoubtedly, the most often quoted passage from all the documents of Vatican II is surely the first sentence of *Gaudium et Spes*, which reads: "The joy and hope, the grief and anguish of the men of our time, especially those who are poor or afflicted in any way, are the joy and hope, the grief and anguish of the followers of Christ as well" (*GS* 1).

Yet even as this passage is almost ritually invoked almost as soon as Vatican II is mentioned, it is still not necessarily always quoted in its entirety because the "grief and anguish" part too often gets tacitly left out. Moreover, those who quote it in this truncated fashion often turn out to be the same people who think that the main point about Vatican II is that it left the "old Church" behind and that we are now launched into a new era where "the followers of Christ" are now pretty much indistinguishable from "the men of our time." Such people have really not assimilated the true teaching of this document, perhaps because they have not even read it in its entirety but are just following what they imagine to be "the spirit of Vatican II."

It does not at all mean, for example, that we should just go over to the modern world and take the latter on its own terms. What the Council meant by this famous first sentence was expressed farther on, where it is noted that "Christians cherish a feeling of deep solidarity with the human race and its history" (*GS* 1), not that Christians should henceforth be just like everybody else. Rather, Christians, by definition, should be committed to following Christ in his Church, and a proper reading and understanding of *Gaudium et Spes*, in fact, does nothing but reinforce such a commitment to Christ.

The second best known and most often quoted passage from the Pastoral Constitution on the Church in the Modern World occurs a bit farther along. It reads as follows: "At all times the Church carries the responsibility of reading the signs of the times and of interpreting them in the light of the Gospel" (*GS* 4). After the Council, however, "the signs of the times" too often turned out to be espousing whatever popular contemporary causes, usually on the political left, had come to be thought appropriate for Catholics to be supporting. Thus, modern secular ideologies such as leftism, liberation theology, environmentalism, feminism, and the like were often embraced by Catholics in the postconciliar years on the grounds that these ideologies represented "the signs of the times." Similarly, Catholic married couples adopting birth control, theologians embracing dissent, religious taking up political activism, politicians promoting abortion, perhaps even bishops and cardinals insisting upon debating birth control at the Council in spite of the Holy Father's decision to reserve the subject to himself—all such people were, again, no doubt just discerning "the signs of the times."

What these and other interpreters of "the signs of the times" also often leave out, though, is the second part of the same much-quoted passage, which specifies that these signs need to be interpreted "in the light of the *Gospel*" (emphasis added). This is a tall order, which entails constantly referring the "signs" in question back to the standards of Christ and his Church. It means the signs are *not* just to be interpreted in the light of fashionable but possibly mistaken ideas of our contemporaries—whose joy and hope, grief and anguish, we should assuredly be sharing but not necessarily also their opinions and prejudices and *partis pris*—positions already adopted in advance—on certain modern questions.

Because of the way *Gaudium et Spes* has too often been misinterpreted and used as a pretext to justify the adoption of practically any modern idea or cause in vogue, it is incumbent upon us to go back to the text of the Pastoral Constitution on the Church in the Modern World and to pay careful attention to what it actually says. This is true of all the documents of Vatican II, of course, but it is especially true of this one. As we have already noted in discussing its development within the Council, *Gaudium et Spes* consists of a part 1 and a part 2, the first part expounding, yes, *doctrine*, and, as it happens, important doctrine, including the Church's teaching on the dignity of the human person, the community of mankind, man's activity in the universe, and the role of the Church in the modern world. Each of these topics rates its own chapter in *Gaudium et Spes.*

Part 2 of the document contains applications of Church teachings to areas of special interest in the modern world: marriage and the family, culture, economic and social life, the political community, and the fostering of peace in the community of nations. Here again, each of these topics rates a chapter in part 2 of *Gaudium et Spes.*

It would have been little short of miraculous if the Council had managed to get everything exactly right on such a wide range of topics. What is remarkable is how well the text does cover most of this territory, especially considering the way it was composed and under the conditions that we have to some extent briefly indicated. This is not to say that the document is without flaws or lacunae, some of which are more obvious after more than forty years than perhaps they were when it was written. We shall mention in passing a few of the places where it seems to fall short or to have missed the mark.

But the document does not compromise in any way the Church's teaching authority, by the way. This is precisely *not* a dogmatic constitution treating of revealed truth and of the truths of faith that immediately follow from it. The Council Fathers in this case consciously decided to issue a new and different kind of teaching document in the hope of bringing Church teaching to bear on a wider range of issues. No doubt the "ready and respectful allegiance of mind" mentioned in *Lumen Gentium* 25 is owed by Catholics to the teaching in part 1, some of which, however, is not irreformable doctrine anyway. Part 2 is more problematical and, as the document itself says, contingent. Some of its "applications" would thus surely not demand strict assent from the faithful. Yet, as Archbishop Wojtyla pointed out at the Council, part 2 also does contain some "doctrine" to which the adherence owed to ordinary teachings of the Magisterium would indeed seem to be called for. Obviously, specific judgments are called for in the case of the materials contained in part 2.

To a remarkable degree, however, *Gaudium et Spes* does contain teaching that has become a permanent part of the Church's patrimony of truth. It contains much of permanent value that might never have been brought out if the Council Fathers had not decided to try. It has influenced the Church enormously and will continue to do so in the future. The pontificate of John Paul II, in particular, owed a great debt to this pastoral constitution. As we saw, Archbishop Karol Wojtyla had a hand in the drafting of it. Thirty years later, in a speech commenting upon it, Pope John Paul II frankly stated: "It is precisely my intimate knowledge of the origin of *Gaudium et Spes* that has enabled me to appreciate its prophetic value and to make wide use of its content in my magisterium, starting with my first encyclical, *Redemptor Hominis*."

Let us look briefly at John Paul II's first encyclical, "The Redeemer of Man," *Redemptor Hominis*, as a way of approaching and appreciating two of the key teachings of *Gaudium et Spes*. Early in this first encyclical of his, issued on March 4, 1979, Pope John Paul II quotes in toto the following passage from *Gaudium et Spes*:

> [I]t is only in the mystery of the Word made flesh that the mystery of man truly becomes clear. For Adam, the first man, was a type of him who was to come, Christ the Lord, Christ the new Adam, in the very revelation of the mystery of the Father and of his love, fully reveals man to himself and brings to light his most high calling. . . .
>
> He who is the "image of the invisible God" (Col 1:15), is himself the perfect man who has restored in the children of Adam that

> likeness to God which had been disfigured ever since the first sin. Human nature, by the very fact that it was assumed, not absorbed, in him, has been raised in us to a dignity beyond compare. For by his incarnation, he, the Son of God, has in a certain way united himself with each man. He worked with human hands, he thought with a human mind, he acted with a human will, and with a human heart he loved. Born of the Virgin Mary, he has truly been made one of us, like to us in all things except sin. (*GS* 22)

When quoting this long passage, which John Paul II characterizes as "stupendous," he italicizes the phrases "fully reveals man to himself" and "in a certain way united himself with each man." Thus, he emphasizes and clarifies at the same time the passage's first sentence—which John Paul II probably quoted more often in his teaching than any other quotation from any other source—that "it is only in the mystery of the Word made flesh that the mystery of man truly becomes clear."

Man can properly understand himself, in other words, only by first understanding who and what Christ was and is. Christ was and is God, yet he became a man, and in taking a human nature, he "elevated it to a dignity beyond compare." This human dignity, which was inherent in the fact that man was created "in the image of God" (Gen 1:26) but which was disfigured by human sin, was then restored by Christ's assumption of a human nature, thus uniting himself to mankind, and "in a certain way . . . with each man." This theme of human dignity restored by Christ proved to be one of the major themes of the pontificate of Pope John Paul II, who regularly based teachings of his, whether on human life, on human work, or even on, for example, women, on the need to respect this inherent human dignity. Even such initiatives, later in his pontificate, as his much publicized campaign against the application of capital punishment go back to his realization that the human dignity conferred by God and restored by Christ remains even in the case of condemned criminals—who in another sense may be thought to have forfeited their human dignity by their crimes. According to John Paul II's understanding, however, while a man may tarnish or diminish his human dignity, he cannot abolish it because he is created in the image of God.

This emphasis on human dignity, so marked throughout the long teaching pontificate of Pope John Paul II, was already a major theme and concern of the Council as well, not only here in this document but, for example, in the Council's teaching on religious liberty, as we saw briefly earlier in considering the very title of the Council's Decree on Religious Liberty, *Dignitatis Humanae.*

The long quotation from *Gaudium et Spes* included above occurs in a full chapter of the document entitled "The Dignity of the Human Person." This chapter represents a major contribution to Christian anthropology. It expounds the Church's teaching on human dignity that follows from man's creation in God's image. This inherent human dignity, however, was followed by the man-imposed disfigurement of sin: "Although set by God in a state of rectitude, man enticed by the evil one, abused his freedom at the very start of history. He lifted himself up against God and sought to attain his goal apart from him" (*GS* 13). (This passage, by the way, contains one of the Council's few explicit references to the devil.)

Although man is therefore "divided in himself" (ibid.), he still retains his essential dignity. The chapter goes on to discuss this dignity in terms of man's intellect and God's truth and, especially, in terms of what the document calls "the dignity of moral conscience": "Deep within his conscience, man discovers a law which he has not laid upon himself but which he must obey. Its voice ever calling him to love and to do what is good and to avoid evil tells him inwardly at the right moment: do this, shun that. For man has in his heart a law inscribed by God. *His dignity lies in observing this law,* and by it he will be judged" (*GS* 16; emphasis added). Human dignity, then, also inheres in the fact that man is a moral being, able to choose between good and evil.

It should already be evident from these few quotations that the discussion of human dignity contained in *Gaudium et Spes* goes far beyond the caricature of certain fashionable modern ideas that the document is sometimes reputed to contain. It contains much more than that: it presents true and quite traditional Catholic teaching on man and his dignity in a true and highly relevant light. And it is here in connection with its treatment of human dignity that its treatment of atheism, so heatedly discussed at the Council, is also included. It seems obvious with the passage of time that the Council was correct in electing to treat of the basic nature of atheism rather than getting caught up in the condemnation of atheistic Communism that so many bishops actually wanted.

It is this fairly detailed discussion of human dignity that leads on to Pope John Paul II's second favorite passage from *Gaudium et Spes*. The next chapter in the document is entitled "The Community of Mankind," but it nevertheless continues on to some extent with the theme of human dignity, placing it in the communitarian context of man in society and, among other things, reviving the very traditional Catholic idea of "the common good." Respect for the human person as well as respect for and love of one's enemies, as Christ counseled, constitute further themes. It is from this second chapter of part 1 that John Paul II derives the second of his favorite passages from *Gaudium et Spes* that he includes in *Redemptor Hominis* (and in not a few other teaching documents of his!). This is the passage: "Man is the only creature on earth that God has wanted for its own sake" (*GS* 24). To this statement the Council immediately added another passage, also often quoted by Pope John Paul II: "Man can fully discover his true self only in a sincere giving of himself" (ibid.). In *Redemptor Hominis*, John Paul II relates this to the fact that "man has become a sharer in Jesus Christ" (*RH* 13), just as he earlier stressed that Jesus united himself in a mysterious way with "each man."

The theme of human dignity really dominates the first two chapters of this "doctrinal" part 1 of *Gaudium et Spes*—just as the same theme would figure prominently in the Magisterium of Pope John Paul II himself. But this part of *Gaudium et Spes* contains many other important points as well. For example, it is here that *human equality* is greatly stressed. It is worth giving the Church's reading here on what she considers to be the basis for human equality, which is so often simply taken for granted in the modern world. But here is the Church's position: "All men are endowed with a rational soul and are created in God's image," says the Council here, speaking for the Church. "They have the same nature and origin and, being redeemed by Christ, they enjoy the same divine calling and destiny" (*GS* 29).

Because of this fundamental equality, the Church teaches that "forms of social or cultural discrimination in personal rights on the grounds of sex, race, color, social conditions, language or religion, must be curbed and eradicated as incompatible with God's design" (ibid.). Thus, the Church at Vatican II did not hesitate to "condemn" discrimination on a number of grounds, in spite of Blessed John XXIII's wish that the Council should not "condemn" anything. In this the Church certainly showed herself to be up with the times. This passage from *Gaudium et Spes* remains the Church's fundamental teaching today on the still burning contemporary issue of discrimination.

It is often alleged that the Church was behindhand and retrograde on the issue, especially when compared with civil society. Equality is supposedly an achievement of modern civil society acting *against* the Church and other traditional institutions. Yet the year this teaching was issued was 1965. Just the year before, 1964, the subject was thoroughly debated at the Second Vatican Council, and Archbishop Patrick A. O'Boyle of Washington (later a cardinal) delivered his memorable address in the name of all the American bishops, declaring, *inter alia*, that "racism is the most important problem of our times. Let us make a solemn declaration to that effect." The future Washington cardinal was loudly applauded for this speech by the assembled bishops in the *aula* of St. Peter's.

It was this same year, 1964, that the U.S. Congress passed the Civil Rights Act (while the Council Fathers were debating the above text, among others). The U.S. Civil Rights Act of 1964 bars discrimination on the basis of race, color, religion, sex, national origin, or reprisal against someone claiming discrimination. The grounds barring discrimination are thus roughly equivalent in the two cases (although the Church lists "social conditions" and "language," while the U.S. law speaks of "national origin" and possible "reprisal"). Significantly enough, though, prohibition of discrimination on the grounds of "sex" is the *first* item in the Church's list. Yet it is a well-known and even notorious fact of history that the U.S. Congress originally had no intention of banning discrimination on the grounds of sex. It came about only because a racial-segregationist legislator from Virginia, Representative Howard Smith, offered an amendment barring discrimination on the grounds of sex as a means of possibly *discouraging* support for the U.S. Civil Rights Act as a whole. It was intended as a proposed "killer" amendment.

Congressman Smith's tactic failed to work, however, and so the U.S. Civil Rights Act of 1964 was passed with "sex" included in the list of things against which discrimination was henceforth to be unlawful. The rest is history, as is so often said. In view of the record, though, the Church should not be hastily criticized or condemned on her human rights record as compared to that of civil society. The Church's record compares very favorably with what formerly segregationist America was able to achieve only in 1964—the same year the Second Vatican Council was debating and moving to enact a similar ban against discrimination. (Interestingly enough, however, Vatican II's Declaration on the Relation of the Church to Non-Christian Religions, *Nostra Aetate*, does *not* include "sex" in its list of items on which there is to be no discrimination; in this list, only "race, color, condition in life, and religion" [*NA* 4] are listed.)

VI.

Among the principal teachings of *Gaudium et Spes* carried forward so creatively by Pope John Paul II was the dual teaching that the mystery of man can be understood only in the light of the mystery of Christ and that man is the only creature created by God for its own sake (cf. *GS* 22 and 24). These are only two of a number of important teachings found in the "doctrinal" part 1 of the document, however. Though these important teachings certainly do underline the document's general theme of "joy and hope," it should not be thought that they constitute the only important notes contained in the document. On the contrary, even while insisting that there is a legitimate "autonomy of earthly affairs" (*GS* 36), in part 1's chapter 3, "Man's Activity in the Universe," the document also includes an entire section on how human activity is nevertheless "infected by sin." "The whole of man's history," *Gaudium et Spes* asserts, "has been the story of dour combat with the powers of evil" (*GS* 37). Hence the Church insists that "human activities, which are daily endangered by pride and inordinate self-love, must be purified and perfected by the cross and resurrection of Christ" (ibid.).

Thus, the Pastoral Constitution on the Church in the Modern World tempers its "joy and hope" note with a healthy realism about the true facts of the human condition and the urgent *need* for redemption by Christ, as well as for the true fulfillment of all human activity in him. The document's list of "crimes" prevalent in the modern world is, by itself, sufficient to refute the charge that the document lacks realism—offenses against human dignity in particular should again be noted in this list:

> The varieties of crime are numerous: all offenses against life itself, such as murder, genocide, abortion, euthanasia, and willful suicide; all violations of the integrity of the human person, such as mutilation, physical and mental torture, undue psychological pressures; all offenses against human dignity, such as subhuman living conditions, arbitrary imprisonment, deportation, slavery, prostitution, the selling of women and children, degrading working conditions, where men are treated as mere tools for profit rather than free and responsible persons; all these and the like are criminal; they poison civilization; and they debase the perpetrators more than the victims and militate against the honor of the Creator. (*GS* 27)

Gaudium et Spes also supplies an emphasis on the supernatural and on man's ultimate destiny in heaven with God. We saw earlier that this dimension was, relatively speaking, somewhat lacking in *Lumen Gentium.* Concentrating on the living Church here and now, the Council's earlier great Dogmatic Constitution on the Church tended to neglect the traditional "Four Last Things," that is, death, judgment, heaven, and hell. *Gaudium et Spes* makes up for this in a way that those who have not read it would hardly suspect, considering the reputation that the document has generally for supposedly expressing only a this-worldly "optimism." But let us take, for example, the following passage, which in its beauty and truth surely tempers—and indeed very severely qualifies—the still widespread idea supposedly stemming from Vatican II that we should henceforth not worry so much about "saving souls" but should simply be working for "a better world." Rather, *Gaudium et Spes* affirms:

> We know neither the moment of the consummation of the earth and of man, nor the way the universe will be transformed. The form of this world, distorted by sin, is passing away and we are taught that God is preparing a new dwelling and a new earth in which righteousness dwells, whose happiness will fill and surpass all the desires of peace arising in the hearts of men. Then with death conquered the sons of God will be raised in Christ and what was sown in weakness and dishonor will put on the imperishable: charity and its works will remain and all of creation, which God made for man, will be set free from its bondage to decay.
>
> We have been warned, of course, that it profits man nothing if he gains the whole world and loses or forfeits himself. Far from diminishing our concern to develop the earth, the expectancy of a new earth should spur us on, for it is here that the body of a new human family grows, foreshadowing in some way the age which is to come. That is why, although we must be careful to distinguish earthly progress clearly from the increase of the kingdom of Christ, such progress is of vital concern to the kingdom of God, insofar as it can contribute to the better ordering of human society. (*GS* 39)

This same theme is pursued in chapter 4 of part 1 of the document, "The Role of the Church in the Modern World," where we learn, *inter alia*, that

> the Church is entrusted with the task of opening up to man the mystery of God, who is the last end of man; in doing so it opens up to him the meaning of his own existence, the innermost truth about himself. The Church knows well that God alone, whom it serves, can satisfy the deepest cravings of the human heart, for the world and what it has to offer can never fully content it. It also realizes that man is continually being aroused by the Spirit of God that he will never be utterly indifferent to religion—a fact confirmed by the experience of ages past and plentiful evidence at the present day. For man will ever be anxious to know, if only in a vague way, what is the meaning of his life, his activity, and his death. The very presence of the Church recalls these problems to his mind. (*GS* 41)

Gaudium et Spes thus cannot be taxed with being too "optimistic," though it has often been taken to be such, as we have mentioned. On the basis of the text as we have been in the process of examining it here, however, it appears to be quite balanced, as would befit a conciliar text. Having established pretty plainly that the Church's real task is a *religious* one, in spite of her continuing interest in the affairs of this world, *Gaudium et Spes* goes on to state this quite plainly and unmistakably: "Christ did not bequeath to the Church a mission in the political, economic, or social orders," the text explains. "The purpose he assigned to it was a religious one" (*GS* 42). Still, the document does not fail to balance this with other statements more in keeping with what people think Vatican II generally stressed, stating very pointedly, for example, that

> it is a mistake to think that because we have here no lasting city, but seek the city which is to come, we are entitled to shirk our earthly responsibilities; this is to forget that by our faith we are bound all the more to fulfill these responsibilities. . . . The Christian who shirks his temporal duties shirks his duties toward his neighbor, neglects God himself, and endangers his eternal salvation. Let Christians follow the example of Christ, who worked as a craftsman. (*GS* 43)

We have now covered enough of the doctrinal part 1 of *Gaudium et Spes* to be able to say with some confidence about the document that it is not only authentically Catholic but is quite original, creative, and imaginative as well. If, like Vatican II generally, this document had been properly read, understood, and followed in the postconciliar years, we would not have had some of the postconciliar problems that we have had. Sadly, though, we are obliged to record that, as far as part 1 is concerned, the document has *not* always been read, understood, and followed in the postconciliar era as it should have been.

VII.

What about part 2 of *Gaudium et Spes*, the part in which the bishops at the Council aimed to apply Catholic teaching to some of what they called the "urgent problems" of today? Did they succeed in doing so in a way that is useful and pertinent to the life of the Church today? To some extent they did, as we shall see. The areas in question include five chapters, which deal with marriage and the family; culture; economic and social life; the political community; and the promotion of peace.

We examined in some detail already the development at the Council itself of the chapter on marriage and the family. We are thus already familiar with some of its provisions, in particular those insisted upon by Pope Paul VI in his key intervention in the Council's proceedings. In the meantime, the tenor and contents of the completed text are relatively easy to summarize. We can assert that the chapter contains an accurate, and, at times, beautiful, description of Christian marriage. In this regard we may cite the following introductory paragraph to a section entitled "The Holiness of Marriage and the Family":

> The intimate partnership of life and love which constitutes the married state has been established by the Creator and endowed by him with its own proper laws: it is rooted in the contract of its partners, that is, in their irrevocable personal consent. It is an institution confirmed by the divine law and receiving its stability, even in the eyes of society, from the human act by which the partners mutually surrender themselves to each other; for the good of the partners, of the children, and of society, this sacred bond no longer depends on human decision alone. For God himself is the author of marriage. (*GS* 48)

The text excels in its description of marriage as it is encountered existentially in the world of today, with attendant problems perhaps undreamed of by earlier generations. The Council did, however, foresee some of the evils that threaten human life and Christian marriage today, and it very clearly taught, for example, that "life must be protected with the utmost care from the moment of conception: abortion and infanticide are abominable crimes" (*GS* 51). This statement was prophetic, since abortion was still illegal in most of the world outside the Communist bloc at the time of the Council, and infanticide was still virtually unthinkable. With nothing less than such horrors as partial-birth abortion today, however, we can see how the situation in society has deteriorated since then.

But part 2 of *Gaudium et Spes* also understands that "the rights of parents to procreate and educate children must be safeguarded" (*GS* 52).

This is not only *not* granted by society today, it is specifically threatened by some disturbing contemporary trends. Interestingly, the text makes no mention of the evil of direct *sterilization*, a preferred method of birth control for many couples, then as now. It would be left to Pope Paul VI in *Humanae Vitae* to reinforce the Church's teaching against sterilization.

Possibly no reference was originally made to sterilization because, as we saw earlier, a fair number of the bishops at the Council were on the verge of abandoning the Church's constant teaching prohibiting the use of artificial birth control. This was apparently an objective of at least some of the members of the drafting commission at the Council, and if it had not been for the personal intervention of Pope Paul himself, as we have seen, the draft text might well have been quite deficient in not specifically excluding birth control. As things turned out, given the additions required by the pope, the text of *Gaudium et Spes* does correctly state the constant teaching of the Church on the transmission of life—a teaching that has endured for two thousand years. The text might have been made even stronger, since the text merely forbids "methods disapproved of by the teaching authority of the Church" (*GS* 51). It does not, however, state explicitly what is in fact the case, namely, that contraception and sterilization are *intrinsically evil* and hence are morally forbidden to everyone by the natural law, not just to the "children of the Church." This truth, however, was not always clearly seen in the climate of the 1960s, or even always today—far from it!

In the climate of the 1960s, the Council similarly did not foresee such contemporary aberrations as so-called same-sex marriage—which came to be imaginable only on the assumption that sexual acts between persons need not be open to the transmission of life, as *Humanae Vitae* would frame the question. The grave moral aberrations of in vitro fertilization, extraction of embryonic stem cells, and cloning were similarly not even imagined at the time of the Council, although in vitro fertilization, of course, was always implicitly condemned by the Church's teaching that conception licitly takes place only as a result of a natural act of sexual congress by persons married to each other. But if the Council did not actually foresee such grave evils, it provided at least one basis for opposing them in the teaching of *Gaudium et Spes* on the subject of human dignity: these practices are clearly contrary to, and seriously violate, human dignity.

All in all, then, the chapter on marriage and the family in part 2, chapter 1, of *Gaudium et Spes* did the job about as well as it could have been done at that particular moment in time. When we turn to the document's next chapter on culture, however, we find a discussion that, while it is probably adequate, is really quite pedestrian. Judging by this text, the Council was really not up to the task of dealing adequately with the problem of modern culture—a topic that engaged Pope John Paul II much more vitally. The text makes valid points, such as that since "scientific methods of investigation . . . are incapable of penetrating to the deepest nature of things, [they] are unjustifiably taken as the supreme norm for arriving at truth" (*GS* 57). Although the text here includes such a gem as Pope Pius XI's statement that "one must never lose sight of the fact that the Church's objective is to evangelize, not to civilize" (*GS* 57, n. 7), we may safely pass on from this chapter without much loss.

Looking at the chapter on economic and social life, we again find a text that is no doubt adequate but that is little more than a concise summary of some of the main points of the social teachings of the Church found much more richly and abundantly laid out in the papal social encyclicals from Pope Leo XIII's 1891 encyclical *Rerum Novarum* on. Of course, it was no doubt considered highly desirable by the Council Fathers that these social teachings of the Church should be confirmed by a general council of the Church; and in this conviction they were certainly not wrong. It surely is appropriate that we should see restated and reaffirmed Church teachings such as that "economic development . . . is not to be left to the judgment of a few individuals or groups possessing too much economic power" (*GS* 64), or that "all kinds of discrimination in wages and working conditions should be avoided" (*GS* 66), or that "remuneration for work should guarantee man the opportunity to provide a dignified livelihood for himself and his family" (*GS* 67), or that "among the fundamental rights of the individual must be numbered the right of workers to form themselves into associations which truly represent them" (*GS* 68), and so on.

The right to own private property is duly upheld, and, interestingly, it is even stated that this constitutes "one of the conditions for civil liberty" (*GS* 71). At the same time, it is held that "God destined the earth and all it contains for all men and all people so that all created things would be shared fairly by all mankind under the guidance of justice tempered by charity" (*GS* 69). Or again: "The Fathers and Doctors of the Church . . . taught that men are bound to come to the aid of the poor and to do so not merely out of their superfluous goods" (ibid.).

When we recall how determined a sizable group of Council Fathers were to have atheistic Communism condemned by the Council, it is interesting that the strongest statement in *Gaudium et Spes* to that effect ended up declaring that "we must denounce as false doctrines [those] which stand in the way of all reform on the pretext of a false notion of freedom"—a rejection of libertarianism—"as well as those *which subordinate the basic rights of individuals and of groups to the collective organization of production*" (*GS* 65; emphasis added). This latter clause is not much of a "condemnation" of Communism, of course, but nobody can say it is not there. Almost certainly, though, it did not satisfy those who wanted to see Communism roundly condemned by name, as some Catholic traditionalists have not failed to try to make us aware since the Council.

In short, the teaching of *Gaudium et Spes* on economic and social life, while it is surely adequate, is hardly exhaustive; nor is it particularly inspired or new. In the chapter that immediately follows, entitled "The Political Community," not too surprisingly, it is the question of human dignity that is again taken up. The text states:

> A keener awareness of human dignity has given rise in various parts of the world to an eagerness to establish a politico-juridical order in which the rights of the human person in public life will be better protected—for example, the right of free assembly and association, the right to express one's opinions and to profess one's religion privately and publicly. The guarantee of the rights of the person is, indeed, a necessary condition for citizens, individually and collectively, to play an active part in public life and administration. (*GS* 73)

Again, not surprisingly, *Gaudium et Spes* affirms that "political authority . . . must be exercised within the limits of the moral order and directed toward the common good" (*GS* 74). Such considerations as these logically led the Council to affirm in principle the value of *democracy.* Vatican II saw clearly and stated officially that the old alliance between "throne and altar"—once thought by some to have been an *essential* feature of the Church's political philosophy—was long since gone (for one thing, there were not too many thrones around any longer for the Church to be allied with!). The same thing was true of the old "confessional" state once favored by the Church. Although the Church is not committed to *any* political order in particular and, historically, has obviously accommodated herself to many different ones, it was also true at the time of Vatican II that the Church had been moving steadily for some time toward an accommodation with, and even an affirmation of, democracy.

This trend could be seen in the successive papal social encyclicals from Pope Leo XIII and later, for example. One of the reasons Blessed Pope John XXIII convoked the Council in the first place was precisely to update and clarify the Church's teaching in vital areas such as the political area. Theories of the relations of "church and state" that in some ways dated back to the era of the "old regime" in prerevolutionary Europe less and less accorded with contemporary reality and practice. The following passage, however, is one of the key passages that reflects the Church's updated understanding of contemporary political reality, with which Church teaching surely had to come to terms. Among other things, it indicates that the Church fully accepts—but does not necessarily prescribe—democracy as a desired form of government:

> It is fully consonant with human nature that there should be politico-juridical structures providing all citizens without any distinction with ever improving and effective opportunities to play an active part in the establishment of the juridical foundations of the political community, in the administration of public affairs, in determining the aims and the terms of reference of public bodies, and in the election of political leaders. Every citizen ought to be mindful of this right and his duty to promote the common good by using his vote. The Church praises and esteems those who devote

> themselves to the public good for the service of men and take upon themselves the burden of public office. (*GS* 75)

At the same time as she accepts democracy as a legitimate form of government, the Church condemns modern totalitarian governments or oppressive dictatorships: "It is inhuman for public authority to fall back on totalitarian methods or dictatorships which violate the rights of persons or social groups" (ibid.).

Whatever the form of government, or even the degree of anarchy, that prevails, however, the Church cannot but be solicitous about the necessity for her own freedom to preach the Gospel. This is an imperative that the Catholic Church has maintained throughout her entire history, whether it was a case of Peter speaking "truth to authority" in Gospel times and declaring that "we must obey God rather than men" (Acts 5:29), or a case of the medieval popes contending against kings and emperors, or of the modern popes defending the freedom of the Church against the incursions of revolutionary, anticlerical, or secularist governments. In one important sense, the entire history of the papacy has been a history of the bishops of Rome struggling to maintain the freedom of the Church against the powers that be. It remains a constant struggle that the Church, by her very nature, cannot evade or renounce. The Church is quite happy to "render unto Caesar the things that are Caesar's," but she can in no way accept the riposte of the old radical French anticlerical politician Georges Clemenceau that "everything is Caesar's." *Au contraire*, as *Gaudium et Spes* declares:

> But at all times and in all places, the Church should have the freedom to preach the faith, to proclaim its teaching about society, to carry out its task among men without hindrance, and to pass moral judgments even in matters relating to politics, whenever the fundamental rights of man or the salvation of souls requires it. (*GS* 76)

We can imagine what some of the doctrinaire American proponents of "the separation of church and state" might think about this last claim by the Church. For them religion is to be relegated entirely to the private sphere. In the nature of the case, however, the Catholic Church cannot accept any such relegation. She is *bound* by her very nature to "pass moral judgments"! It should be evident from the quotations we have included here that the basic teachings of *Gaudium et Spes* fall within the same long tradition and represent an important, indeed an indispensable, *development* of Catholic social doctrine. The Council was right on the mark in this area, and was quite conscious of being so.

However, this cannot be said in the same degree of the last chapter of part 2 of the Pastoral Constitution on the Church in the Modern World. This chapter is entitled "Fostering of Peace and Establishment of a Community of Nations." It is not that there is anything false or mistaken in it. On the contrary, it contains sound and authentic Catholic teaching. However, except for the Council's moral condemnation of "every act of war directed to the indiscriminate destruction of whole cities or vast areas with their inhabitants" (*GS* 80)—which after Hiroshima and Nagasaki (and Dresden!) was a pretty obvious step to take for anyone giving the slightest thought to the nature of modern warfare, especially nuclear war—there is very little in the text that is at all new. Moreover, some of the points that are made are sometimes obscure or not fully developed.

For example, it is stated—quite prophetically!—that "in many cases terrorist methods are regarded as new strategies of war" (*GS* 79). But there is virtually nothing else about how we are supposed to cope with morally, or to combat, these "new strategies of war" employed by terrorists. These are precisely the strategies we are faced with in combating terrorism today in the post-9/11 world. How can we go about combating terrorists and their typical methods while remaining within the boundaries of what the Church considers to be sound and moral?

Perhaps because of the nuclear "balance of terror" between the United States and the Soviet Union that prevailed at the time of the Council, the text is perhaps understandably preoccupied with such horrendous strategies of that day as "mutually assured destruction" (MAD). Confronted with such strategies, some observers could not but be tempted to reject the idea of war entirely if it entailed them. The very destructiveness of modern warfare raised the question in many minds of whether war itself did not have to be outlawed completely (whether this was possible or not was another question). Nor were these moral concerns without foundation. We still suffer the threat of nuclear destruction with the continuing proliferation of nuclear weapons—perhaps even into the hands of terrorists. Nor has the concept of the "balance of terror" disappeared today, as between India and Pakistan, for example, or Israel and Iran.

In this volume, we did not cover the Council debates on the subject of fostering peace because, with our limited space, we had to spend so much time discussing the intervention of Pope Paul VI in the drafting of *Gaudium et Spes.* At the Council itself, however, there was a pronounced pacifist tone among many of the Council Fathers, not a few of whom declared in the course of the debates that the very idea of a "just war" was obsolete today. War ought simply to be condemned, many bishops thought. Even as conservative a bishop as Curia cardinal Alfredo Ottaviani shared this sentiment to a large extent. On October 8, 1965, he noted in a speech that "several Fathers have said that war should be condemned absolutely. I am in entire agreement. I would like to see the *schema* treat at greater length the means of promoting and maintaining peace and resolving international conflicts." (It was only one month earlier, in September 1965, that Pope Paul VI had famously declared at the United Nations in New York: "No more war! War never again!")

Such were the sentiments of the time. For virtually all of the Fathers of Vatican II, the unprecedented destructiveness of World War II had been one of the principal experiences of their adult lives. Perhaps they really were too close to the unhappy facts of modern war as these had been manifested during World War II to be able to judge the whole question of war and peace for the Church in a really optimal way. It was probably inevitable, in fact, that the Council Fathers were strongly tempted by simple pacifism, given the experience of their generation. It would have been surprising if these tendencies had not been reflected somewhat in this chapter. But it is noteworthy that, just as Cardinal Ottaviani had suggested, this chapter of *Gaudium et Spes* is not about "war and peace" but simply about "the fostering of peace." Remarkably, the Church's traditional "just war" teaching is not treated, as such, at all, and this is certainly a deficiency.

In the end, though, the Council Fathers realized that they had to deal with the fact of war as well as with fostering peace. They themselves explicitly included the statement: "Insofar as men are sinners, the threat of war hangs over them and will so continue until the coming of Christ" (*GS* 78). They were not, therefore, unrealistic. They knew they had to fall back on some of the Church's traditional *dicta* concerning war. The Council's teaching on war can actually be summarized in a sentence, in fact: *Defensive* war can be licit; *offensive* war is condemned as a means of resolving conflicts among nations; and *total* war, especially nuclear, is condemned out of hand. In some ways, the document they fashioned is a compromise between the affirmation of the peace they wanted to foster and the problem of war they knew they had to deal with, at least in certain essentials. Nor is the end result of what they decided without merit or pertinence.

On the contrary, if we turn to the *Catechism of the Catholic Church*, we discover an interesting fact. It is this: virtually the entire treatment of war and peace in the *Catechism* (*CCC* 2302–17) is based on this chapter of *Gaudium et Spes.* Except for one reference concerning anger from St. Thomas Aquinas and one reference to St. Augustine's famous definition of peace as "the tranquility of order," every citation in the *Catechism* is either to a passage in sacred Scripture or to one in this document. Unlike *Gaudium et Spes* itself, however, the *Catechism* does summarize the elements of a just war but without referring to any previous Church statement or authority.

Thus, we cannot underline the importance and influence of *Gaudium et Spes* more effectively than by quoting some of the passages from it that found their way into the *Catechism of the Catholic Church*—the Church's authoritative statement of her own essential teaching for our times. They include the following:

> Peace is more than the absence of war. . . . It is the fruit of that right ordering of things with which the divine founder has invested human society and which must be actualized by man thirsting after an even more perfect reign of justice. (*GS* 78)
>
> All Christians are earnestly to seek the truth in love (cf. Eph 4:15) and join with all peace-loving men in pleading for peace and trying to bring it about. In the same spirit we cannot but express an admiration for all who forgo the use of violence to vindicate their right and resort to those other means of defense which are available

> to weaker parties, provided it can be done without harm to rights and duties of others and of the community. (*GS* 78)

Although the Church of Christ—who is the Prince of Peace (Isa 9:5)—obviously and understandably prefers peace, realism dictates that defense against aggression may nevertheless be necessary and hence must be considered legitimate. *Gaudium et Spes* thus plainly states:

> As long as the danger of war persists and there is no international authority with the necessary competence and power, government cannot be denied the right of lawful self-defense, once all peace efforts have failed. State leaders and all who share the burden of public administration have the duty to defend the interests of the people. (*GS* 79)

It is at this point that the *Catechism* lists the conditions of a just war that *Gaudium et Spes* omits. Significantly, the *Catechism* then adds another essential point that, again, is unfortunately lacking in the conciliar document: "The evaluation of these [just war] conditions for moral legitimacy belongs to the prudential judgment of those who have responsibility for the common good" (*CCC* 2309). In other words, decisions concerning war and peace belong to established, legitimate political authorities (and not, in concrete cases, to the Church). The conciliar document also does go on to affirm that military service is good and honorable:

> All those who enter the military service in loyalty to their country should look upon themselves as custodians of the security and freedom of their fellow countrymen; and when they carry out their duty properly, they are contributing to the maintenance of peace. (*GS* 79)

Finally, as we should have expected, *Gaudium et Spes* does not fail to affirm an essential of the Church's traditional teaching on war and peace, which the *Catechism* duly adopts, namely, that once war breaks out, it must be waged morally; the moral law is not suspended because two parties are at war:

> [I]t is one thing to wage a war of self-defense; it is quite another to seek to impose domination on another nation. The possession of war potential does not justify the use of force for political or military objectives. Nor does the mere fact that war has unfortunately broken out mean that all is fair between warring parties. (*GS* 79)

In summary, chapter 5 of part 2 of *Gaudium et Spes* contains much that is useful to understand Catholic teaching on war and peace. It is not completely adequate as a guide today, however, especially in the era of "regional wars," such as in Bosnia in the 1990s, or of suicide bombers, terrorist attacks against innocent civilians, and the like, which we have increasingly seen since September 11, 2001. The Council Fathers had the best of intentions, but in this case they did not always see as far as they needed to.

VIII.

Vatican Council II met and deliberated and issued its sixteen documents before what in those days was called "women's liberation" had really gotten under way. The influence that the ideology of feminism—and, indeed, *radical* feminism—would come to have on our society was still largely in the future. The Council itself, in fact, had very little to say about women as such. The Council's Decree on the Apostolate of Lay People, *Apostolicam Actuositatem*, speaks in passing about the fact that women in our day "are taking an increasingly active share in the whole of life and of society," and this decree on the laity thus says they should also participate "in various sections of the Church's apostolate" (*AA* 9), without, however, specifying which ones.

Gaudium et Spes, for its part, speaks very mildly, again in passing, about what it calls "new social relations between the sexes" (*GS* 8); and a little farther on, it mentions that "women claim parity with men in fact as well as of rights where they have not already obtained it" (*GS* 9). Many radical feminists in America today, of course, forty years later, would hold that women are far from having obtained "parity" *yet*, even in advanced Western countries!

In a key chapter entitled "The Dignity of the Human Person," *Gaudium et Spes* mentions, with hardly a glimmer of a suspicion of what is coming, that "the partnership of man and woman constitutes the first form of communion between persons" (*GS* 12). Again, in its chapter on culture, this pastoral constitution says that women "ought to be permitted to play their part . . . in all spheres of life . . . according to their own particular nature" (*GS* 60), not realizing how soon any such reference to a woman's "own particular nature" would come to be deeply resented and regularly excoriated by convinced ideological feminists. And yet again, in a chapter entitled "The Community of Mankind," which explicitly condemns discrimination on the basis of sex and which affirms "the essential equality of all men" (*GS* 29), modern feminists would object to the very use of the word "men" here and would claim that its use in this generic sense did not *include* them!

What *Gaudium et Spes* enumerates as among the principal rights being denied to women in some places today includes merely "women who are denied the chance freely to choose a husband, or a state of life, or to have access to the same educational and cultural benefits as are available to men" (*GS* 29). *That's it!* These are the only instances of discrimination against women actually mentioned in the Council documents. There is nothing about the "demeaning" condition of being confined to work in the home; nothing about discrimination in the workplace; nothing about equal pay for equal work; nothing about "glass ceilings"; nothing about the denial of opportunities or the stifling of initiative; nothing about the "cultural conditioning" of little girls; and, it surely goes without saying, nothing about the ordination of those women who believe themselves "called" to the priesthood!

In the United States today, of course, where some *60 percent* of all students enrolled in postsecondary education are females, the idea that a major problem exists with regard to female "access to the same educational and cultural benefits" as males is more than slightly risible. As for choosing husbands or a state of life, young women in America not only suffer no disabilities in this regard but are typically forward and even aggressive in such matters, especially by comparison with many of today's young men. The typical modern nonaggressive male "wimp," for example, is almost certainly one of the unforeseen by-products of the modern radical feminist movement, about which the Council was entirely silent for the simple reason that it hardly even conceived of such a thing.

In short, the Council simply did not turn out to be very prophetic where the subject of women was concerned. We have quoted virtually all of the passages in the Council documents where women are singled out for special mention. It is obvious that there were not very many mentions of them. Almost as an afterthought, Vatican II did issue to the world a series of "closing messages" on the last day of the Council, December 8, 1965—the Closing Message to Rulers; to Men of Thought and Science; to Artists; to the Poor, Sick, and Suffering; to Youth; to Workers. And among them also was the Council's Closing Message to Women.

It is not at all a bad statement. In it the Church takes credit for having "glorified and liberated women," among other things, and it is surely true that women have fared better historically under Christianity than with, for example, Hinduism or Confucianism or Islam. But the statement must nevertheless have grated on incipient radical feminist ears already back then in the 1960s, since it placed such strong emphasis on woman as *wife and mother. Inter alia*, the Council's Closing Message to Women said:

> You women have always had as your lot the protection of the home, the love of beginnings and an understanding of cradles. You are present in the mystery of a life beginning. You offer consolation in the departure of death. Our technology runs the risk of becoming inhuman. Reconcile men with life and above all, we beseech you, watch carefully over the future of our race. Hold back the hand of man who, in a moment of folly, might attempt to destroy human civilization.
>
> Wives, mothers of families, the first educators of the human race in the intimacy of the family circle, pass on to your sons and your daughters the tradition of your *fathers*.

It does not take much imagination to realize the contempt and derision with which such a statement as this would be greeted by many today. From a modern radical feminist point of view, the Fathers of the Second Vatican Council simply did not "get it" as far as modern women were concerned. Perhaps because the Council itself failed to take the measure of and deal adequately with what would turn out to be the growing and proliferating modern feminist movement, Church authority in the postconciliar era has similarly often failed to take its measure and deal with it adequately from the standpoint of authentic Catholic teaching. Examples of this could be cited in the realms of the sacred liturgy, the religious life, and, especially, the ordination question, about which so many feminist and feminist-influenced voices have expressed such bitter disappointment over Pope John Paul II's nevertheless "definitive" statement that the Church has no power to ordain women. The whole question of women thus remains a critical issue for the Church today, especially when the Catholic bishops, and even the Holy See, sometimes continue to see as merely "justice for women" certain feminist-inspired issues and imperatives that, if allowed to be carried to their logical conclusions, could result in the undermining of both doctrine and discipline in more than a few instances.

This remains the case even though one of the best of the documents from Pope John Paul II's remarkable twenty-six-year teaching pontificate carefully laid out the theoretical basis for seeing the question of women both steadily and wholly and seeing it also from an authentic Catholic standpoint. Even though the Council failed to deal with the question of women adequately—at the time that the radical feminist train was just picking up the speed with which it would shortly come thundering rapidly down the tracks—John Paul II, nevertheless, once again produced a document on his own that largely remedies what was lacking from the Council. This document of John Paul II's, an apostolic letter entitled On the Dignity and Vocation of Women, *Mulieris Dignitatem*, as it is called, was issued on August 15, 1988. It is of special interest to us here because of the degree to which it goes back to *Gaudium et Spes* in its basic message.

Mulieris Dignitatem still remains to be understood and assimilated by the Church, though, perhaps especially by some of our contemporary Church leaders, who sometimes appear to be disoriented and even intimidated by almost anything having to do with women—at least as the contemporary radical feminist movement has typically portrayed "women." In being taken in by this, some of our Catholic leaders may not be all that different from some of the other leaders of our contemporary society. We need only think, in this connection, of politicians, journalists, newspaper editors, news anchors, media moguls, college presidents, corporate CEOs, army generals, navy admirals, and so on down the list; many such people in our society today have tended to "cave" virtually as soon as they are ever challenged by the radical feminists. Catholic bishops, however, ought to know better and to do better, since the Catholic Church, again, teaches truly on the subject of men and women and on why and how "male and female he created them" (Gen 1:27).

John Paul II's *Mulieris Dignitatem* helps to remedy the Church's deficient postconciliar record with respect to the question of women. It is one of John Paul's best efforts, and it is hard to see how any woman reading this document could fail to be greatly affirmed in her womanhood as well as in her faith. Of course, John Paul II more than once addressed the question of women in the course of his pontificate. In his Letter to Women of June 29, 1995, for example, he was widely reported in the press as "praising feminism" and "apologizing" to women, which was only a slight exaggeration of the pope's position: he truly did wish to reconcile disaffected modern women to the Church and to the Church's truths about the human condition. He even prompted the Congregation for the Doctrine of the Faith to issue the Letter on the Collaboration of Men and Women in the Church and in the World, which came out as recently as May 31, 2004. So it is not that the Church's leadership has not been trying. During his pontificate, John Paul II never ceased thinking of ways at least to try to address what for him was the burning question of women. No doubt he was keenly aware of the harm done to the faith and the Church by radical feminism.

His best effort on the subject, however, was his apostolic letter On the Dignity and Vocation of Women, *Mulieris Dignitatem.* This document seems to have grown out of the 1987 Synod of Bishops on the subject of the laity. Although a postsynodal apostolic exhortation on the laity, *Christifideles Laici,* was duly written and published, Pope John Paul II seems to have felt that special treatment of the subject of women was also called for, and hence he produced this apostolic letter as well, pegging it to the Marian Year.

As with the pontiff's "theology of the body," which he developed and set forth in a series of Wednesday audiences over several years, beginning in September 1979 and extending into the early 1980s, Pope John Paul II seems to have been particularly inspired by the need to get it right about women on what by then had become our current era of virulent radical feminist ideology that was leading so many astray. Just as the pope realized that something had to be done about sexuality in marriage, following the sexual revolution in general and the rebellion within the Church against *Humanae Vitae* in particular—which led him to develop his "theology of the body"—so he realized that the challenge of a radical feminism that was almost unopposed in modern society at large had to be countered with the Church's true and positive teaching on the subject of women.

That *Mulieris Dignitatem* was also inspired by *Gaudium et Spes* and its emphasis on human dignity is evident from the apostolic letter's very title. John Paul II twice quotes or refers to *Gaudium et Spes* 22 on our being able to understand the mystery of man only in the light of the mystery of the Incarnate Word, Jesus Christ; and he similarly refers to the teaching of *Gaudium et Spes* 24 that man is the only creature willed for its own sake—and one who can achieve self-realization only through a sincere gift of self—no less than *four times*!

For John Paul II, "both man and woman are human beings to an equal degree, both are created in God's image" (*MD* 6). This is the source of the human dignity of both. The pope quotes Scripture and the Fathers extensively to show that this has been the constant teaching of the Church. Sin, of course, affected (and affects) both men and women, as it has adversely affected the condition of women in many places down through history. But sin could not destroy human dignity or cancel it out.

In marriage, the woman's "sincere gift of self" should be

> responded to and matched by a corresponding 'gift' on the part of the husband. Only on the basis of this principle can both of them, and, in particular, the woman, 'discover themselves' as a true 'unity of the two' according to the dignity of the person. The matrimonial union requires respect for and a perfecting of the true personal subjectivity of both of them. *The woman cannot become the 'object' of 'domination' and male 'possession'*. (*MD* 10; emphasis in the original)

Showing his deep respect for women as they are—as they have been created by God—John Paul II gets to the heart of the principal mistake of modern radical feminism, which sees equality as requiring that women need to be *exactly the same as men.* Thus, to take the most extreme example of this attitude—which is nevertheless very influential in society today—if men do not have to bear children, then women should not have to bear children either! Legalized abortion thus becomes a necessity. It is no accident that the affirmation of a woman's so-called right to abortion—in America called her "right to choose"—is the most consistent of all the claims of modern radical feminism.

No, John Paul says:

> In the name of liberation from male domination, women must not appropriate to themselves male characteristics contrary to their own feminine 'originality.' There is a well-founded fear that if they take this path, women will not reach fulfillment, but instead will *deform and lose what constitutes their essential richness.* . . . In the biblical description, the words of the first man at the sight of the woman who had been created are words of admiration and enchantment, words which fill the whole history of man on earth. (ibid.; emphasis in the original)

But even though Eve was different, Adam immediately recognized that she was "bone of my bones and flesh of my flesh" (Gen 2:23). Man and woman possess the same but a complementary human *nature*, enjoy the same and equal *dignity*, and are ordered by their complementarity to love one another. "A woman's dignity is closely connected with the love which she receives by the very reason of her femininity; it is likewise connected *with the love that she gives in return*" (*MD* 30; emphasis in the original). It is worth quoting *Mulieris Dignitatem* at some length on this point:

> Only a person can love and only a person can be loved. This statement is primarily ontological in nature, and it gives rise to an ethical affirmation. Love is an ontological and ethical requirement of the person. The person must be loved, since love alone corresponds to what the person is. This explains the *commandment of love,* known already in the Old Testament (cf. Deut 6:5; Lev 19:18) and placed

> by Christ at the very center of the Gospel *ethos* (cf. Mt 22:36–40; 12:28–34). This also explains the *primacy of love* expressed by Saint Paul in the First Letter to the Corinthians: "the greatest of these is love" (cf. I Cor 13:13).
>
> Unless we refer to this order and primacy we cannot give a complete and adequate answer to the question about women's dignity and vocation. When we say that the woman is the one who receives love in order to love in return, this refers not only or above all to the specific spousal relationship of marriage. It means something more universal, based on the very fact of her being a woman within all the interpersonal relationships which, in the most varied ways, shape society and structure the interaction between all persons—men and women. In this broad and diversified context, *a woman represents a particular value by the fact that she is a human person*, and, at the same time, this particular person, *by the fact of her femininity*. This concerns each and every woman, independently of the cultural context in which she lives, and independently of her spiritual, psychological, and physical characteristics, as for example, age, education, health, work, and whether she is married or single. (*MD* 29; emphasis in the original)

All this is a pretty far cry from the war of the sexes that radical feminism helped launch in our society. It was intended to be. The emphasis on love and personhood, profoundly Christian, is simply at opposite poles from the harshness and egotism of radical feminism. The Church could never endorse the radical feminist ideology—which truly does entail putting the two sexes into conflict with one another—any more than the Church could ever have endorsed the Marxist ideology of inevitable conflict between social classes. Radical feminism, on its face, should immediately be seen as an unchristian and even anti-Christian ideology. Christian charity, or love, as St. Paul teaches, "does not insist on its own way" (1 Cor 13:5; emphasis added). Radical feminism, on the contrary, insists upon nothing else *except* "its own way"! By itself, this should serve to expose the profoundly unchristian character of feminism.

Fortunately, in such a document as Pope John Paul II's apostolic letter *Mulieris Dignitatem*, the living Magisterium of the Catholic Church turned out to be capable of countering this ideology at the time of what may have been the height of feminism's influence in our society, the 1980s and the 1990s. Since then, there have been a few signs that radical feminism may have perhaps begun to decline, although it is still very, very far from being a spent force. The likelihood is that the Church will be obliged to continue to counter it for years to come. What remains puzzling and sometimes not a little dismaying, though, as we have remarked before, is that the American Catholic bishops in the postconciliar era have been slow to grasp that the Church *does* have to counter radical feminism. Too often they have uncritically accepted feminist imperatives on feminist terms as simply "justice for women." We can only hope that, as time goes by, the bishops will be more and more influenced by the cogency and clarity of such a document as *Mulieris Dignitatem.*

IX.

One of the patterns that quite consistently characterized the actions of the U.S. Conference of Catholic Bishops in the postconciliar era, and still does to a great extent, was the continued recognition of and support for groups or elements such as religious orders reorganized in defiance of Church norms, or societies such as the Catholic Theological Society of America even after the latter had demonstrated by its official actions that a majority of its members were in open rebellion against Church teachings. The same thing was true of associations such as the Association of Catholic Colleges and Universities, which actively lobbied and aided and abetted its member institutions in resisting the acceptance and application of John Paul II's *Ex Corde Ecclesiae* on the Catholic university and of the canon law that plainly pertained to Catholic universities. However, none of this ever seemed to have any negative effect on the way the organizations in question were viewed by the bishops' conference: such organizations still seemed to be accepted as fully "Catholic," "in good standing," and perhaps "in dialogue" with the bishops. The conference was no more going to get into the business of correcting such organizations than it was ever very seriously in the business of correcting individuals.

At the same time, the conference was consistently reluctant to acknowledge even the existence of, much less provide support or encouragement to, groups such as Catholics United for the Faith, the Fellowship of Catholic Scholars, Women for Faith and Family, or the Society of Catholic Social Scientists, whose very raison d'être lay in their loyalty to Church teaching and discipline. A few individual bishops accepted and encouraged these latter groups, but never the conference itself. To have done so would no doubt have meant acknowledging the existence of the widespread disloyalty, disobedience, and dissent in the Church that had called these loyalist organizations into being in the first place. The conference was never able to acknowledge this, however.

One of the most remarkable manifestations of postconciliar dissent and disloyalty, though, came about as a result not just of toleration but of active sponsorship on the part of the American bishops' conference. This was the decade-long (1973–1983) American Catholic Bicentennial Program. We need to take a brief look at it since it was to a large extent *inspired* by *Gaudium et Spes*, even though it proved to be one of the more unfortunate examples of how the Council's teachings and directives were sometimes greatly distorted in the process of being implemented in the postconciliar era.

Perhaps the principal manifestation of how the American Bicentennial Program went astray came as a result of its notorious Detroit Call to Action Conference. This gathering took place in October 1976. It consisted of an assemblage of Catholic "delegates" from all over the country that became a national forum in which liberal elements in the Church openly challenged Church authority on a number of key issues and called for drastic changes in Church doctrine and discipline. The conference became a huge embarrassment for the American bishops, who had themselves set the machinery in motion that resulted in the conference. It demonstrated to the whole world that, at least for the time being, they had lost effective control of some of their own institutions. When one looks back upon the whole process from the perspective of more than thirty years, it is difficult to believe that any conference of Catholic bishops anywhere could ever have knowingly sponsored such folly to the detriment of the institution they were supposed to be leading.

Yet the American Bicentennial Program started out as a positive effort by the Church in America to respond to the legitimate call to justice set forth in *Gaudium et Spes* (cf. *GS* 63, among other texts). An advisory council to what was in those days called the National Conference of Catholic Bishops/United States Catholic Conference (NCCB/USCC) initiated the program, choosing the theme "Liberty and Justice for All" from the American Pledge of Allegiance. Another inspiration for the program, in addition to *Gaudium et Spes*, was a 1971 apostolic letter of Pope Paul VI entitled "A Call to Action," which endeavored to deal with the problem of how to apply Catholic social teachings to concrete problems encountered in the world. Paul VI surely never imagined how some of his ideas were going to play out in Detroit five years later; certainly he never dreamed that the title of his apostolic letter would later be adopted as the name of one of the most radical dissident Catholic groups in America.

In addition to the pope's apostolic letter, there was also the important document that had been issued by the Synod of Bishops, "Justice in the World," dated November 30, 1971, in which the Synod Fathers, scrutinizing "the signs of the times" in accordance with *Gaudium et Spes* 4, declared that "action on behalf of justice and participation in the transformation of the world fully appear to us a constitutive dimension of the preaching of the Gospel" (Introduction). Thus, the question of justice was a live one for the Church in the immediate postconciliar years. Not just radical elements, but the official Church herself, at the highest levels of her leadership, was concerned about the issue of justice and convinced that the Church had a role to play in helping to bring about justice in the world. How all the principles enunciated by the Council and the Synod and the Holy Father could be translated into practice, however, was another question, indeed a series of questions. If anyone could succeed in translating them, however, would it not perhaps be the very practical Americans? It turned out that the American bishops were prepared to try.

In the three years leading up to the American bicentennial in 1976, a massive effort was mounted involving the USCC bureaucracy, many individual dioceses and parishes, and Catholic organizations of all kinds. Over 830,000 individual responses were elicited in numerous meetings in over half of the nation's dioceses, identifying "justice" issues considered important by the participants in the meetings. Seven regional "justice hearings" were held, in which more than five hundred priests, religious, and laity presented testimony. Eight writing committees prepared working papers and proposals on a variety of subjects, including the Church; ethnicity and race; neighborhood; family; personhood; work; nationhood; and humankind. Only in America, it would seem, would such an extraordinary response be mounted in response to the ferment caused by the issuance of a number of Church documents.

All of these efforts were preparations for the 1976 Detroit Call to Action Conference proper. This conference was attended by 1,340 delegates from 150 of the 170 dioceses in the country. Fifty-three percent of them were clergy and 47 percent were laity. No less than 110 of the nation's 300 bishops themselves attended. Nevertheless, it should not be thought that the conference was representative of "Catholic opinion" generally. On the contrary, one quite extraordinary fact about this Detroit Call to Action Conference was that some two-thirds of the participants were *employed by the Church*! The conference was primarily a conference of, by, and for what Catholic sociologist Joseph A. Varacalli has aptly called "the new Catholic knowledge class"—Church "professionals" of all kinds, whether bureaucrats, theologians, teachers, catechists, or other experts operating on the basis of their acquired training and their degrees and diplomas and not necessarily on the basis of what was still nevertheless presumed to be their commitment to the faith of the Church. The fact that so many of them were actually employed by the Church made it all the more astounding that they could have passed some of the radical conference resolutions that they did pass. There were 182 such resolutions voted in all, not all of them radical; but the number of them that *were* radical, and in some cases plainly contrary to the established teaching and discipline of the Church, was only too revealing of the state of mind of a significant portion of the Catholic Church's working "personnel" generally. They seem to have pretty much laid aside, perhaps as irrelevant, major features of the Catholic faith as taught and guaranteed by the Church; instead they seemed to have largely adopted a revisionist kind of this-worldly "faith" not easily distinguishable from contemporary secular humanism.

The original idea had been that the resolutions voted by the Detroit bicentennial conference would be presented to the NCCB, which would consider them at its summer meetings over the next several years and decide which proposals should (1) be studied further; (2) be acted on immediately by an appropriate organization or element of the Church; (3) be supported in connection with an existing Church activity; or (4) be responded to in the light of the universal law of the Church. As things turned out, this fourth and last category would prove to be more important than perhaps anyone had originally imagined, since a disturbing number of the 182 proposals turned out to be *incompatible with*, and, in some cases, actually *contrary to*, "the universal law of the Church."

In fact, the resolutions or proposals as a whole proved to be a farrago or grab bag of practically everything that liberal, disgruntled, or dissenting Catholics had ever imagined up to that point. Many of them continue to be hot-button issues today. Even if they were not immediately subversive of Church teaching or discipline, many of them were otherwise impractical or even utopian. Proposals on the Church called for the selection of bishops and pastors by the "local Church" (4) and the sharing of their responsibilities with "the Catholic population" (5); the ordination of married men (12) as well as the ordination of women (13); the allowing of priests to marry (14) and of laicized priests to continue in various ministries (11). Discrimination of all kinds was to be eliminated, including against homosexuals (6). "Sexist language" was to be expunged from all Church documents (18). Women were to be accorded completely "equal status" in the Church (17). Ironically in view of the later clerical sex abuse scandals, a National Review Board was to be set up to oversee the work of the bishops (2). Remember: all these things were being proposed by an officially convoked national Church body back in 1976!

As regards ethnicity and race, it was proposed that American Indian liturgies be admitted (48) and that the NCCB/USCC bureaucracies be expanded to include "secretariats" for blacks, Hispanics, Indians, and other ethnics (66). Church "policy" should be made on the basis of "proportional representation of racial, ethnic, and cultural groups" within the Church (32). This was only one of the ways in which a rather total "democratization" of the Church was evidently envisaged by the radical Catholics who dominated the conference in Detroit.

With regard to the family, "discrimination" against the divorced and remarried was to cease, and the sacraments were to be allowed to them (78). Some of the real problems of the family today, for which Catholic teaching (e.g., fidelity, indissolubility) might have helped provide remedies, however, were hardly considered. Authentically Catholic viewpoints on issues were apparently of little or no interest for most conference participants. On the subject of humankind, it was proposed that the Church in her investment policies should follow the "guidelines" of the Protestant National Council of Churches, which already in 1976 was busy transforming itself into the leftist pressure group that it seems to be today (95). Amnesty was to be granted to all illegal aliens in America (100). Among the things to be promoted by the Church under the category of nationhood was the then proposed Equal Rights Amendment to the U.S. Constitution, as well as "unconditional amnesty" for all resisters to the Vietnam War (114, 147, 170, and 176).

Such were the demands of "justice," as seen by the delegates to the 1976 Detroit bicentennial Call to Action Conference. These were only some of the proposals, of course. Not all of them were bad. Some of them even represented commonsense ideas on social justice. But enough of them approached or even the crossed the line into leftist ideology and extremism to make clear that radical ideological elements were strongly entrenched, if not dominant, within many of the Church's official structures. These elements did not scruple to recommend changes in Church teaching, sanctioning, for example, the common view of contemporary dissenting theologians that Catholics should "form their own consciences and . . . discover what is morally appropriate regarding contraception" (155)—presumably without reference to the fact that the Church had already, authoritatively and definitively, decided well before 1976 that contraception was *morally wrong*; it was not something individual Catholics *could* decide on their own. Similarly, sex education "from an early age" was frankly counseled (156), and "discrimination" against homosexuals was castigated (157).

Even proposals affirming authentic Catholic teaching in matters of social justice were too often couched in partisan or absolutist terms that made it unlikely that they could ever be implemented in any fruitful way. Thus, the NCCB/USCC was supposed to "critically challenge both the U.S. Government and corporations with regard to their promotion of human rights" (101). Again, the NCCB/USCC was called upon to "mobilize the international conscience on behalf of all political prisoners under repressive governments in any country of the world" (103).

What happened at this 1976 Detroit bicentennial Call to Action Conference, of course, was the same thing that had happened at many similar Church meetings and general congregations of religious orders in the postconciliar years, namely, that radical ideologically committed partisans gained control of the conference machinery and then engineered outcomes in accordance with their own ideological aims—aims not only revolutionary but also often of the type that would later be styled "politically correct." That the bishops in attendance at the Detroit conference stood by while all this was happening before their very eyes constituted a sort of model or paradigm of how they had stood by generally in the postconciliar years while dissenters and ideologues in their employ were allowed to carry on and promote their own alien agendas within and through official structures of the Church. One assumes (and hopes) that the bishops in Detroit were deceived and blindsided in much of this; but the fact remains that, as far as the Detroit meeting was concerned, they had freely though perhaps naïvely put themselves into a situation where they *could* be outvoted by radical partisans and extremists on every issue that came before the conference.

The embarrassment for the bishops was considerable, owing especially to the great interest of the media in gleefully reporting many of the instances where the Detroit conference was clearly going beyond what was widely understood to be legitimate in the Church. Even newspaper and television reporters understand it when delegates call for the acceptance of, say, contraception or female ordination at the same time that the pope has obviously excluded these things. The bishops themselves, however, did not allow the embarrassment that they could not help but incur to deflect them from their original plans. They formed an Ad Hoc Committee on the Call to Action within the NCCB/USCC; eventually this committee responded in one way or another to all of the 182 proposals voted, either by slating them for further study, assigning them to other existing Church activities, or, in some cases, actually explaining, *mirabile dictu*, how they diverged from Church teaching. Some criticisms were voiced by some bishops at the end of the whole affair, but by and large the original bicentennial process ground on as it had been programmed to do and as if nothing untoward had occurred in Detroit.

In 1978, two years after Detroit, the bishops produced a follow-up Call to Action plan, which was brought out in an official USCC publication entitled *To Do the Work of Justice*. In 1979, there was a follow-up miniconference in Washington, D.C. In no way, apparently, were the bishops capable of simply *rejecting* or *repudiating* what Detroit had brought about in the Church, even though so much of it had turned out to be in conflict with Church teaching and practice. A number of official bicentennial activities actually continued after that, still sponsored by the bishops.

John Cardinal Dearden of Detroit, the first president of the NCCB/USCC, and the host of the Detroit conference, was unapologetic about how things had turned out. He had earlier explained that the purpose of the whole affair was "trying to begin a new way of doing the work of the Church in America." After the conference, when nothing resembling any such new way had emerged—all that had emerged was massive evidence that many of the "employees" of the Church had evidently gone over to frankly secular liberal ways of seeing and doing things—Cardinal Dearden was nevertheless able to include the following remarks in an official report:

> The results of the bicentennial process may at this point seem hasty, untidy, careless, even extreme. But on closer examination, it seems to me that far more often the working papers and conference resolutions demonstrate a warmth and sympathy for the problems of Church leadership on the part of our people, their enthusiastic affirmation of Christian faith and hope, their sincere willingness to share in building a stronger Church and their firm resolve to fulfill a Christian ministry to the world. No one expects us to endorse all that transpired at Detroit. People do expect us to continue the process by responding with decisive action where it is called for, and with honest disagreement where that seems necessary. The key to our actions in the future is to continue the process, to build on the

> hopes that have been awakened, to act upon our clear responsibility for the unity, fidelity, and vision of the Catholic community.

That was certainly one way to put it. I myself, however, remember visiting Rome early in 1977, not long after the Detroit conference, when Franjo Cardinal Seper, then prefect of the Congregation for the Doctrine of the Faith, asked me: "What has happened to Cardinal Dearden?" When Roman officials are reduced to asking visiting laymen about what may have happened to prominent members of the hierarchy in their countries, we may conclude that Rome itself has surely lost at least temporary "control" over the hierarchies in question (if indeed "control" is the proper term to express the necessity of Roman and papal oversight over the authenticity of acts and statements of national hierarchies). Cardinal Dearden's colleague and contemporary (and successor as NCCB president), John Cardinal Krol of Philadelphia, was probably closer to the truth, as well as more candid, when he remarked that the Detroit conference had obviously "fallen into the clutches of rebels." He felt obliged to add that the conference was clearly not "a legislative body."

It was left to the then NCCB president, Archbishop Joseph Bernardin of Cincinnati—the future cardinal archbishop of Chicago—in his opening address to the American bishops at their meeting in May 1977, to observe that, "amidst the controversy of the Call to Action, people have forgotten that the role of bishops as guardians of the faith, is to lead and guide the rest of the Church." But what the Detroit conference had served to demonstrate was that the bishops were precisely *not* entirely in control any longer in leading and guiding the Church. Nor were they showing themselves to be very effective "guardians of the faith." A conference consisting of "delegates," a majority of whom, though "employed" by the bishops, were quite openly attempting to move the Church down other paths besides those already approved by the Church's Magisterium, was, in fact, the real situation here. What this indicated about the state of mind of large numbers of the very people upon whom the bishops were depending to do the official work of the Church should have been troubling to all of the bishops; but, in fact, it does not seem to have been very troubling to very many of them. Rather, the watchword seemed to be "business as usual."

There can scarcely be any doubt, however, that the 1976 American Bicentennial Program cannot be considered to have been anything else but a huge, regrettable mistake. It was never in the cards that any such large, bureaucratic program as the Bicentennial Program was ever going to be anything but a façade or was ever going to result in any improved social justice in any real sense. It was never anything but a highly utopian initiative. The remote legacy today of all this is an unofficial organization of aging radicals that adopted the slogan "Call to Action" as its name. The organization still holds annual conferences featuring radical, revisionist, and dissenting speakers. Fortunately, the participants at its meetings grow grayer with each passing year; nor does there seem to be very much of an infusion into the organization of any new blood. *Gaudium et Spes*, however, surely deserved better than this.

X.

In the forty years since the end of Vatican Council II, the Pastoral Constitution on the Church in the Modern World, *Gaudium et Spes*, has been misunderstood and misapplied in more ways than one. In this respect, it has perhaps been the quintessential document of a Council that itself has been misunderstood and misapplied in so many ways. The Council Fathers themselves did not wholly understand all the dimensions of what they were launching with this "new" kind of teaching document. Moreover, the generation that followed the Council proved mostly incapable of compensating for what the document itself lacked at the same time that it proved unable to understand and apply the document in its proper meaning and depth.

Nevertheless, as we have seen—and in spite of some of the unfortunate missteps and other questionable results that have stemmed from it—*Gaudium et Spes* remains a very significant and even profound document that still needs to be fully assimilated in the life of the Church. The extent to which Pope John Paul II made use of it in his remarkable teaching pontificate is just one indicator of its continuing importance. The "anthropology" of *Gaudium et Spes* alone represents a permanent acquisition in the Church's self-understanding. Taken along with

Lumen Gentium, this pastoral constitution definitely marks Vatican II as the Council of the Church's self-understanding.

More than that, though, it should not be forgotten that *Gaudium et Spes* also *did* issue a "call to justice." This was the theme of a conference in Rome organized in honor of the fortieth anniversary of the document by the Pontifical Council for Justice and Peace. Held in March 2005, the conference examined in particular the document's teaching that peace is the work of justice (cf. *GS* 78). In one of the last substantive messages of his pontificate before his death, Pope John Paul II told the participants (in a message read by Secretary of State Angelo Cardinal Sodano) that peace is more than just the work of justice: "*Gaudium et Spes* does not reduce its teaching to this," the pontiff declared. "In this Constitution the Council maintains that 'peace is also the fruit of love, for love goes beyond what justice can ensure.'" John Paul II went on to state even more precisely:

> To say it in other words: the theme of justice does not exhaust the social doctrine of the Church. The virtue of love that leads to forgiveness and reconciliation and motivates Christian commitment to justice must never be forgotten. It nevertheless remains unquestionable that the topic of justice is the basis for "the right ordering of human society." (*GS* 78)

Joseph Cardinal Ratzinger, very soon to become Pope Benedict XVI, although he did not know it at the time, also preached to the participants at this fortieth-anniversary *Gaudium et Spes* conference in Rome. Of special interest in his homily for our purposes here was his concise statement of the purpose of the pastoral constitution itself: "*Gaudium et Spes* sought to address," he said, "the significance of the Christian contribution to the improvement of human welfare, through works of mercy and justice, *within the overall mission of the Church*" (emphasis added). This last phrase describes what was too often forgotten in the postconciliar years with respect to *Gaudium et Spes*, namely, that authentic Catholic social action can properly be carried out only "within the overall mission of the Church."

This is exactly what was *not* done at the 1976 Detroit bicentennial Call to Action Conference, of course, where the participants more or less disregarded the overall mission of the Church—acted as if there were no existing teachings or practices of the Church in particular that they needed to respect—while heading off heedlessly in pursuit of their own cock-eyed modern ideas of what they thought the requirements of justice were.

In giving his own interpretation of how Christians should understand *Gaudium et Spes*, Cardinal Ratzinger turned, significantly, to the beautiful text of *Gaudium et Spes* 39:

> As Christians we must constantly be reminded that the call of justice is not something which can be reduced to the categories of this world. And this is the beauty of the Pastoral Constitution *Gaudium et Spes*, evident in the very structure of the Council's text; only when we Christians grasp our vocation as having been created in the image of God and believing that "the form of this world is passing away . . . [and] that God is preparing a new dwelling and a new earth, in which justice dwells" (*GS* 39), can we address the urgent social problems of our time from a truly Christian perspective.

This, then, is the true legacy of *Gaudium et Spes*, which it is to be hoped will be continued during the pontificate of Pope Benedict XVI and his successors.

CHAPTER FOUR

Orientalium Ecclesiarum

I.

VATICAN COUNCIL II'S Decree on the Eastern Catholic Churches, *Orientalium Ecclesiarum*, the third Council document on the subject of the Church herself, was the fifth and last of the Council's documents to be approved at the end of the Third Session. This meant that no less than eleven of the Council's eventual sixteen documents would have to be approved the following year at the end of the Fourth (and final) Session of the Council. In keeping with the hope that all of the Council's official documents would be approved by large majorities, the final text of *Orientalium Ecclesiarum* was indeed approved by a favorable vote of 2,110, while only 39 *non placet* votes were registered. It was promulgated on November 21, 1964.

Up until the very end, though, there was considerable dissatisfaction with the actual text of this document. This was the case for various reasons, and the dissatisfaction in question was exhibited by bishops from both the East and the West. In certain ways, the document was recognized by nearly everyone to be a not entirely complete or finished document; nor was the situation of the Eastern Catholic Churches such that perhaps a complete or finished document could be produced. It was equally widely recognized, however, that some provisions concerning the Eastern Catholic Churches needed to be put in place by the Council, if only to reflect the profound change of Catholic attitudes that the progress of the Council had already brought out toward Eastern Christians, whether or not their churches were united with the Roman Apostolic See. These changes were evident in some of the already approved Vatican II documents, namely, the Dogmatic Constitution on the Church, *Lumen Gentium*, and the Decree on Ecumenism, *Unitatis Redintegratio*.

In its conclusion, *Orientalium Ecclesiarum* thus actually contains the statement that all its "arrangements are made in view of present conditions, until such time as the Catholic Church, and the separated Eastern Churches, unite together in the fullness of communion" (*OE* 30). Such was the optimism that reigned at the time of Vatican II: it was sincerely believed by many that reunion with the Eastern Orthodox Churches, separated from the time of the schism of 1054, would actually be coming about soon—and this in spite of all the obstacles and setbacks that had been experienced at the Council itself.

This optimism, if indeed it was not actually euphoria, was encouraged by the passage of the Decree on Ecumenism, *Unitatis Redintegratio*, which roundly endorsed the new ecumenism, as we have very briefly noted earlier in this book. The Council Fathers evidently believed that at least some degree of Christian unity could be, and was going to be, achieved quite soon, once the basic decisions they had made to enter into ecumenical dialogue could begin to be implemented.

The reality would prove to be somewhat different. Forty-plus years later it is easy to see this. In the meantime, though, the Decree on the Eastern Catholic Churches was approved to show, once again, the practical unanimity regularly exhibited by the Council Fathers on the general directions being taken by the Council, even when some doubts or dissatisfactions remained.

But it must also be recognized that the whole issue of the Eastern Catholic Churches and their proper status within the universal Church never did get properly debated at the Council. This was the case, at least in part, as a result of the sheer weight and impetus of the whole ecumenical question, dealing as it did, among other things, with those Christians separated from formal union with the bishop of Rome. As a result, those Eastern Catholics already in union with the Catholic Church tended to get treated rather too briefly and, unfortunately, sometimes too superficially.

A *schema* on Church unity was originally drawn up by the Preparatory Commission for the Oriental [Catholic] Churches, headed by Amleto Cardinal Cicognani. This document, however, soon got swallowed up when the whole question of ecumenism got assigned to the new Secretariat for Promoting Christian Unity headed by German cardinal Augustin Bea. The debate then shifted to the very extensive deliberations and decisions pertaining to ecumenism. The question of the Eastern Catholic Churches—those Eastern Churches already in communion with the Holy See and hence already an integral *part* of the Catholic Church—got pushed to one side, as it were. Another *schema* was prepared on them, but it never got even a fraction of the attention given to *De Oecumenismo* but was rather rushed through because everybody understood that there had to be a document dealing with the Eastern Catholic Churches. Father Ralph Wiltgen, S.V.D., wrote in his history of the Council, *The Rhine Flows into the Tiber*, that "no other Council document had so short a conciliar life span, from the time it was first discussed on the Council floor to its solemn promulgation as the Decree on the Eastern Catholic Churches."

It was not that the Eastern Catholic Churches were accorded no attention at all at the Council. On the contrary, already during the debate on the *schema De Ecclesia* that became *Lumen Gentium*, that is, during the Second Session, in October 1963, the Catholic Coptic bishop of Thebes in Egypt, the Most Reverend Isaac Ghattas, delivered a major intervention that rather dramatically called attention to the situation of the Eastern Catholic Churches. He pointed out with respect to the *schema* on the Church that "though it is universal in intention, [it] is decidedly Latin in execution. The treatment seems to regard the universal Church as being only the Latin Church. . . . This identification of the Latin Church with the universal Church is the root of all difficulties with the Orientals. They cannot accept any such mentality." It was, he said, as if the Eastern Catholic Churches were "ecclesiastical oddities or exotic creations" instead of "sister Churches which together with the Latin-rite Church make up the universal Church."

Bishop Ghattas also wondered why the *schema* on the Church made no mention at all of the ancient institution of the patriarchate, which, after all, was not merely an Eastern institution: the pope himself was considered the patriarch of the West, as the *Annuario Pontificio* itself regularly confirmed each year (although Benedict XVI dropped this title following his election to the chair of Peter).

That these kinds of questions could be raised by a Catholic Coptic bishop (and also by others) no doubt figured among the reasons why the Council found it necessary to prepare and issue a separate document on the Eastern Catholic Churches. Yet, ironically, some of the Eastern Catholic bishops themselves were opposed to issuing any such separate document, as if it were all just a matter of conceding, as they saw it, and in the words of Bishop Ghattas, "so-called privileges to a minority group, the Eastern Churches."

However that may be, on Monday, October 14, 1963—following the intervention of Bishop Ghattas on the previous Thursday, all the patriarchs of the Eastern Catholic Churches, who had formerly been seated in the *aula* of St. Peter's *after* the cardinals and among the archbishops, were suddenly found to have been accorded a special place of their own in the *aula* and were seated directly across from the cardinals—and hence were now seen to be equal in rank to the latter. It was a significant gesture, and it seemed to have been directly brought about by the spirited intervention of Bishop Ghattas.

Father Ralph Wiltgen reported, though, that this change had actually been in the making for a number of years. The fact that it was put into effect only after Bishop Ghattas spoke out could perhaps be attributed to typical Roman slowness in moving or changing. But the idea itself went back to a letter that the elderly but still vigorous Melchite patriarch Maximos IV Saigh had addressed back in 1959 to Pope John XXIII, not long after the latter had announced the convoking of the Council.

Patriarch Maximos in his letter pointed to the plain fact that the cardinals really were the pope's *auxiliaries* in the Western Church; they were honorary clergy of the See of Rome, appointed primarily to assist the bishop of Rome in his capacity as head of the universal Church. As such they were also, of course, empowered to elect his successor in his primatial (and universal) Apostolic See. However, the other ancient patriarchal sees of Constantinople, Alexandria, Antioch, and Jerusalem also went back to ancient times. If the Church was to be truly "Catholic" in the original sense of "universal," these patriarchates also needed to be recognized more publicly. The Eastern Orthodox Churches would be watching, Patriarch Maximos told Pope John, "to see from our example what place the Roman Church would give to their patriarchs in case of reunion."

So the ground had already been prepared for the rather dramatic gesture of the reseating of the Eastern Catholic patriarchs in a place of greater honor. As it happened, though, when during the following year the *schema* on the Eastern Churches was being debated on the one and only occasion that it ever came before the full Council—this was in October 1964—the same Bishop Ghattas favored jettisoning the whole document and inserting any essential parts of it into other *schemata*. According to the position he had championed all along, this Coptic Catholic bishop believed that the Eastern Catholic Churches were already an integral part of the Catholic Church, and hence there should not be any separate document concerning them!

The Council Fathers, however, did not accept this logic. Although the Eastern Churches were indeed integral parts of the Catholic Church, they nevertheless had their own special histories and liturgies; they exhibited various special features; and, as had been brought out in the debate about them, they sometimes posed special problems. Hence, a separate document devoted to them did seem necessary, if they were to be given their due—as well as proper recognition within a Church otherwise so heavily oriented toward the Western and Latin tradition.

Amleto Cardinal Cicognani mentioned some of the special problems of the Eastern Catholic Churches when introducing the debate on the *schema* that had been prepared on them: these problems included whether converts to the Catholic Church from Orthodoxy needed to remain in their corresponding Eastern Church; under what conditions marriages between Eastern Catholics and Eastern Orthodox were both valid and licit; and to what extent Eastern Catholics could avail themselves of Orthodox sacraments and vice versa. These issues would be dealt with in the approved document.

Franz Cardinal König, archbishop of Vienna and one of the most influential of the Council Fathers, speaking as the ordinary for Eastern Catholics in Austria, probably reflected the views of many when he made the debate on this *schema* the occasion to express some even perhaps exaggerated opinions about the less than first-class past and present position held by the Eastern Catholic Churches within the overall Catholic communion. He hoped the final document would rectify their position where necessary. What was needed was a change of attitude, he thought. He believed these ancient communions were not sufficiently honored within the larger Church, and he thought they should be viewed more for what they shared in common with Western Catholics than for what made them different.

The Vienna cardinal also, and emphatically, did not think the Eastern Catholic Churches should be viewed primarily as possible instruments for the "return" of the Eastern Churches not in communion with the Holy See. A tendency to think of them in this way had no doubt been quite strong in the past; the origins of some of them went back to instances where groups originally within the Orthodox fold *had* sought reunion with the Catholic Church. Especially in view of the Council's embrace of the new ecumenism, the *schema* on the Eastern Catholic Churches surely needed to be in complete harmony with the one on ecumenism that the Council was moving to adopt.

Numerous Eastern bishops spoke during the debate; and some, such as the Ukrainian archbishop Josyf Slipyi of Lviv—who had been released from a Soviet concentration camp only on the eve of the Council—deplored the long-standing tradition within the Church to try to "Latinize" the Eastern Churches. Not all the Eastern bishops were dissatisfied, however, nor did all of them stress the importance of the patriarchates. Speaking for the Chaldean Catholic bishops, Bishop Raphael Bidawid—who himself lived to become the patriarch of Babylon of the Chaldeans in Baghdad and as such vigorously opposed the launching of the Iraq War by the United States in the spring of 2003 (before dying himself in the course of that same war)—went on record as the young bishop he was back at Vatican II by declaring that the patriarchates were human, not divine, institutions and that they should be as subject to normal development and reform as any other Church institution.

Melchite patriarch Maximos IV Saigh, so prominent throughout the Council in so many ways, made some of the same points during this debate in the *aula* that he had earlier made in his 1959 letter to Pope John XXIII. This letter, it will be recalled, was about the importance of upgrading the position of the Eastern Catholic Churches within the universal Church. This should absolutely not be neglected, he repeated to the assembled Council Fathers, "if it is wished to offer our Orthodox brothers a preliminary draft of the charter of union."

Following this one single debate that was held on the *schema* in October 1964, the document was returned to the conciliar Commission on the Eastern Churches for revision in the light of the comments made during the debate. In truth, it seems that very few changes were actually made in the draft text—which accounted for at least some of the dissatisfaction with the document that continued to be expressed even after it was approved. Still, the sentiment was quite strong that something needed to be put in place on the subject of the Eastern Catholic Churches as at least a tangible step forward. This document undoubtedly accomplished that. And so, when the final vote came on November 21, 1964, the usual huge majority of Council Fathers was found to be in favor of adding the Decree on the Eastern Catholic Churches, *Orientalium Ecclesiarum*, to the growing collection of the official enactments of Vatican II.

II.

Before looking at the final version of the document that the Council approved on the Eastern Catholic Churches, we need to consider briefly a much more basic question: What are the Eastern Catholic Churches? Most Catholics are aware that there are, in fact, what were commonly called "Eastern-rite" Catholic Churches, though it was actually Vatican II that began the now present custom of speaking about Eastern Churches instead of Eastern "rites." These Eastern Catholic Churches possess their own languages, liturgies, and traditions but nevertheless remain firmly in communion with, and under, the bishop of Rome, the pope. Most of them—except, notably, the Maronites of Lebanon—correspond to an existing Eastern Church not in communion with the bishop of Rome, whether one in the Byzantine-Slavic Orthodox tradition or one in the tradition of one of the Ancient Eastern Churches in communion with neither the Eastern Orthodox Churches nor the Catholic Church.

Most of the Eastern Catholic Churches originated as groups within these established Eastern traditions that had sought at various times to return to the fullness of Catholic faith and practice and had thus applied to Rome to be admitted into communion with the Catholic Church. Sometimes these reunions came about as a result of Western missionary efforts; in other cases, the interested groups had approached the Holy See on their own seeking reunion.

Six of the existing Eastern Catholic Churches are headed by patriarchs—the Armenian, Chaldean, Coptic, Maronite, Melchite, and Syrian Catholic Churches. Others are headed by metropolitans or major archbishops. These Church leaders normally rule their Churches along with an ecclesiastical synod or council. Some smaller Eastern Churches are organized differently, depending upon their particular situations. Eastern Catholic Churches are generally composed of or divided into "eparchies" or "exarchates" instead of dioceses.

Eastern Catholic patriarchs, archbishops, and other Church heads normally are elected and enthroned by the bishops of each particular Church—who themselves are appointed and installed by their Church synod from a list of candidates approved by Rome. This is the reverse, of course, of the procedure now followed in the Western Church, where as a result of historical developments in the West bishops are now selected and appointed by the Holy See from lists of candidates submitted by the metropolitans of the national Catholic Churches. When a patriarch or other Eastern Catholic Church leader is selected by that Church's synod, he then normally appeals to the Holy Father for continuance of the ties with the Holy See. The pope then grants "ecclesiastical communion."

Most of the patriarchs or heads of Eastern Catholic Churches are not members of the College of Cardinals (though some are). Some

Eastern Catholic churchmen, in fact, entirely oppose the idea that they should ever be named cardinals, since the latter, after all, are honorary "clergy" of the Western, or Latin, diocese of Rome. This position is an eminently logical one, of course, although in accordance with its logic, the Eastern Churches could then never have any role or say in the election of the supreme head of the Church. But then too it follows quite logically that, whatever else might be said about it, because the supreme head of the universal Church is the bishop of a Western, Latin-rite diocese, who is theoretically elected by his "clergy" (the cardinals!), it could even be argued that the pope *ought* to be strictly a Latin-rite bishop, even though the Church herself is "universal."

Most of the Eastern Catholic Churches continue to exist in their country of origin, but most of them have also experienced a "diaspora," where, as a result of emigration, and sometimes of actual persecution, they now have members living far from their original homelands, especially in the New World. This has sometimes made for difficulties with regard to worship and the administration of the sacraments. In the past, some Eastern Catholics have had reason to be dissatisfied with their reception by the Roman Catholic dioceses in which they came to find themselves. One of the reasons *Orientalium Ecclesiarum* was thought necessary at Vatican II was to help change the attitudes of Western Catholics toward their Eastern brethren; to regularize the situations of these Eastern Catholics now living in diaspora; and, finally, to set forth some principles in accordance with which Eastern Churches might continue to exist and, hopefully, to flourish within the larger Catholic Church.

There may be no more than about twenty million Eastern Catholics in all—only a few more than a half million of them are currently living in the United States. These numbers do not add up to even 2 percent of the total Catholic population of the world. Obviously the vast majority of Catholics worldwide do belong to the Roman rite. This is an inescapable fact, as it was at the time of the Council, and as a result certain consequences have stemmed, and stem, from that fact. Still, the Eastern Catholic Churches have played an important part in the history of Christ's Church, just as they represent a legitimate Catholic Church claim to "diversity" today—supposedly something badly lacking in the Church. There is no doubt at all that they represent an important factor in the total Catholic reality. The Catholic Church is not just "the Roman Catholic Church," as cannot be too often repeated, but is a diverse worldwide communion in more senses than just the geographical.

For a long time, of course, it was thought and hoped that the Eastern Catholic Churches would constitute a kind of natural "bridge" leading to the "return" to full Catholic unity of their often larger Orthodox and Ancient Eastern Church counterparts. This hope has generally not been realized up to now. On the contrary, in some ways, the very existence of these Eastern Catholic Churches has been seen as an obstacle to full unity, since the Eastern Orthodox in particular have tended to resent them very strongly as disloyal "uniates" subservient to the Western Church.

The "uniate" question has long been a sore point in ecumenical relations, as a matter of fact. For example, the Joint International Commission for Theological Dialogue between the Orthodox Church and the Catholic Church sponsored a major conference on the subject at the Balamand School of Theology in Lebanon in 1993, at which most of the autocephalous Byzantine Orthodox Churches were represented. From this conference there issued a major paper, "Uniatism, Method of Union of the Past, and the Present Search for Full Communion." The very title of the paper conveys an idea of how strongly the Orthodox evidently disapprove of those Christian communities that, in the past, had sought the fullness of Catholic truth and practice as "uniates" (that is, as *Eastern Catholic Churches*, the subject of our present chapter!). Presumably in the interests of a greater ecumenical good, the Catholic participants at the Balamand conference seem to have allowed this negative attitude to stand pretty much unchallenged. Even so, however, the Catholic–Eastern Orthodox dialogue that had been going on virtually since the time of the Council broke down at its meeting in Baltimore in 2000 over questions relating to "uniatism" and did not resume again for five years, following the election of Pope Benedict XVI. This is obviously an ongoing problem, and one that cannot be ignored.

The 1993 Balamand paper had nevertheless contained two central affirmations: first, that the "method" that has been called "uniatism" was henceforth to be rejected because it was found to be "opposed to the tradition of our Churches"—presumably, the Eastern Churches, not the Catholic Church. Second, the paper did affirm, however, that the Eastern Catholic Churches do "have a right to exist and to act in response to the spiritual needs of their faithful."

So there was something of a compromise, after all: the Eastern Catholic Churches were at least going to be allowed to exist, in spite of some of the rhetoric with which they have regularly been treated and occasionally been excoriated in the Eastern Orthodox world! Still, the Catholic Church was described as no longer pushing for "uniatism"—which had once seemed to be her major policy regarding the East, and that for not a few centuries.

The recognition by the Catholic partners in an important official ecumenical dialogue that the "method" of "uniatism"—that is, welcoming Eastern splinter groups into full Catholic unity—should no longer be pursued by the Catholic Church was surely required by the spirit of the new ecumenism. Indeed, the Church *should* now eschew that "method" (as it is, curiously, styled). It hardly represents the way reunion should be actively sought, in any case.

However, at the same time, the Church should in no way be *blamed* for having admitted in the past into her full communion Eastern Christians who themselves sought that communion. The Holy See, in particular, was never going to refuse or reject—and certainly will not do so now—any *bona fide* group or community of Christians prepared to return to the full unity of the Catholic Church, accepting the conditions laid down by the Holy See.

At the same time, though, looking carefully at the Balamand paper, it must be granted that the dialogue partners on the Eastern Orthodox side have now at least recognized the *legitimacy* of the Eastern Catholic Churches. However much the Orthodox may have resented them in the past, they are now seen to be definitely present, and legitimate, in the relations between the Churches. This is a step forward. It would even seem, in the light of the Balamand paper, that there might be some way in which the Eastern Catholic Churches *could* yet play a role in helping to restore Christian unity, contrary to the way in which they have typically been described and treated by the Eastern Orthodox up to now.

Of course, the very same "uniate" question has continued to be a major bone of contention between the Russian Orthodox Church and the Ukrainian Catholic Church. As a consequence, many problems and mutual antagonisms still remain to be worked out. In many respects, though, the strong post–Vatican II outreach of the Catholic Church has left the Eastern Catholic Churches sidelined to a certain extent. This does not mean, however, that they may not in the future constitute some kind of a bridge to Christian unity, once the antagonisms, prejudices, and misunderstandings of the centuries have been cleared away. As was repeatedly stressed at the Council, the Eastern Catholic Churches provide a practical demonstration of how Churches with a history and traditions not necessarily consonant with the Roman tradition and practices nevertheless *can* fit within the unity of the Catholic Church.

In 1995, Pope John Paul issued his apostolic letter *Orientale Lumen*, written to commemorate the one-hundredth anniversary of Pope Leo XIII's *Orientalium Dignitas.* In this latter document, Leo XIII had affirmed the Catholic Church's will to uphold the dignity and venerable traditions of the Eastern Catholic Churches. In the ensuing one hundred years, though, the Church did not have a perfect record in this regard—as she did not have any such perfect record prior to Pope Leo XIII's letter, either. Still, the attention devoted to the subject at the Council could not but be a pledge of the Church's continuing good intentions. John Paul II, more than once, firmly indicated that he intended to continue that tradition in the post-conciliar period, and it appears that he pretty consistently did precisely that. His successor evidently intends to do the same. Much will now depend upon how well the Church keeps her promises in this regard in the future.

Thus, it was both necessary and salutary that Vatican Council II should have addressed, and, in an important degree, regularized, the situation of the Eastern Catholic Churches within the larger Church—and this, not only for its own sake, but precisely because the hoped-for reunion with the separated Christian Churches has not yet, in God's Providence, been brought about. If and when this becomes a more active possibility—or if and when it actually comes about—

these Ancient Churches that have celebrated and handed down their venerable rites and sacraments from apostolic times will surely come to be seen as important witnesses to the unity of the Church of Christ. Meanwhile, the traditions they embody and represent are valuable not only in their own right but as a vibrant part of "the Catholic Church that comes to us from the apostles."

III.

What kind of document, then, is Vatican II's Decree on the Eastern Catholic Churches, *Orientalium Ecclesiarum*? It is not a long document. It begins by declaring:

> The Catholic Church values highly the institutions of the Eastern Churches, their liturgical rites, ecclesiastical traditions, and their ordering of the Christian life. For in those Churches, which are distinguished by their venerable antiquity, there is clearly evident the tradition which has come from the apostles through the Fathers, and which is part of the divinely revealed, undivided heritage of the Universal Church. (*OE* 1)

Because of this, the Council declares that it "has a special care for the Eastern Churches . . . and wishes them to flourish" and hence has produced this document containing "some guiding principles for these Churches," meanwhile "leaving all else to be cared for by the Eastern synods and the Apostolic See" (ibid.).

Orientalium Ecclesiarum states that "the Catholic Church wishes the tradition of each particular Church or rite to remain whole and entire" (*OE* 2). It also states that the Eastern Catholic Churches "are of equal rank, so that none of them is superior to the other because of its rite" (*OE* 3). No doubt one of the intentions of the Council Fathers here, in view of the often-voiced complaints of some Eastern Catholics, was to establish the principle that the Roman rite itself, though as a practical matter it is massively predominant throughout the world, is not thereby "superior" to the other rites either. The other Churches must be given the chance to "flourish" in the measure that their history, their numbers, and their present situations allow. This very idea marked a distinct break with some past practices. Catholic missions, for example, had up to then been pretty much an affair of the Western Church or the Roman rite alone; priests of other rites wishing to work in the missions were obliged to adopt the Roman rite.

The document also maintained the principle that "each and every Catholic, as also the baptized members of any non-Catholic Church or community who come to the fullness of Catholic communion, must retain each his own rite wherever he is, and follow it to the best of his ability" (*OE* 4). The text goes on to affirm that "the Churches of the East, like those of the West, have the right and duty to govern themselves according to their own special disciplines . . . guaranteed by ancient tradition" (*OE* 5). This affirmation seemed to be particularly important in view of any possible future reunion with non-Catholic Eastern Christians, since an often expressed fear of the latter contemplating reunion has been that they would lose their autonomy under the Roman primacy.

Like Pope John Paul II in his 1995 encyclical *Ut Unum Sint* ("That They May Be One"), though, *Orientalium Ecclesiarum* does not envisage any kind of reunion that would entail the same kind of direct, operational papal authority over them that has developed in the history of the Western Church. Rather, the principal model following reunion would be the normal practice of the first millennium of Christianity, when the pope's supreme authority and jurisdiction came into play only in cases where the regular Eastern synodal and collegial ecclesiastical machinery had proved unable to decide and settle particular questions, and an "appeal" to Rome therefore had to be made. Even now, as we have just seen above, the governance of the Eastern Catholic Churches is left to be "cared for by the Eastern synods and the Apostolic See."

Not surprisingly, the Decree on the Eastern Catholic Churches affirms the ancient institution of the patriarchate and establishes that "the rights and privileges" of the Eastern patriarchs should be "restored" where necessary "in accordance with the ancient traditions of each Church and the decrees of the ecumenical councils" (*OE* 9). The same principles apply to the major archbishoprics. Moreover, the document provides that new patriarchates could be established by the supreme pontiff or by an ecumenical council.

Orientalium Ecclesiarum goes on to endorse the traditional sacramental disciplines of the Eastern Catholic Churches, reaffirming such customs as that priests of the Eastern Churches can validly confer confirmation and that the Eastern Catholic faithful are obliged to take part in the Divine Liturgy on Sundays and feast days. The document urges that the diaconate be restored where it may have fallen into disuse. It decrees that marriages between Eastern Catholics and Eastern Orthodox are valid if the sacred minister is present. It basically confirms the Eastern traditions in liturgical matters as well as those pertaining to the Church calendar and such.

It was probably inevitable in the ecumenical climate that prevailed at the Council that the Eastern Catholic Churches should have been given "the special duty of fostering the unity of all Christians" (*OE* 24). Perhaps the decree even helped that enterprise along by stating that "nothing more should be demanded of separated Eastern Christians who come to Catholic unity under the influence of the grace of the Holy Spirit than what the simple profession of the Catholic faith requires." More than that: "Since a valid priesthood has been preserved among them, Eastern clerics who come to Catholic unity may exercise their own orders, in accordance with the regulations laid down by competent authority" (*OE* 25). Or yet again:

> Eastern Christians who are separated in good faith from the Catholic Church, if they are rightly disposed and make such request of their own accord, may be given the sacraments of Penance, the Eucharist, and the Anointing of the Sick. Moreover, Catholics also may ask for those same sacraments from non-Catholic ministers in whose Church there are valid sacraments, as often as necessity or true spiritual benefit recommends such action, and access to a Catholic priest is physically or morally impossible. (*OE* 27)

In short, no matter how much the Council Fathers may have wished to treat the Eastern Catholic Churches separately, and apart from the question of ecumenism as such, it is obvious that its actual treatment nevertheless kept edging over toward the ecumenical question. This is not necessarily a contradiction, though—at least not a fundamental one. *Orientalium Ecclesiarum* is really in basic agreement with *Unitatis Redintegratio* throughout. Yet it is significant that the Council did so often end up seeing the whole question of all the Eastern Churches, Catholic and non-Catholic, in the light of ecumenism and the quest for Christian unity.

Moreover, the fact that the Catholic Church, in a solemn conciliar decree such as this, does recognize and affirm the rightful and legitimate place of the Eastern Catholic Churches within the larger Catholic communion means that the ecumenical question, on the Catholic side, actually does admit of a solution in principle: there is a place for non-Roman "autonomous" Churches desirous of Christian unity to fit in within the Catholic system; the continuing existence of, and even in some cases, the current flourishing of, the Eastern Catholic Churches proves that this is eminently possible.

The same thing does not appear to be true on the other side, however: it would seem that the Eastern Orthodox Churches, for example, have not yet worked out an ecclesiology that would enable them to agree to such a restored unity as currently obtains between the Apostolic See and the various Eastern Catholic Churches. The development of such an ecclesiology would seem to be an important priority for the Orthodox Churches. Theoretically, this would seem to be possible; but it certainly does not appear to be on the immediate horizon.

Nevertheless, the Decree on the Eastern Catholic Churches did succeed in setting forth valid guiding principles that, if followed—and it seems that they generally have been followed in the postconciliar era—surely do allow the Eastern Catholic Churches to function and even flourish in accordance with their own venerable traditions. What the Eastern Catholic Churches will make of this, and what their futures will ultimately be within the larger Catholic universe, ultimately now depends pretty much on them—and upon the blessings God will see fit to bestow upon them.

The Decree on the Eastern Catholic Churches rounded out the five documents of Vatican II that were completed and promulgated by the end of the Third Session in the fall of 1964. These documents on the liturgy, the media, the Church herself, ecumenism, and the Eastern Catholic Churches would by themselves stand up quite creditably with the productions of practically any other previous ecumenical council. Yet these five documents constituted only the beginning of what the Council would debate and in the end decide.

Back in 1959, nobody had remotely imagined that Blessed Pope John XXIII's Council would go on for so long or do so much. He himself had originally thought and hoped that the Council would complete its work within the year that proved to be the final year of his own pontificate and his own life. The preparatory work carried out by the commissions between 1959 and 1962 were, in his opinion, so thorough and excellent that, as he remarked in April 1962, "the consent of the bishops will not be difficult to obtain and their approval will be unanimous." This was not the only respect in which this beloved pontiff's habitual optimism was not to be borne out by the actual events!

Nevertheless, the Council *did* successfully pursue some of the major lines laid down for it by John XXIII. This was especially true as regards ecumenism. His yearning for Christian unity was as strong as John Paul II's would later prove to be. Although he still thought in terms of a simple "return" of the *errantes*, as he explicitly said in his first encyclical, *Ad Petri Cathedram* (*APC* 80), he was certainly prepared to go far to achieve it. Having served as a papal nuncio in Bulgaria and Turkey in the 1930s and 1940s, he was especially interested in reunion with the Eastern Orthodox, with whom he had personally come into such close contact. In 1939, for example, the then archbishop Angelo Giuseppe Roncalli actually prefigured the famous later mutual embrace, in 1965, of the ecumenical patriarch Athenagoras I and Pope Paul VI when he publicly and lavishly embraced the ecumenical patriarch Benjamin I on the occasion of one his visits to the latter in connection with courtesies being exchanged in Istanbul on the occasion of the election of Pope Pius XII.

So the Council, in truth, accomplished much of what John XXIII had hoped it would accomplish—and much, much more besides. Once it got under way, and even though the Council itself soon rejected almost out of hand much of the preparatory work that John XXIII had regarded so highly, the Council henceforth seemed determined to cover almost every important aspect of the Church's life and practice. The Council Fathers had a sense of what Pope John Paul II many times emphasized afterward, namely, that in God's Providence, the Council was almost consciously preparing the Church for the advent of the third millennium of Christianity.

The Fourth Session, which convened in the fall of 1965 and which would prove to be the final session, would turn out to be even more productive than the first three: eleven documents would be voted on and promulgated during its course—documents that are in many ways as important as the three documents on the Church that we have been able to cover in this book. One thing is certain, though, and that is that the three documents that we have been able to "reread" in the course of these pages, *Lumen Gentium*, *Gaudium et Spes*, and *Orientalium Ecclesiarum*, all represent uniquely important teachings of the Church on the Church. They constitute the principal reasons why Vatican Council II is rightly called "the Council *of* the Church." And as we noted about *Lumen Gentium* in chapter 1, "few or no Church teaching documents have contributed more to the Church's own self-understanding."

CHAPTER FIVE

Vatican II Lives

TO GO through seriously and carefully even one of the actual documents of the Second Vatican Council is usually to acquire a different and hopefully much richer view of the Council than the one many people hold today on the basis of their experience of the distinctly "mixed results" of the aftermath of the Council. That is surely one of the reasons why Pope Benedict XVI, upon his election, recommended a "rereading" of the Council's documents. The discovery from such a rereading of some of the many things the Council "did right" can help us to understand why the recent popes have all been so convinced of the great importance of the Council in the life of the Church. This remains true in spite of the many abuses, missteps, and errors of the postconciliar era, which this book has not attempted to pass over or evade.

Abusus non tollit usus ("Abuse does not nullify use"). The fact that many abuses have been perpetrated in the name of the Second Vatican Council does not cancel out the truths the Council taught and the positive good it has brought about in other ways. Time after time in looking at the conciliar and postconciliar documents, I have discovered things I could hardly have imagined were actually there. Our understanding of the truths of Christ's revelation, as they have been preserved, developed, and handed down in the Church is enormously enhanced and strengthened when viewed in the perspective of what the Council contributed to Catholic teaching and to the Catholic tradition. Our faith can be greatly fortified by a knowledge of what the Council taught; certainly mine has been.

Nevertheless, it is still often argued, especially by Catholic traditionalists, and by many conservatives as well, that regardless of what the Council documents might say, however true and right they might be, the bitter fruits of the Council and the postconciliar years have nevertheless been such that the Council can only be judged to have been a mistake and a failure. After all, documents are only documents, words on paper. What counts is how things get worked out in the "real world," and here nobody can deny the grave crisis in which the Church finds herself today and which she has been passing through virtually from the time of the Council.

Indeed, nobody *can* deny the seriousness of the present crisis of the Church, but we should beware of falling too easily into the *post hoc, ergo propter hoc* mode of imagining that because the crisis seems to have followed so closely upon the Council, it was necessarily caused by the Council. The facts are really otherwise. There is no way that the Catholic Church could have escaped being bathed in the acids of modernity over the last forty years whether or not the Council had taken place. Those acids already before the Council had begun to eat relentlessly away at the confident edifice the Church seemed to present in the immediate preconciliar years. The Council was the occasion, rather than the cause, of much that was imported into the Church from the world in the revolutionary 1960s. That same world would have had a significant effect on the Church regardless of the Council. We live in an era of a decline in faith across the board; it has affected all Christian Churches, denominations, and communions, and not just the Catholic Church. Indeed, the Catholic Church comes out *better* on that score than most other Christian bodies.

It is also not true that documents are merely words on paper. Documents represent what an organization such as the Catholic Church is willing to commit to paper and hence be reminded of, be called back to, and be bound by. Documents help save us *from* the worst effects of our mistakes and the mistakes of our leaders. They constitute as permanent a record of what the Church believes and teaches as anything we are likely to see in this world. Even where the conciliar documents have not been properly understood or implemented, or have even been disregarded or set aside, they are still there when the time comes to go back to them and make necessary corrections. In this sense, Vatican II still remains to be implemented properly in more than a few respects—as, progressively, in fact, now actually seems to be happening in some areas, *Deo gratias.*

In the official acts and documents of the Council—although not *only* in them—Vatican II *lives*! Today, from a perspective of more than forty years, we can now discern more than a little Providence in the fact that the Council took place when it did. It dealt with and decided questions of principle that have only now emerged and are being worked out in that highly touted "real world"—and that Pope John Paul II, for example, in the course of his long pontificate, often exploited so creatively. In doing so, he was following the trail blazed by his predecessor, Pope Paul VI. Nor can there be any doubt that Pope Benedict XVI—a man of the Council par excellence, though also one who has never hesitated to criticize false postconciliar outcomes, and not only in his famous 1985 *Ratzinger Report*—has been engaged in doing the same thing from the first day of his pontificate. All three of these popes must be considered to be preeminently "men of the Second Vatican Council," in which all three of them participated significantly.

The evidence after the fact too is that in a mysterious way, the Holy Spirit *did* preside over the Council, as the Church has always believed has been the case with all of her ecumenical councils. Nor is it any less true that the same Holy Spirit presided over the conclaves that elected three such men of the Council as Paul VI, John Paul II, and Benedict XVI. Certainly all of *them* believed, or believe, this to be the case. Pope Paul VI, elected during the Council and destined to carry it to completion, scarcely ever spoke or wrote anything that did not have some reference to the Council that loomed so large in his own pontificate. This is certainly true of those words or writings of his that we have had the occasion to look at in this book.

Pope John Paul II, for his part, constantly invoked, referred to, explained, or quoted Vatican Council II throughout his entire twenty-six-year pontificate, as to some extent we have been able to show in these pages. Almost all of those so-often-remarkable productions of his go back to the Council in one way or another. The marvel would be to find a work of John Paul II's that did not in some way go back to Vatican II.

As for Pope Benedict XVI, the writing of this book was moving toward completion around the same time that he was elected to be the successor of Peter. Yet there was no way of knowing beforehand that he would actually be elected pope. Looking back over what I had written, though, I was simply amazed at how many times he was mentioned. Either as a theologian, a former Council *peritus*, or the prefect of the Congregation for the Doctrine of the Faith, it was inevitable that Joseph Cardinal Ratzinger would have to figure prominently in any book about Vatican II. And so it proved.

A point to be underlined here is that all three of these supreme pontiffs have believed in, affirmed, and promoted what we may call a "conciliar Church." Extreme traditionalists, such as the Lefebvrites, of course, use this very term to denote what they consider to be a false, wayward, and misguided Church, a Church corrupted by the Council, as they see it. Many conservative Catholics do not go quite that far, but they nevertheless have little enthusiasm for the Council and believe it to have been ultimately bad for the Church. They point to its "bitter fruits" all around us—the misconceived experiments, the watered-down doctrines, the bad catechetics, the radical religious orders, the touchy-feely enthusiasms, the uncritical ecumenism, the wimpy and sometimes spineless churchmen. The Council failed, in the view of many conservatives, and hence it must be more or less disregarded today.

What we must hold to, according to them, is apparently a strictly "papal" Church. Whether or not they actually look back to the imagined golden days of a Pope Pius XII, they seem to consider the Church of his day stretching back into history under the leadership of a long succession of supreme pontiffs to be the real and proper model of what "the Catholic Church" should be like. The "conciliar Church," in their view, turned out to be an embarrassing mistake and an aberration. Blessed Pope John XXIII, though undoubtedly a sincere and holy man, was surely also a naïve optimist and perhaps even an unrealistic utopian into the bargain if the convoking of Vatican II is supposed to be his great legacy. If the Council was not entirely mistaken, it certainly represented a considerable deviation from the traditional model of the historically more sound and consistent "papal" Church that represents the way the Church ought to appear and function.

Somehow, and in some way that is never very clear in the minds of those Catholics who think along these lines, the bad dream that was Vatican II is just going to have to go away. We can then all go back to the real and authentic "papal" Church that worked so well for so long, as all the statistics attest. Hardly anybody ever tries to spell out or explain how it might possibly be that we *could* ever today have a Church *sans* the Council, especially considering the fact that the Council *did*, after all, take place. Very probably nobody has really tried to think this through very carefully. People of a certain persuasion just know that the Council was bad for the Church, and hence the less said about it now, the better.

This is not an inaccurate description of how some who consider themselves to be "orthodox Catholics" see things today. They really do think the Church is somehow going to go on without the Council. This is not, of course, true of all who consider themselves "orthodox Catholics." Probably a very large majority of the latter understand perfectly well that the Council did take place, that its acts and documents henceforth do represent an integral part of the Church's tradition, and that the Church cannot back away from them even if that really were desirable. But a fair number of them nevertheless see little or no positive good stemming from the Council; and many of them just wish its unwelcome reforms and initiatives somehow just *would* go away.

The sad thing about people of this cast of mind is that they are generally sincerely believing Catholics who profess the creed, affirm the supernatural faith, and love the Church. They are not religious liberals, and most of them correctly see that it has been mostly liberal ideas and initiatives that have devastated the Church in the postconciliar era.

Indeed, they tend to ascribe the liberal ideas that have proven so destructive in the postconciliar years to the Council. Hence their solution to the current crisis in the Church lies in an abandonment of the defective "conciliar Church" and a return to the tried and true "papal Church."

(When speaking of religious "liberalism," by the way, we are thinking of the definition that Venerable John Henry Newman gave to it in his famous "Biglietto Speech" on the occasion of his being made a cardinal, namely, that "liberalism in religion is the doctrine that there is no positive truth in religion, but that one creed is as good as another." But this is the precise opposite, of course, of Vatican II's actual teaching, which is that the Catholic Church is the "teacher of truth"!)

Any view of the Catholic Church that disregards or downplays the Council, however, cannot be sustained in the light of what we have examined in this book *about* the Council's teaching on the Church herself. Another problem that immediately leaps to the eye as well is this: how could we ever possibly have any such thing as a purely "papal" Church when none of the *popes* involved believed or believes in any such thing? The popes have believed in and taught and promoted, precisely, the "conciliar Church" that is so readily belittled by some conservatives. The respective agendas of *all* of the post–Vatican II popes have entailed implementing Vatican II as an important, if not the first, order of business for them. At the beginning of this book, it was noted how each one of the post–Vatican II popes announced at the beginning of his pontificate that the implementation of Vatican Council II would be among his top priorities.

Forty years after the end of the Council, Pope Benedict XVI announced the same priority upon his election in April 2005. In his first Latin sermon to the College of Cardinals, the day after his election, the new pope stated that he wanted to "forcefully affirm the strong desire to continue in the task of implementing the Second Vatican Council." The fact that he could say this *meant*, of course, that he does not consider it to have been fully implemented to date!

In the course of this book, we have been able to see and judge and take the measure of a few examples of just *how* relevant Vatican II has been, and is, and will no doubt continue to be in the life of Christ's Church. If it was not the most important event in the twentieth century, as French president Charles de Gaulle is said to have believed, it was one of the most important events. It is unfortunate that this has not been more evident to more people. The postconciliar chaos has unfortunately taken its toll. We should not forget that roughly two generations of chaos and turmoil also followed the Council of Nicaea. Although conditions in the contemporary Church have improved recently—even to a rather considerable extent in some cases—the postconciliar chaos continues to exact its toll in some other cases. The reputation of the Council still suffers in the minds of many average, sensible Catholics, even while many Catholic liberals continue to ascribe to it a mystique that sees it as having granted carte blanche for practically anything and everything anyone ever imagined the Church ought to be or wished she were: *they* certainly do not seem to accept that the Catholic Church is the teacher of truth!

Disloyalty, disobedience, and dissent remain with us, meanwhile, to a much greater extent than most institutions could tolerate, much less the institution that is supposed to be proclaiming the Word and extending the work of Jesus Christ in the world. The Church continues to do these things anyway, of course, in spite of the troubles that came upon her following the Council. She continues to do these things because she cannot *not* do them, being what she is. She is going to go on doing these things primarily because the faith of a billion people gathered into the world's largest and longest continually existing institution is *true*—and compelling. She is going to go on doing these things in spite of the setbacks of the postconciliar years because these setbacks represent nothing more than temporary deviations from the path of her true earthly pilgrimage.

So the Church is going to go on doing what she has always done, regardless. Yet it remains true that sometimes she does it better than at other times. The Second Vatican Council aimed to provide, and did provide, the theoretical basis to enable the Church to do it better still. Instead, the first postconciliar generation of Catholics, including its hierarchical leadership, apparently did not fully understand either the Council itself or its principal teachings and acts. Like the first generation of the Chosen People in the Exodus from Egypt, the first postconciliar generation was destined to remain forty years in the deserts of false renewal and watered-down faith—truly a "faithless generation" (Mk 9:19) caught up in the temptations of the so-called spirit of Vatican II. The world was too much with them.

More attention should thus have been paid to the *letter* of Vatican II, as we have tried to do in this book. Only on the basis of what the Council actually *taught* and *said* can we go forward with the *true* renewal originally envisaged by Blessed Pope John XXIII and provided for by the Council itself in the documents it issued—of which we have been able to "reread" at least a few of the more important ones to some purpose here.

Selected Bibliography

Abbott, Walter M., S.J., general editor. *The Documents of Vatican II.* New York: Herder and Herder/Association Press, 1966.

Amerio, Romano. *Iota unum: Studio delle variazioni della Chiesa cattolica nel secolo XX.* Milan/Naples: Riccardo Ricciardi Editore, 1989.

Bunson, Matthew, general editor. *2008 Catholic Almanac.* Huntington, IN: Our Sunday Visitor Publishing Division, 2007 (and similar volumes from previous years).

Code of Canon Law. Latin-English edition (a translation of *Codex Iuris Canonici*). Washington, DC: Canon Law Society of America, 1983.

Congregation for the Doctrine of the Faith. Declaration on the Unicity and Salvific Universality of the Church, *Dominus Iesus.* August 6, 2000. In *Origins: CNS Documentary Service,* September 14, 2000, vol. 30, no. 14.

———. Instruction on the Ecclesial Vocation of the Theologian, *Donum Veritatis.* May 24, 1990. In *Origins: CNS Documentary Service,* July 5, 1990, vol. 20, no. 8.

Curran, Charles E. *Faithful Dissent.* Kansas City: Sheed and Ward, 1986.

Fesquet, Henri. *The Drama of Vatican II: The Ecumenical Council—June, 1962–December, 1965.* New York: Random House, 1967.

Flannery, Austin, O.P., general editor. *Vatican Council: The Conciliar and Post Conciliar Documents.* Northport, NY: Costello Publishing Company, 1975.

———. *Vatican Council II: More Post Conciliar Documents* (volume 2). Northport, NY: Costello Publishing Company, 1982. (Contains a number of the official Church postconciliar documents mentioned in the text.)

Hales, E. E. Y. *Pope John and His Revolution.* New York: Doubleday Image Books, 1965.

Häring, Bernard. *The Johannine Council: Witness to Unity.* New York: Herder and Herder, 1963.

Hebblethwaite, Peter. *Pope John XXIII: Shepherd of the Modern World.* New York: Doubleday and Company, 1985.

———. *Paul VI: The First Modern Pope.* New York/Mahwah, NJ: Paulist Press, 1993.

———. *Pope John Paul II and the Church.* Kansas City: Sheed and Ward, 1995.

John Paul II, Pope. Encyclical Letter on the Redeemer of Man, *Redemptor Hominis.* March 4, 1979. Washington, DC: U.S. Catholic Conference Publications Office, 1979.

———. Encyclical Letter on the Mother of the Redeemer, *Redemptoris Mater.* March 25, 1987. Boston, MA: Daughters of St. Paul, 1987.

———. Apostolic Letter on the Dignity and Vocation of Women, *Mulieris Dignitatem.* August 15, 1988. Boston: Pauline Books and Media, 1988.

———. Apostolic Constitution on Catholic Universities, *Ex Corde Ecclesiae.* August 15, 1990. Washington, DC: USCC Publications, 1990.

———. Encyclical Letter on the Splendor of Truth, *Veritatis Splendor.* August 6, 1993. Boston, MA: St. Paul Books and Media, 1993.

———. Encyclical Letter on the Church's Commitment to Ecumenism, *Ut Unum Sint.* May 25, 1995. Boston: Pauline Books and Media, 1995.

———. Apostolic Letter *Motu Proprio Ad Tuendam Fidem.* May 28, 1998. In *L'Osservatore Romano* (English edition), July 15, 1998.

———. Apostolic Letter on the Most Holy Rosary, *Rosarium Virginis Mariae.* October 16, 2002. Washington, DC: USCCB Publishing, 2002.

Kaiser, Robert. *Inside the Council: The Story of Vatican II.* London: Burns and Oates, 1963.

Kasper, Walter. *That They May All Be One.* London/New York: Burns and Oates, 2004.

Kloppenburg, Bonaventure, O.F.M. *Ecclesiology of Vatican II.* Chicago: Franciscan Herald Press, 1974.

Küng, Hans. *Infallible? An Inquiry.* New York: Doubleday Image Books, 1972.

Küng, Hans; Yves Congar, O.P.; and David O'Hanlon, S.J., eds. *Council Speeches of Vatican II.* Glen Rock, NJ: Paulist Press, 1964.

Küng, Hans, and Leonard Swidler, eds. *The Church in Anguish: Has the Vatican Betrayed Vatican II?* San Francisco: Harper and Row, 1986.

Marchetto, Agostino. *Il concilio ecumenico Vaticano II: Contrapunto per la sua storia.* Vatican City: Libreria Editrice Vaticana, 2005. (An English translation is to be published by the University of Scranton Press.)

Neuner, J., S.J., and J. Dupuis, S.J. *The Christian Faith in the Doctrinal Documents of the Catholic Church.* Westminster, MD: Christian Classics, 1975.

A New Catechism: Catholic Faith for Adults, with supplement ("authorized edition" of the Dutch Catechism). New York: Seabury Press, 1969.

Novak, Michael. *The Open Church: Vatican II, Act II.* New York: Macmillan Company, 1964.

Paul VI, Pope. Encyclical Letter on the Paths of the Church, *Ecclesiam Suam.* Boston: St. Paul Editions, 1964.

Prendergast, Michael R., and M. D. Ridge. *Voices from the Council.* Portland: Pastoral Press, 2004.

Quinn, John R. *The Reform of the Papacy: The Costly Call to Christian Unity.* New York: Crossword Publishing Company, 1999.

Ratzinger, Joseph Cardinal, *Church, Ecumenism and Politics: New Essays in Ecclesiology.* New York: Crossroad Books, 1987.

Ratzinger, Joseph Cardinal, with Vittorio Messori. *The Ratzinger Report: An Exclusive Interview on the State of the Church.* San Francisco: Ignatius Press, 1985.

Rynne, Xavier. *Vatican Council II.* New York: Farrar, Straus and Giroux, 1968.

Stacpoole, Alberic, O.S.B., ed. *Vatican II Revisited: By Those Who Were There.* Minneapolis: Winston Press, 1986.

Varacalli, Joseph A. *Toward the Establishment of Liberal Catholicism in America.* Lanham, MD: University Press of America, 1983.

———. *Bright Promise, Failed Community: Catholics and the American Public Order.* Lanham, MD: Lexington Books, 2000.

Weigel, George. *Witness to Hope: The Biography of Pope John Paul II.* New York: HarperCollins, 1999.

Whitehead, Kenneth D. *The New Ecumenism: How the Catholic Church after Vatican II Took Over the Leadership of the World Ecumenical Movement.* Staten Island, NY: St. Paul's/Alba House, 2009.

Wiltgen, Rev. Ralph M., S.V.D. *The Rhine Flows into the Tiber: The Unknown Council.* New York: Hawthorn Books, 1967.

Wojtyla, Karol (Pope John Paul II). *Sources of Renewal: The Implementation of Vatican II.* San Francisco: Harper and Row Publishers, 1979.

About the Author

KENNETH D. WHITEHEAD is a former career Foreign Service officer who served in Rome, the Middle East, and North Africa but later completed his federal government career in the U.S. Department of Education as President Ronald Reagan's assistant secretary of education for postsecondary education. He now works as a writer, editor, and translator in Falls Church, Virginia. He is the author, among other books, of *One, Holy, Catholic, and Apostolic: The Early Church Was the Catholic Church* (Ignatius Press, 2000), and is the coauthor (with James Likoudis), most recently, of *The Pope, the Council, and the Mass* (revised edition, Emmaus Road Publishing, 2006). He has authored, coauthored, edited, or translated a number of other books, mostly of Catholic interest; most recently, he has edited *The Church, Marriage, and the Family* (St. Augustine's Press, 2007) and has translated Archbishop Agostino Marchetto's *Il concilio ecumenico Vaticano II.*

Mr. Whitehead was educated at the University of Utah and the University of Paris and holds an honorary D.Litt. degree in Christian Letters from the Franciscan University of Steubenville. He serves on the boards of directors of the Catholic League for Religious and Civil

Rights, the Fellowship of Catholic Scholars, and the *Review of Metaphysics.* Mr. Whitehead is married to the former Margaret O'Donohue, a parish director of religious education, and they are the parents of four grown sons.

Index